Published & Drawn by L.R. BURLEIGH, Troy, N.Y.

BECK & PAULI, Litho, Milwaukee, Wis.

Copyright 1884 by L.R. BURLEIGH, Troy, N.Y.

1. Presbyterian Church
2. Methodist "
3. Baptist "
4. Episcopal "
5. St. Mary's Roman Catholic Church
6. French " "
7. Friends' Church
8. West Street Mission
9. Glens Falls Academy
10. Union School

11. Opera House
12. Post Office
13. Railroad Station
14. American House, Geo. Pardo, Prop
15. Mansion " Sweeny & Lynch, Prop
16. New Hall " James Brown, "
17. Windsor Hotel, J. B. Powell
18. Rockwell House
19. Glens Falls Republican
20. Weekly Messenger

21. Daily & Weekly Times
22. Daily & Weekly Star
23. Finch, Pruyn & Co
24. Glens Falls Paper Mill Co
25. Morgan Lumber Co.
26. Lapham & Co., Grist and Flouring Mill
27. J. L. & S. B. Dix, Machine Shop
28. LaSalle's Carriage Mufy.
29. Joints Lime Works
30. Glens Falls Hub & Spoke Co.

31. Glens Falls Transportation Co.
32. Cashion Brothers Carriage Mufy
33. S. D. Kendrick's Planing & Lumber Mill
34. J. L. Libby's Shirt and Collar Mufy
35. Carriage Mufy., Geo. W. Ferris
36. Sleights Wagon Mufy., South Glens Falls
37. Baptist Church " "
38. Methodis Chapel " "
39. Union School " "

Bridging the Years

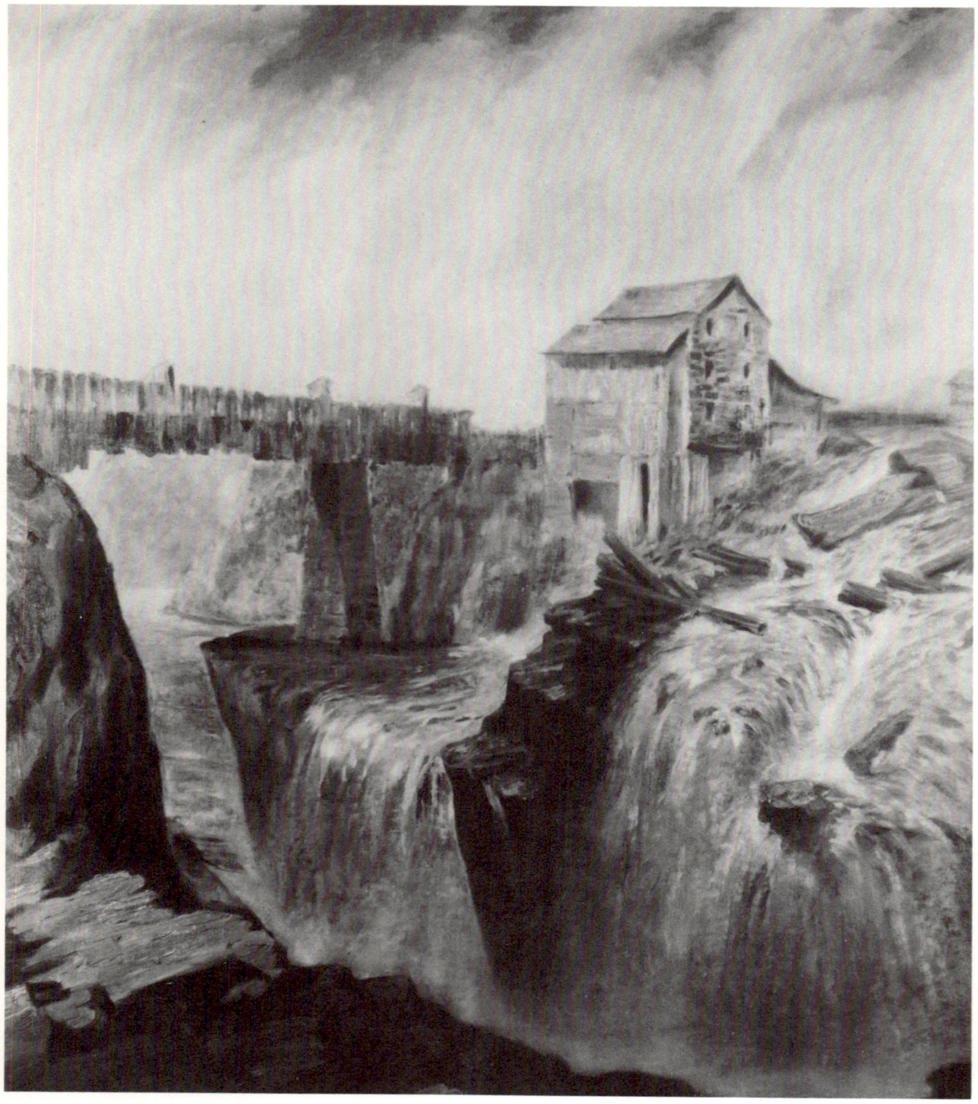

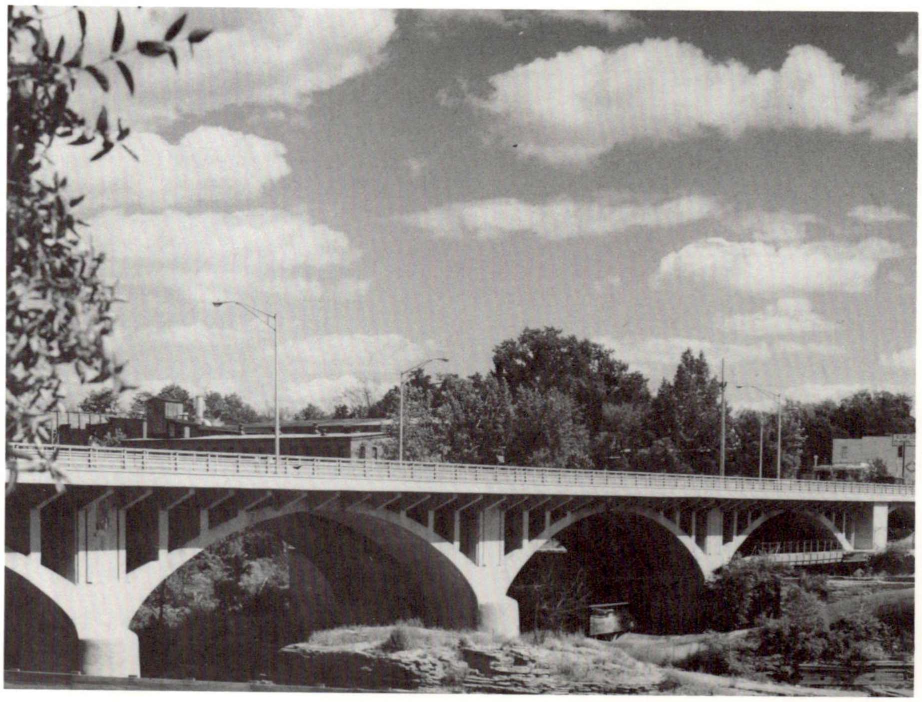

Bridging the Years
Glens Falls, New York
1763-1978

Published by
The Glens Falls Historical Association
in cooperation with
Crandall Library

Bridging the Years

Glens Falls Historical Association

Publications Committee

Robert N. King, Chairman
John D. Austin Jr.
Susan E. Buffington
Arthur S. Fisher
Florence M. King
Elizabeth S. McAndrew
Pauline S. Smith

This edition is dedicated to
FRANCIS X. DEVER, M.D.,
for his many years of service to
the Glens Falls Historical Association

Copyright © 1978 by the Glens Falls Historical Association, 348 Glen Street, Glens Falls, New York. All rights reserved. No part of this publication may be reprinted or reproduced in any form or manner without express permission in writing from the publisher, except for brief quotations embodied in critical reviews or articles.

Printed in the United States of America by Excelsior Printing Company, North Adams, Mass., on paper manufactured in Glens Falls by Finch, Pruyn & Co., Inc. The type used in this book is mainly twelve point Baskerville; the paper is Finch Opaque White Vellum, basis 70; end papers, 100 lb. Uncoated Offset.

First Printing 1978
Second Printing 1979
Third Printing 1980

Contents

	Page
Introduction	11
Our Bridges	23
Under the Hill	47
Downtown	71
All Around the Town	145
Acknowledgments	238
Index	241

"Spirit of Glens Falls" lift-off in City Park July 4, 1977

To the People of Glens Falls

*May their spirit always rise
to meet the challenge of change.*

Part of
the Counties of
Charlotte and Albany.
in
the PROVINCE of
NEW YORK;
being the Seat of War
between the King's Forces
under
Lieut. Gen. Burgoyne
and the Rebel Army.
By Thos. Kitchin Senr.
Hydrographer to his
Majesty.
British Statute Miles 69 to a Degree.
1 2 3 4 6 8 10 12 14 16 18 20
Longitude W. from London.
N.B. Situations uncertain have
a Line drawn under the
Name.
PART OF CHARLOTTE COUNTY
PART OF ALBANY COUNTY
Wilderness Lands
Wilderness Lands of the Crown not yet appropriated
Limits not settled by the Crown
Pt. of NEW ENGLAND
Manour of Ranslaerwick
TICONDEROGA
Mt. Independence
Lake Champlain
LAKE GEORGE
Sugar Hill
Fort George
Fort Anne
Ft. Amherst
Fort Edward
Ft. Miller
Ft. Hardy
Saratoga
Still Water
Scorticoke
Half Moon
Skenectady
ALBANY
Green Bush
Skeensborough
Castletown
Huberton
Bennington
Hosick
Massachusets Fort
Dunmore Lake
Otter R.
Hudsons River
South River
Wood Cr.
Mohawk
Fish Kill
Saratoga L.
Long L.
Round L.
Hosick R.
Mohawk Hill
Wynants Kill
Batten-kill
White Creek
Moses Cr.
Snook Creek
Kayadrossera Cr.
Sacondage River
Scaron Lake
Putnam Creek
Sabbath Day Pt.
Pleasant Pt.
South Bay
Blockhouse
Saw Mill
Falls
Great Falls
Queensbury
Kingsbury
Halfway Cr.
East Br.
South Branch
Bagly Br.
Stoney Cr.
Cohoes Falls
Moon Kill
North Branch
West R.
Black R.
Long Cr.
Road fr. Crown Point to No. 4 or Charlestown 72 m.
Road from Ticonderoga to No. 4 or Charlestown 60 m.

1763 – "Hardly had the sounds of warfare died away, than the pioneer's ax and saw were heard resounding among the yellow pines in this vicinity, as clearings were made and homesteads started."

James A. Holden

Half Way Brook

"The Crossing" of Half Way Brook on the Lake George road from 1755 to 1760, was one of the most important military halting places in North America, being on the direct route from Montreal to Albany, and midway between Fort Edward and Fort William Henry.

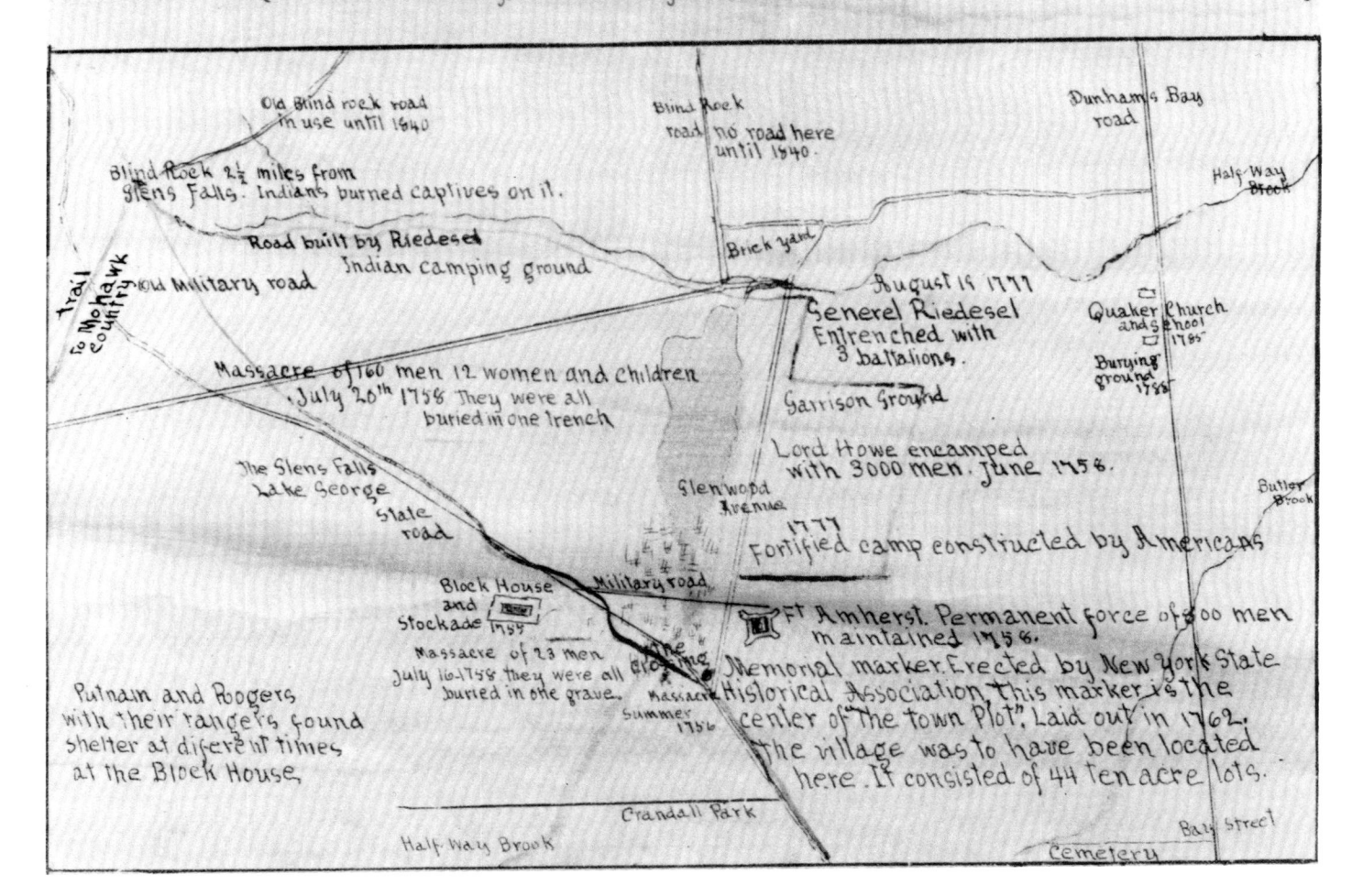

- Old Blind rock road in use until 1840
- Blind Rock road no road here until 1840
- Dunhams Bay road
- Blind Rock 2½ miles from Glens Falls. Indians burned captives on it.
- Half Way Brook
- Road built by Riedesel
- Brick yard
- Trail to Mohawk Country
- Old Military road — Indian camping ground
- August 14 1777 General Riedesel Entrenched with 3 battalions.
- Quaker Church and school 1785
- Massacre of 160 men 12 women and children July 20th 1758. They were all buried in one trench
- Garrison Ground
- Burying ground 1785
- The Glens Falls Lake George State road
- Glenwood Avenue
- Lord Howe encamped with 8000 men. June 1758.
- 1777 Fortified camp constructed by Americans
- Butler Brook
- Block House and Stockade 1754
- Military road
- Ft. Amherst. Permanent force of 300 men maintained 1756.
- Massacre of 23 men July 16, 1758 they were all buried in one grave.
- Massacre Summer 1756
- Memorial marker. Erected by New York State Historical Association. This marker is the center of the "town plot". Laid out in 1762. The village was to have been located here. It consisted of 44 ten acre lots.
- Putnam and Rogers with their rangers found shelter at different times at the Block House.
- Half Way Brook
- Crandall Park
- Bay Street
- Cemetery

The Falls at Glens Falls

Introduction

As our republic begins its third century, the historian has only now begun to examine the small community, its everyday life, its people, for answers to the riddle of America's success.

Glens Falls resembles many such communities in the pattern of its development, yet the facts that intertwine to produce the fabric of history are its very own.

The community focuses on waterfalls in the Hudson River as it flows southward from high in the Adirondacks to the Atlantic. About halfway between the urban centers of New York and Montreal, Glens Falls is also midway between two sites of early military importance: Fort Edward, downriver on the Hudson, and Fort William Henry, at the head of Lake George. Flowing north from the community and eventually into Lake Champlain, the St. Lawrence River and the Atlantic is Halfway Brook.

These waterways played a major role in the French and Indian War (1754-1763) and in the Revolutionary War (1775-1783). The site of the future village of Glens Falls was on a height of land blocking direct water passage between the lakes and the Hudson. Known by Indians as the Great Carrying Place, this site was recognized as important long before the white man established Fort Edward. Ferris Greenslet, man of letters, in his autobiography *Under the Bridge* called it the "bottleneck and hotspot" of the ancient water route from the St. Lawrence River, along Lake Champlain and Lake George, to the Hudson and the sea.

Halfway Brook bisected the fifteen dangerous miles between Fort William Henry and Fort Edward. During the French and Indian War this brook was noted as a halting place and rendezvous for passing troops and convoys of supplies between the two forts. Because its crossing was so familiar to the warring parties, many a bloody ambush, surprise or savage foray took place here.

Thus, military activity dominated the scene before courageous pioneers built the first homes in this great northern wilderness. While Indians maintained no large permanent sites in the immediate area, their presence in the region contributed substantially to a delay in settlement until long after civilized man had established himself in New England and southern New York.

In 1760 a group of Connecticut residents joined in the land-speculation fever that characterized colonial New York by making application for 23,000 acres west of a patent that only recently had been granted to their brethren and called Kingsbury. The application was approved in 1762 and the new town, a part of the empire of King George III of England, was named Queensbury in honor of his bride.

This Connecticut group almost immediately sold its interest in the land to Abraham Wing and fellow Quakers from The Oblong in Dutchess County, New York. Wing, founding father of the community, journeyed here that summer with a surveyor, Zaccheus Towner of New Fairfield, Connecticut, to subdivide the patent. The only permanent resident at that time was a recently mustered out military man, Jeffrey Cowper, who maintained a small way station on Halfway Brook near the present Upper Glen Street crossing.

Between fact and fancy, we gather that this first known resident was not really a community-building pioneer. The war was over and the Halfway blockhouse was being abandoned. Far from being daunted by the area's recent bloody past, the Lieutenant could think of no better place to settle down and enjoy living than near the brook where trout were so plentiful. General Amherst granted Cowper's request for permission to occupy the post, maintain the barracks and other buildings and offer convenience for travelers. So, perhaps as the originator of an Adirondack tradition, he became a caretaker, farmer, fisherman and, on occasion, an innkeeper.

We learn from Abraham Wing's notebook diary that Jeffrey Cowper's first encounter with our shrewd Quaker founder came on August 28, 1762, about the middle of that "showery" day. Wing and his surveyor rode in from the south on the old military road and probably interrupted Cowper cleaning fresh-caught trout for his noon meal. They were "doubtful of some trouble" but explained their expedition and "after a short consideration" Cowper gave them rooms and storage for their supplies. The next day they "set forward early in the morning" and "went to surveying the town plot."

Such activity in the quiet of his angler's paradise must have distressed Cowper, but it was not a permanent invasion. In the original survey, Wing's selection for the Home Plot, or center of town, was the blockhouse area where Halfway Brook crosses the old military road, presently Route 9 to Lake George. This chosen site was ignored, however, when the great falls of the Hudson with its useful water power was recognized as the prime site for development. Surveying and distribution of land followed, and the first log buildings were erected near the river. Cowper was left undisturbed in his blockhouse by the brook. Permanent settlement by the Quakers occurred probably in 1763, and the first town meeting was held May 6, 1766. Abraham Wing was chosen moderator and supervisor.

By the onset of the American Revolution a pioneer outpost had grown around the sawmill and grist mill built by Wing at the falls. Along with the mills, the settlers had built about a dozen log homes and cleared a few rough roads and bridle paths. Where the old military road came in near the top of the hill, now the corner of Warren and Ridge Streets, stood the legendary Wing's Tavern, a log building which was a store as well as an inn and a popular gathering place.

At Wing's Tavern, undoubtedly, lively debates over trouble with the Crown occurred nightly around the log fire, but in 1775 the news of Lexington and Concord must have shocked the group gathered in the evening listening to some member read the account from a weeks-old newspaper.

Hardships far greater than those of pioneer life were faced during the Revolution. Because of their religious beliefs the Quakers did not participate as fighting men, but they suffered repeatedly from military requisitions. With its location between the waterways, the settlement became deeply involved in the conflict. After their homes and mills had twice been ravaged by fire, the settlers withdrew to Dutchess County in 1780. Most returned within three years, and less than a month after official cessation of hostilities the usual town meeting was held.

General George Washington passed through the community during the summer of 1783 on his tour of northern battlefields and fortifications. In the old Glens Falls Insurance Company's collection of area historical scenes J.L.G. Ferris, noted American painter-historian, portrays Washington as stopping at the Halfway Brook for a drink of water. According to Dr. A.W. Holden, writing in 1874, the halt was made not at Halfway Brook but at Butler Brook, "a small affluent of the Halfway Brook, made up of three small streams which have their origin in the swamps and swales west of the village. It was at the upper branch, still a much resorted to watering place, just north of the Warren County fair ground [on Glen Street between Lincoln Avenue and Crandall Park], where General Washington with his staff stopped to drink while on his way to Crown Point in 1783. Walter Briggs, who was at work in an adjoining field, was hailed by the party, and he brought his pail and tin cup and dipped up water for the entire party." The stopping place, then, must have been about where the pond in Crandall Park opposite Lake Avenue now provides a pleasant stopping place for visitors.

Although fires of the Revolution had destroyed more than a decade of progress, the settlers returned to their lands in the spring of 1783 and promptly set about rebuilding homes and mills.

Holden tells us, "The fruits of a permanent peace soon became apparent, and the wilderness border again put on the aspect of culture and thrift. The first clearing (at Glen's Falls) was limited to the hill which rises from the falls, and in the year 1783 presented only a wheat field, with a solitary smoke on its border, and two other dwellings in the vicinity of the forest. These houses were built after the architecture of the first settlers, of a few rough logs, placed one upon another, the interstices filled with straw and a mixture of mud and clay."

In 1784, however, the first frame house was built by Abraham Haviland, a blacksmith, in "the upper part of the village," today's Monument Square area. It stood on what is now Glens Falls National Bank and Trust Company's landscaped corner at Glen and South Streets. This was soon followed by a home modeled after a Massachusetts country house, built by Edward Wing, the founder's younger brother, on the northeast corner of Glen and Bay Streets. Later known as the Sisson place, it was a landmark in the community for over a hundred years until it was torn down in 1888 to make way for a new home for the Glens Falls Insurance Company.

Washington at Halfway Brook
AUGUST 1783   GLENS FALLS, N.Y.

From the Glens Falls Insurance Company Collection of Historical Paintings

The year 1784 also marked a surge of growth that would continue for more than a century and a half. Joining the Quakers were Yankees, many from Connecticut, in a migration that went on unabated until nearly 1850. For many of these sojourners, residence here was temporary as families continued a westward trek, often to the Genesee country of New York or to Michigan. Beginning in the 1840's there was a substantial migration of French-Canadians from Quebec who were attracted by economic opportunities in the industries then developing. A famine and bitter political strife in Ireland resulted in the addition of a large population from the 1850's, many coming as single men and women and later establishing families here. In the late 19th and early 20th centuries a variety of national and ethnic groups further contributed to community growth. Additions to the citizenry for most of the present century have been fewer in number and have generally been associated with corporate relocations or a desire to move here to enjoy the advantages of the Glens Falls region.

Our community has had several names. At first, it was called simply The Corners. Then, in honor of its founder, the settlement became Wing's Falls. In 1788, a transfer of the name of the falls was made to Col. Johannes Glen of Schenectady who owned water rights on the south side of the river. Col. Glen spent some weeks every summer at a cottage near the falls. Quoting Holden again, "Here, if tradition be of any worth, he maintained a state and style of opulence and splendor superior to any in all the vicinity. It was during one of these visitations, that in a convivial moment, it was proposed by him to pay the expenses of a wine supper for the entertainment of a party of mutual friends if Mr. Wing would consent to transfer his claim and title to the name of the falls. Whether the old Quaker pioneer thought the project visionary and impracticable or whatever motive may have actuated him, assent was given, the symposium was held, and the name of Glen's Falls was inaugurated.

"Mr. Glen hastened to Schenectady, and ordered some hand bills printed, announcing the change of name. These were posted in all the

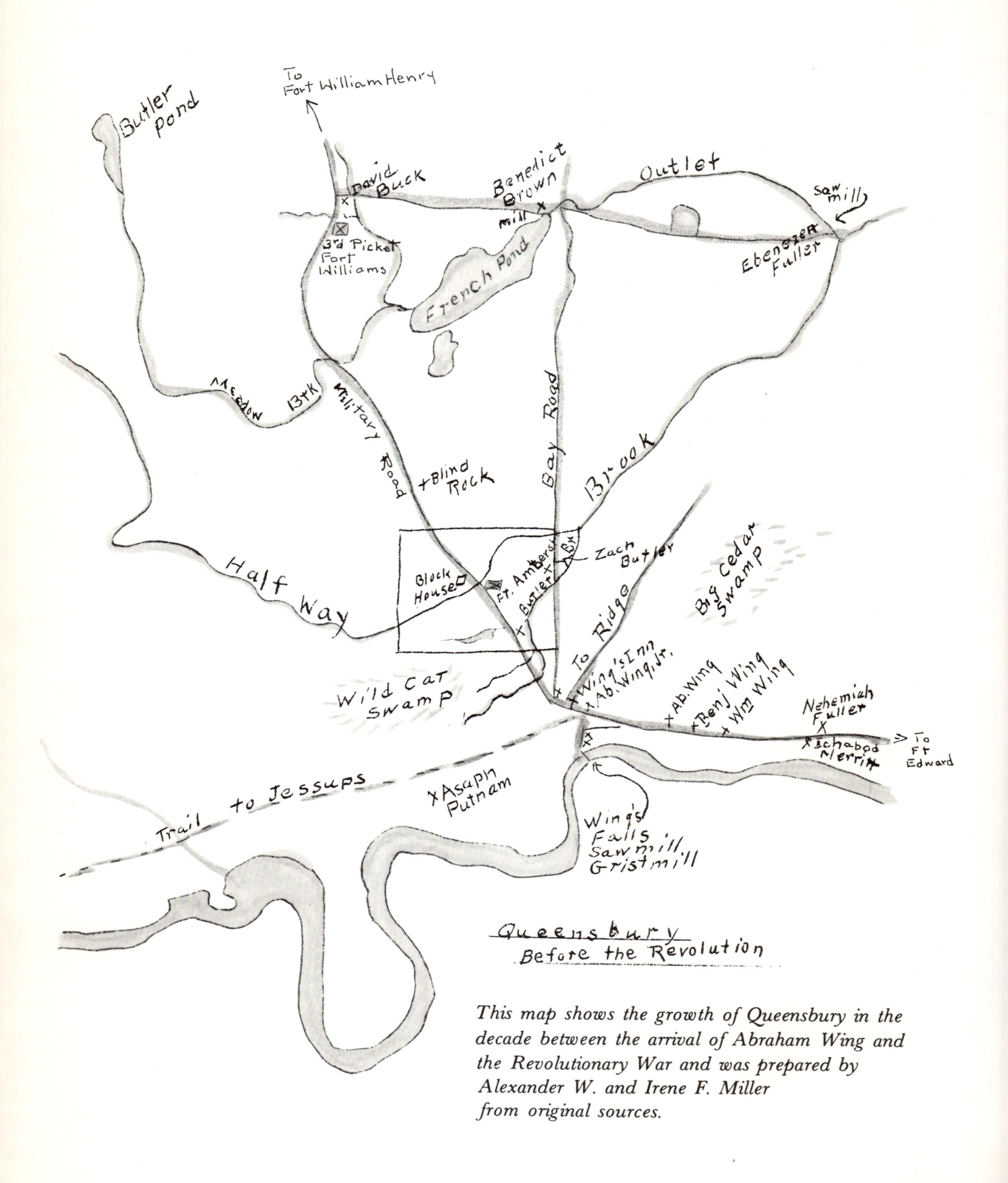

This map shows the growth of Queensbury in the decade between the arrival of Abraham Wing and the Revolutionary War and was prepared by Alexander W. and Irene F. Miller from original sources.

14

taverns, along the highway, and bridle paths from Queensbury to Albany, and the change of name was effected with a promptitude that must have been bewildering to the easy going farmers of the town in those days."

The Indian name for the falls was Chepontuc, meaning "a difficult place to get around." In the 1790's and early 1800's there had been unsuccessful attempts to fasten the name of Pearl Village or Pearlville to the community. Early publications gave it such names as Glenville or simply Glenn's. When a post office was established in 1808, the hamlet was referred to as Glen's Falls. The apostrophe was later dropped.

All of the first settlers farmed at least a portion of their land in order to survive. As the forest was cleared and homesteads established, the community was substantially agricultural until the middle of the 19th century. Many early families achieved prosperity and prestige with successful farming. With an increasing growth of population, however, farms within what is now the city of Glens Falls were subdivided and lots sold for homes. Farms flourished on the outskirts until World War II, but since that time, many of the orchards, woodlots, pastures and cultivated acres have become home developments such as Montray Heights, Cottage Hill, Twicwood, Westland and Rolling Ridge. Today less than half a dozen commercial farms operate in all of Warren County.

Foremost in time and importance, however, was the lumber business which began with Abraham Wing's sawmill at the falls. Other mills soon sprang up, utilizing the water power, not only of the Hudson, but of any small pond or brook which could operate saws. As nearby forests were depleted, and the timber frontier with its sawmills moved farther and farther north, the cost of hauling lumber to big markets from Albany to New York increased. Lack of cheap transportation threatened the growing industry. A crisis faced the struggling village of Glens Falls.

The answer to the problem came in 1822 when construction of the Glens Falls Feeder Canal was approved by the State Legislature. Completion of the canal for navigation in 1832 resulted in an economic boom which buoyed the community into an era of outstanding enterprise. The riches of Adirondack timberlands, as well as other distinctive area products, could now meet competition in metropolitan markets.

In the late 1820's, Abraham Wing III, the pioneer's grandson, foresaw the canal's potential and initiated an Adirondack waterways system of sluices, river drives and booms for floating the logs into the Hudson and thence to sawmills on or near the Feeder. With the resulting river drives, Glens Falls was on its way to becoming the lumber capital of the nation.

This might not have been possible, however, without construction of the Big Boom in 1849. As each spring river drive brought more and more logs down the Hudson, the little spar booms envisioned by Wing were inadequate to hold them until needed by the mills. The high water of every freshet carried logs into the main channel and distributed them along the river banks as far south as Albany. To avoid repeated disaster, mill owners and lumbermen between Fort Edward and Feeder Dam organized the Hudson River Boom Association and built the Big Boom a few miles west of Glens Falls on the big bend of the Hudson. This was a convenient place for holding and sorting the logs belonging to all of the mills along the river. Their annual supply of raw material assured, the sawmills continued to increase production.

The lime industry, second in importance only to that of the lumber business, began in 1832. Deposits of limestone and black marble along the river were extensively quarried, and with low-cost canal transportation readily available, products were shipped to world markets. Glens Falls was noted for the superior quality of its lime, and the black marble was much in demand for its beauty and workability. Gone today is the black marble business, but the limestone deposits continue to be quarried for the manufacture of cement.

Other early industries included the manufacture of mill machinery which began in 1884 and still flourishes in the area. Several shirt, collar and cuff manufacturers located here after an adequate water supply was developed in 1872.

When the souvenir booklet *Glens Falls, New York, "The Empire City"* was published in 1908, the introduction was written by James A. Holden, who later became New York State Historian. His account of local industry was knowledgeable as well as enthusiastic: "For nearly a hundred years Glens Falls has been noted as a manufacturing place. Here are established some of the largest and finest plants of their kind in the world, and it is estimated that from 10,000 to 12,000 hands are employed by the various establishments. The principal industries and manufactures of the city and its environs at the present time are paper, pulp, wallpaper, Portland cement, lime, lumber, collars, cuffs and shirts, ladies' shirt waists, flour, lath, Joubert & White buckboards, lanterns, machinery and foundry products, ale brewing, brick (ordinary and artificial), paper boxes, cigars, confectionery, gold and silver refining, while various minor but in their way no less important enterprises help swell the grand chorus of our prosperity."

Many of these older industries, along with tanning, extraction of potash from ashes, and shingle making, have disappeared. Shirt making has diminished over the years although a few factories remain in operation. Newer to the scene is the manufacture of lace and tricot fabric which provides substantial employment.

While today we hesitate to claim a "grand chorus of prosperity," Glens Falls is still worthy of note as "a manufacturing place." In addition to paper, pulp and cement, industries now providing jobs include the manufacture of chemical pigments; catheters, artificial arteries and other medical devices; accessories for pulp and paper making processes; paperboard building and packaging materials; wooden giftwares; and the conversion of paper for consumer products. Again, "various minor but in their way no less important enterprises," each employing less than 50 workers, add to the local economy.

As manufacturing has adapted to meet changing product requirements, so too has business enterprise expanded.

Many of the pioneers turned to commercial dealings with their fellow citizens. Banks, stores and offices proliferated around the corners of Bank Square and Monument Square in what later became downtown Glens Falls. The Glens Falls Insurance Company, organized by local investors in 1849 as the Glens Falls Dividend Mutual Insurance Company, eventually spread the name of the community worldwide. That company's successor, The Continental Insurance Companies, continues to serve an international clientele.

Some retail business has moved from the downtown area over the last two decades. Shopping centers have been built in Queensbury just north of the city, and the hub of such activity is not far from the very site designated by Abraham Wing for the village center. Inns, taverns and hotels have flourished from the community's inception. More recently tourism has resulted in extensive development of area motels and restaurants.

The settlement at Wing's Falls has been within the jurisdiction of three counties over its history. Originally an outpost of Albany County, it was part of the territory set off in 1772 as Charlotte County, soon renamed Washington. In 1813, Warren County was created from Washington and included Queensbury. In fact, the bounds of the original Town of Queensbury had included all of the territory later set off as Warren County until 1792, when Queensbury was reduced to dimensions not far different from those of today.

Glens Falls has been the hub of Queensbury from earliest days and was incorporated as a village in 1839. Originally about one half of today's size, it was enlarged to present boundaries in 1886. At the end of the 19th century the village was one of the wealthiest and most populated in New York State. A movement for incorporation as a city by legislative act began, and on March 13, 1908 Governor Charles Evans Hughes, a native son, signed the City Charter. When the news was received, whistles in the new city started blowing and people, young and old, raced into the streets waving flags and dancing. One less jubilant result was a drastic loss of population and identification for the Town of Queensbury. By the stroke of a pen that town was reduced to a decentralized rural area nearly surrounding the city. Since World War II, however, commercial sprawl, suburbanization and highway improvements have brought dramatic growth and development for Queensbury.

Over the years transportation improvements have included a series of bridges across the Hudson beginning in 1792, establishment of a street system by deed in 1848 and construction of the Plank Road to Lake George that same year, enactment of a sidewalk requirement in 1851, opening of a railroad connection to Fort Edward in 1869 and to Lake George in 1882, and establishment in 1885 of a local horsecar system, later electrified and extended. The trolleys were converted into a bus system in 1928, but local service was discontinued in the early 1960's. The Floyd Bennett airfield was developed northwest of Glens Falls in 1928 and abandoned in 1946, since the Warren County Airport had been constructed northeast of the city in 1942 as a national defense facility. Perhaps the most significant recent occurrence has been construction of the Adirondack Northway, the Albany-Montreal superhighway passing just west of the city. Opened at the same time in 1961 was Quaker Road, the important east-west bypass named for Queensbury's founders.

Early newspapers answered a growing need for information. The first issue of *The Warren Republican* in 1813 started a succession of weeklies struggling for existence. By 1843 at least two or three were regularly offered area readers. *The Glen's Falls Republican* and *The Glen's Falls Messenger* were two weeklies outstanding for their long records of publication. The first daily newspaper, *The Glens Falls Times,* was established in 1879 and continued publication until February 13, 1971. The only daily newspaper currently published in Glens Falls, *The Post-Star,* was formed by a merger of *The Morning Star* and *The Morning Post* in 1909. Today two commercial radio stations and two cable television firms provide additional news coverage.

Early 1920's – The Big Bend of the Hudson filled with logs.

The Big Boom Area

Since 1960 – The Adirondack Northway crosses the area.

Fire protection has concerned the community for more than a century. The first municipal fire engine was purchased in 1842, and the first hook and ladder company was organized in 1845. The need for a reliable water system was emphasized by a disastrous fire on May 31, 1864, that destroyed 112 buildings, including most of the village center. The construction of the Wilkie Reservoir on the slopes of West Mountain in 1873 and subsequent storage developments have met this need to the present day.

A step toward modernization occurred in 1854 with the introduction of gas and gaslights. Electricity was first generated about 1880 in a sawmill near Feeder Dam. Increased demand for electricity led to the formation of the Hudson River Water Power Company in 1899 and the completion of Spier Falls Dam and hydroelectric station in 1903. Other improvements initiated about this time were a sewer system begun in 1892 and telephone service provided by two competing firms, the Hudson River Telephone Company and New Union Telephone Company.

Religious life of the community began with Quaker meetings in the earliest days. Other religious groups followed: the Presbyterians organized in 1803; Methodists, 1824; Baptists, 1832; Episcopalians, 1840; Catholics, 1849; and French Catholics, 1855. Churches and synagogues of many other faiths have conducted services here over the past century.

Public school education in Glens Falls was accomplished in one and two-room schools until 1881, when a union free district was organized. A school which later became the high school was built in 1884 on the site of the present Glens Falls Junior High, and seven large schools have been constructed by the district since that time. In 1881, the east end of the community chose to maintain its own school on Walnut Street, and today, known as the Abraham Wing School District, is unique in the state as a separate district within the bounds of a city. In 1948 many one-room districts surrounding the city were consolidated into what is now the Queensbury school system. Private schools at both primary and secondary levels have been sponsored since 1803. The most significant of these was the Glens Falls Academy which existed from 1841 to 1937. Parochial education has included two schools still operating today: St. Alphonsus School from 1873 and St. Mary's Academy from 1883. Higher education in the community over the years has been provided by commercial institutes, teacher training courses, nursing schools, a local division of Skidmore College and more recently by University extension courses. Adirondack Community College, operated jointly by Warren and Washington Counties, opened in 1961 at Hudson Falls and in 1967 moved to a permanent campus four miles north of Glens Falls on Bay Road.

Voluntary associations have had their impact on the community from an early day. Undoubtedly the first groups to meet for mutual assistance were church oriented. The women's societies, with their sewing circles, bazaars and lawn socials, helped to finance church and community needs. Since that time numerous service, veterans, youth and senior citizen groups have contributed time and energy to community activities. Today an effective Voluntary Action Center helps coordinate volunteers in nearly 80 local agencies and organizations.

A harbinger of the trade union movement, a Mechanical Association, was meeting in 1813 at John Derby's Hotel, the old Wing's Tavern on the corner of Ridge and Warren Streets. The oldest union in the city is said to have been the cigarmakers, organized in 1883. Other workers later formed locals, including typographical workers, musicians, iron workers, masons, transit employees, papermakers, electrical workers, barbers, plumbers, garment workers and machinists. The Glens Falls Trades and Labor Assembly, an umbrella group, dates from 1901, and a Chamber of Commerce was organized in 1914.

The local militia was organized in 1876 and still functions as an Army National Guard unit, perhaps best remembered as Company K with infantry service in both World Wars.

Fraternal organizations in the locality began with Masonic meetings in 1805. Since that time such groups as Knights of Columbus, Elks, Odd Fellows, Grange and various ethnic lodges have flourished. In 1868 the Citizens Association promoted the county fair in Glens Falls, later the Warren County Agricultural Society. The Billy J. Clark Division of Sons of Temperance organized in 1867, and from the 1880's, the city had two rival women's temperance groups, the Central W.C.T.U. and the Mission W.C.T.U. The Glens Falls Club, an exclusive men's group formed in 1887, disbanded after 1906 with many of the members joining the Elks. The Woman's Club, organized in 1908, later became the Woman's Civic Club. A forerunner of the present Glens Falls Historical Association was the Old Glens Falls Club, founded informally in 1935 by "old timers" researching local history.

Cultural and entertainment facilities, so eagerly sought and so handsomely provided over the years, form a lively portion of our history. As prosperity rewarded many a struggling en-

Around 1900

Glen Street North from Bank Square

July 1954

Monument Square About 1970

terprise, acceptance of hardship gave way to a yearning toward "the pursuit of happiness" and a more gracious way of living. Alexander W. Miller, one thoroughly versed in the lore of the community, writes in the sesquicentennial *History of Warren County:* "By 1860 Glens Falls could point with pride to the accomplishments of the past twenty-one years [since incorporation as a village in 1839]. The population in 1860 was 3,780 and along with the growth in population had come the feeling that a firm foundation had been laid for even better times to come in lumber, lime, leather, transportation, mercantile establishments, banks, churches and schools. During this period and for some time previously a very active organization called the Glens Falls Lyceum existed where the men, and sometimes women, could debate and match their wits and speaking ability. The most responsible men had served the village as trustees and president. The hogs had been penned up, the streets cleaned, some plank sidewalk had been laid, and the trees, set out about 1840, were now of good size and enhanced the appearance of the village."

It was time to enjoy living in Glens Falls. From the early 1830's, when the Glens Falls Thespian Association was formed, theater presentations were popular with area residents. The Lyceum programs, originated before 1860, attracted audiences for many years. Entertainment and cultural highlights of the following years included relocation of the Warren County Fairgrounds here in 1869, opening of the Glens Falls Opera House in 1871, development of the famous Mile Track in 1890, establishment of Crandall Library in 1892, opening of the Empire Theatre in 1899, and expansion of playground and sports facilities at Crandall Park. A French Cornet Band entertained from 1881 to 1883 and was the predecessor of our Glens Falls City Band.

In the early 1900's the Glens Falls Oratorio Society was presenting prestigious works with the assistance of out-of-town artists. Glens Falls Outing Club theatricals started about 1930, and in 1936 today's Glens Falls Operetta Club first performed.

Two more recent developments of cultural stature have brought pleasure and pride to residents of Glens Falls: founding of the renowned Hyde Collection of art in 1952, and of the distinguished Lake George Opera Festival in 1962.

Let it never be supposed, however, that entertainment in our community has always been on a cultural level. Those respectable Victorian citizens who were pleased that Glens Falls "had arrived" perhaps were ignoring another side of village life. Taverns and hotels flourished "under the hill" and a rollicking rowdyism pervaded the "Five Points" area of the west end, particularly when lumberjacks and rivermen came to town.

Glens Falls has nurtured individuals of national prominence. Among them are Governor and Chief Justice Charles Evans Hughes, Governor John A. Dix, Secretary of War Robert P. Patterson, *Atlantic Monthly* editor Ferris Greenslet, telephone scientist Dr. Francis F. Lucas, artists Douglass Crockwell and John Bradshaw Crandell, philanthropist Charles Reed Bishop, who married an Hawaiian princess and became the power behind the throne, and the Rev. Thomas W. Goodspeed, credited with restoring prestige and economic stability to the University of Chicago. Perhaps most prominent of many local benefactors was Henry Crandall, the lumber king who gave his community two parks and a library. During World War II all citizens gained prominence when *Look* magazine designated the city as Hometown, USA.

While much of the lore of Glens Falls is local and self-sufficient, the community has played its part in the nation's conflicts, in the swings of the economic pendulum, in the vagaries of state and national politics. Our hometown has developed from its Quaker infancy as a pioneer sawmill settlement, through its industrial and cultural coming-of-age in the 19th century, to its present maturity as an attractive and enterprising small American city.

Seeking the good life in our distinctive Adirondack foothills setting has been a constantly changing, often rewarding challenge. People have come. People have gone. They have worked. They have played. This photo essay highlights that panorama.

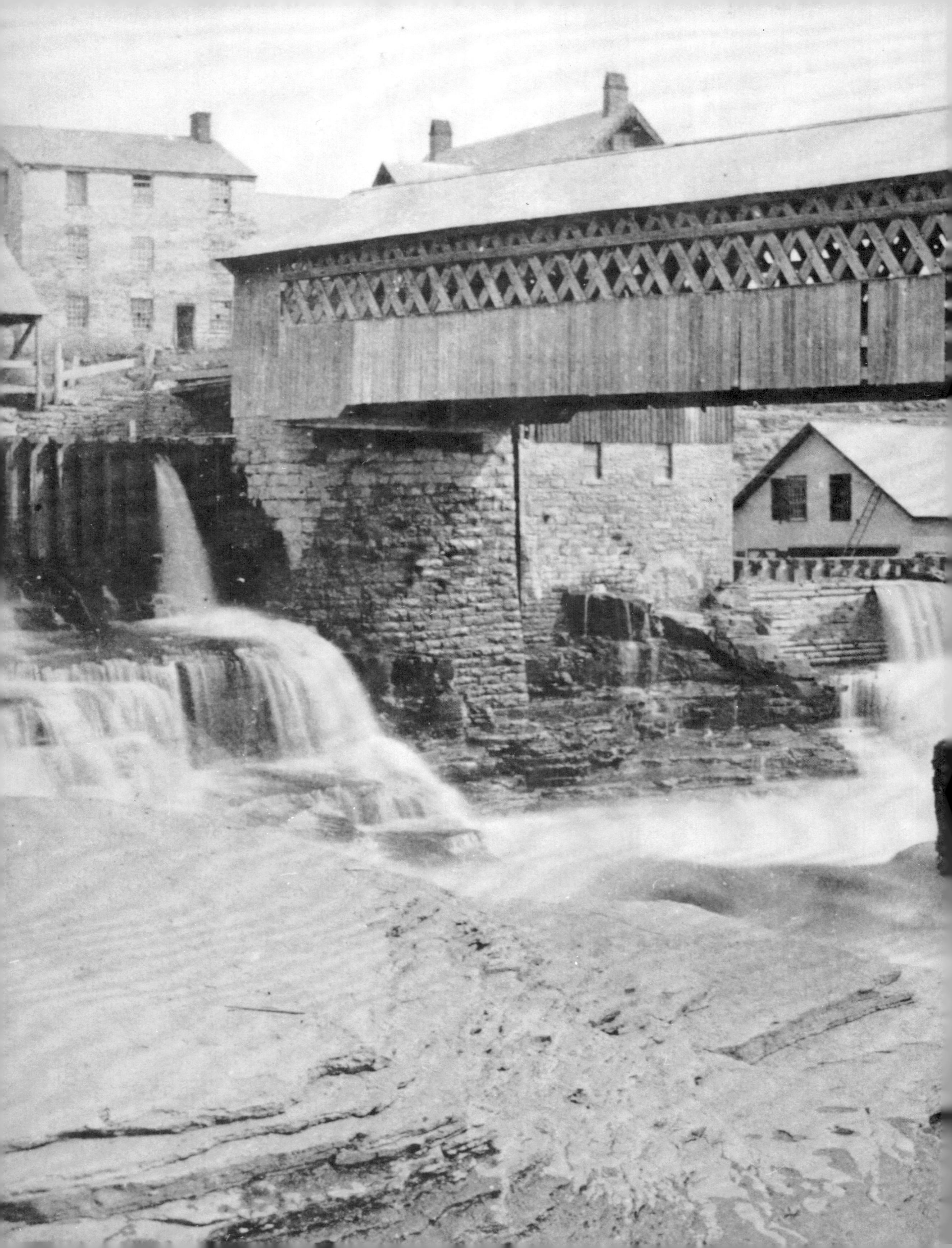

Our Bridges

There were no bright lights in 1763 welcoming travelers to this great northern wilderness. But travelers came, some to settle, some simply to see. We had an attraction... our beautiful and powerful waterfall. Word of its splendor spread, and the lanterns of Wing's Tavern offered warm hospitality.

In the winter of 1780, the Marquis de Chastellux came to see our celebrated falls and recorded in his journal: "Arrived at the height of the cataract it was necessary to quit our sledges, and walk half a mile to the bank of the river. The snow was fifteen inches deep, which rendered this walk rather difficult, and obliged us to proceed in Indian file in order to make a path. Each of us put ourselves alternately at the head of the little column, as the wild geese relieve each other to occupy the summit of the angle they form in their flight. But had our march been still more difficult, the sight of the cataract was an ample recompense."

Increased use of roads called for better bridges, especially the Glens Falls bridge. By 1842 progress had changed the scene considerably. Of his visit to us, historian Francis Parkman wrote: "With an unmitigated temper, I journeyed to Glens Falls, and here my wrath mounted higher yet at the sight of that noble cataract almost concealed under a huge, awkward bridge, thrown directly across it, with the addition of a dam above, and about twenty mills of various kinds. Add to all, that the current was choked by masses of drift logs above and below, and that a dirty village lined the banks of the river on both sides, and some idea may possibly be formed of the way in which New Yorkers have be-devilled Glens."

It is generally acknowledged that Glens Falls has had six bridges crossing the river at the foot of the hill. Actually, there have been seven. Rarely mentioned, a bridge spanned the Hudson from 1913, when the Iron Bridge went out in the flood, until 1915, when the concrete viaduct became passable. Our present bridge is the renovated and modernized structure of that viaduct, our only span to be so improved as to permit continuing use for 63 years to date.

A key to the design of one of our earliest bridges is revealed in a story that Ferris Greenslet's great-aunt Amanda delighted in telling about her grandfather, Abraham Wing. On the morning after the famous wine supper which changed the name of Wing's Falls to Glen's Falls, Wing, "driving down to his stone mill by the river, observed that one track of his sleigh, made just as a light snow of the night before had ceased, was within half an inch of the unguarded edge of the new bridge across the chasm, and how he thereupon took a pledge which was not broken for several months."

In 1788, then, Amanda's morning-after bridge could have been more than string pieces extending from the island to either shore. Improvement followed shortly. In 1792 a bridge capable of supporting the normal weight of traffic was erected. It was carried away by a freshet in 1802. We have no visual record of this span nor of the "normal weight of traffic" it carried in 1792. Our first pictured bridge, the Toll Bridge, was built in 1803 with strict specifications that it be "not less than 16 feet wide, with a strong railing on each side thereof and, built in so substantial and workmanlike manner, as that laden carriages may safely travel thereon."

That traffic "may safely travel thereon" has been the credo of our bridge builders since that time.

The TOLL BRIDGE (1803-1833) saw us grow, not quietly like Thoreau's "corn in the night," but neither with all work and no play.

William Guy Wall, a Dublin artist, made watercolors from which were engraved the twenty aquatints known as the Hudson River Portfolio *published in New York about 1823. Glens Falls is plate 6. Similar views were painted by French artist Jacques-Gerard Milbert and by Alvan Fisher, an American artist.*

According to an 1834 report, "The old toll bridge was six feet nearer the surface of the stream than the present bridge." What parents may not have known, a "daring feat performed when the old bridge was in existence, (that structure being uncovered) was to walk upon the boarded handrail (about five inches wide) from end to end." Dangers of the seething waters are well documented, and stories are myriad. It is said that "An Indian, for a trifling reward, paddled his canoe to the brink of the precipice and then shot like lightning into the gulf to disappear forever." And there's the remarkable escape of a young girl, a member of the family then living in the tollhouse, who was sent out for a pail of water. Dipping her pail into the cataract where it foams over in one unbroken sheet, she was instantly drawn over the brink. Buoyed up by her clothing, she floated down below the mills and was rescued uninjured by men at work there.

James Fenimore Cooper and a party of friends used the Toll Bridge in about 1824, coming "from Saratoga, by the medium of the clumsy old stagecoaches of the day." On that visit he planned details of his novel, *The Last of the Mohicans,* which immortalized our area and brought world-wide fame to Cooper's Cave. In 1933 a ninety-year-old resident remembered the tollhouse and flat rock well: "As a boy I used to go down during the summer and be on the flat rock when the stages would go by from Moreau Station to the Lake. At the time of the writing of *The Last of the Mohicans* a great many people got off the stages and came down to look at the cave and the boys acted as guides. I earned many a ten cents. In my time, about halfway up the ledge on the north side, was the remains of a cedar scrub and we boys used to point it out as what was left of the tree Hawkeye shot the Indian out of."

William Henry Bartlett, English artist and author, journeyed to America four times between 1836 and 1852. He made drawings for the steel engravings which illustrate two volumes of N. P. Willis's American Scenery, *published in 1840 and internationally circulated. This plate,* Bridge at Glens Fall *(sic), is in volume two.*

John Bradshaw Crandell's painting of the bridge. Famous for his Cosmopolitan *magazine cover girls, Crandell constantly sought to depict his ideal of American beauty, the face of a Glens Falls girl he knew in his boyhood.*

People crossing the FREE BRIDGE (1833-1842) probably were unaware that the recently invented camera would soon picture future bridges.

The Free Bridge stood for only nine years and is often mistakenly identified as our first span across the Hudson. Appearing more primitive than artists' versions of the Toll Bridge, Bartlett's approach created a lasting impression. His romanticized drawing so caught Victorian fancy that it was copied in all manner of reproductions. The Queensbury Hotel's original service plates carried a maroon design of the Bartlett bridge. At the Glens Falls Historical Association Museum is a small writing case with a copy of the bridge painted in oil on leather. Mother-of-pearl overlay emphasizes the grandeur of Bartlett's gorge. That this painting truly captured the actual scene is confirmed by reports of early travelers. And even today a watercolor in the Bartlett tradition by native artist John Bradshaw Crandell seemed an apt choice to represent our theme, *Bridging the Years.*

25

Lattice work sides provided light for the interior making the bridge a convenient place to post advertisements and notices. Pedestrians and teamsters formed a captive audience for a sales pitch. The faces of aspiring politicians became familiar and public notices could hardly be missed. These old posters, the billboards of covered bridge days, have become treasured collector's items.

Then came the COVERED BRIDGE (1842-1890) with the roar of gang saws on both sides and stories of lumber barons all around.

A decision to build the Covered Bridge was made in 1839 since repairing the Free Bridge was determined impractical. The old tollhouse on the island, at the upper or west side of the road, was torn down after New York State loaned Warren and Saratoga Counties $2,500 each to complete the work. Moreau spent its share in building the stone work at the south end of the bridge and the arch over the gulf. Warren County awarded a $1,500 contract to construct the span, agreeing to furnish all materials except the round pins for fastening the timbers together. With large sawmills on both sides of the river, the wooden truss bridge was required to support heavy traffic during this period when Glens Falls became the lumber capital of the nation.

"At first there was no pier to support it in the center," it was recalled in 1886 by the son of the man who supervised construction of this substantial bridge. "But we stuck up two white ash poles and put in a crosspiece under the girders to strengthen the bridge. Those poles were carried away twice by high water and the bridge settled down about a foot in the middle. We kept driving over it just the same and finally built the stone pier that now stands on the flat rock. The bridge was lower than it is now. The water used to run down on it and rot the timbers, so we raised it up about a foot." During the flood of 1869 which swept away the Wing Saw Mill, the bridge was chained to the banks and survived the raging torrent.

Framing the mood of the river was a favorite approach for early photographers. Some caught the torrent of spring roaring over the falls while others reflected the repose of summer when water was low.

Indicating the river's working role is this choice photograph, opposite page, upper right, of the old wooden grist mill at the south end of the arch. It was originally built by Cheney and Arms and later occupied by Lapham and Parks until razed in 1906.

The ARCH, a memorable feature from covered bridge days, inspired images.

The arch, internationally known for many years as the trademark of the Glens Falls Insurance Company, was a popular subject for photographers of the day.

The busy traffic of lumber days was adequately supported by the arch, but by 1903 heavy trolley cars had weakened the stone bridgeway, and the arch was condemned. After Moreau authorities built an iron replacement, James Holden lamented a loss of picturesqueness "around which had hung the glamor of romance and the genius of eventful enterprise."

With a beginning even more calamitous than its ending the Iron Bridge may rightly be called the Disaster Bridge.

Tragedy struck on March 15, 1890, during its first weeks of construction. Stringers and framework had been laid from the Moreau side to the central pier. Workmen began tearing away the lattice work of the old bridge so that stringers might be continued to the north side of the river. Trusses placed underneath the floor timbers for support proved inadequate. Workmen had nearly finished cutting the lattice work from the floor timbers and were about to push it over into the gulf beneath when it suddenly toppled over, knocking away the temporary trusses. The whole structure, with its load of human freight, was hurled into the gulf of seething waters below. Two men lost their lives. Five others were injured.

In the violent destruction of the Iron Bridge during the record-making flood of 1913, trusses again were the cause of disaster. Around 1910, in order to support heavy trolley cars, an elaborate underslung system of steel reinforcement had been installed, an incredible error in engineering. When a spar boom below the Big Boom broke, thousands of 13-foot sawlogs were released on the floodtide, swirling and crowding for passage under the bridge. Trapped by a barricade, the logs furiously battered the underpinning, which finally gave way. The bridge crashed into the roaring waters at 9:50 on the evening of March 27. Had there been no trusses, the structure would have survived the flood, for no water touched the floor of the span.

The flood of 1913 caught everyone unaware. Little snow had fallen that winter, but the ground was frozen when it started to rain. It rained for almost a week. There was no place for the quick runoff except the river. Ice above the dam broke up. As James A. Holden recalled, "in the North woods the melting snows and accumulated surface waters swelled the streams more than bank-full, and at last, bursting bounds, the waters came down with a rush in ever swelling volume."

The "ever swelling volume" is evident in records of that week. On March 21, the river was running 16,400 cubic feet per second. It rose and held at 22,000 on March 22 and 23. During the next four days, readings showed 35,500, then 49,000, 62,400 and on to 76,200. It peaked at 84,200 cubic feet per second on March 28.

By March 27, spectators were watching the flood with helpless awe. Trolley car traffic across the bridge was suspended in the morning when a curve in the rails was noticed. Police were stationed at each end to warn pedestrians that they were crossing at their own risk. Throughout the day, as the raging mass of logs increased their onslaught in the rising current, the bridge shook violently. Catastrophe was inevitable.

We lost our bridge but we were fortunate. Newspapers of the day were headlining the floods that swept seven states as the most disastrous in history. While fatalities throughout the flood zone exceeded 4,000, no lives were lost here and we escaped the fire and pestilence desolating many areas. The bridge was our calamity.

The IRON BRIDGE (1890-1913) stood through action-packed years spanning the disastrous panic of '93, the San Francisco earthquake and the first Model T Ford.

At 6:00 p.m., March 27, the log-filled torrent was buckling the trusses.

The boom of its crashing was heard many blocks from the scene of disaster. People knew when the bridge went out.

Next morning, March 28, photographers were everywhere. Stories of personal experience, of inconvenience, and of narrow escapes abounded. A visiting commercial man's description was especially vivid: "A few seconds before the bridge fell, I had crossed over from South Glens Falls and all the way I could feel the swaying of the structure. Hardly had I left the bridge when I heard a creaking noise. Looking backward, I saw the big bridge heave upward in the middle and drop into the river below, taking with it dozens of electric light wires which, when short-circuited, made the place as light as day. Fearing that I might come in contact with some of the fallen wires, I stood still probably for three or four minutes until a watchman with a lantern piloted me to a place of safety."

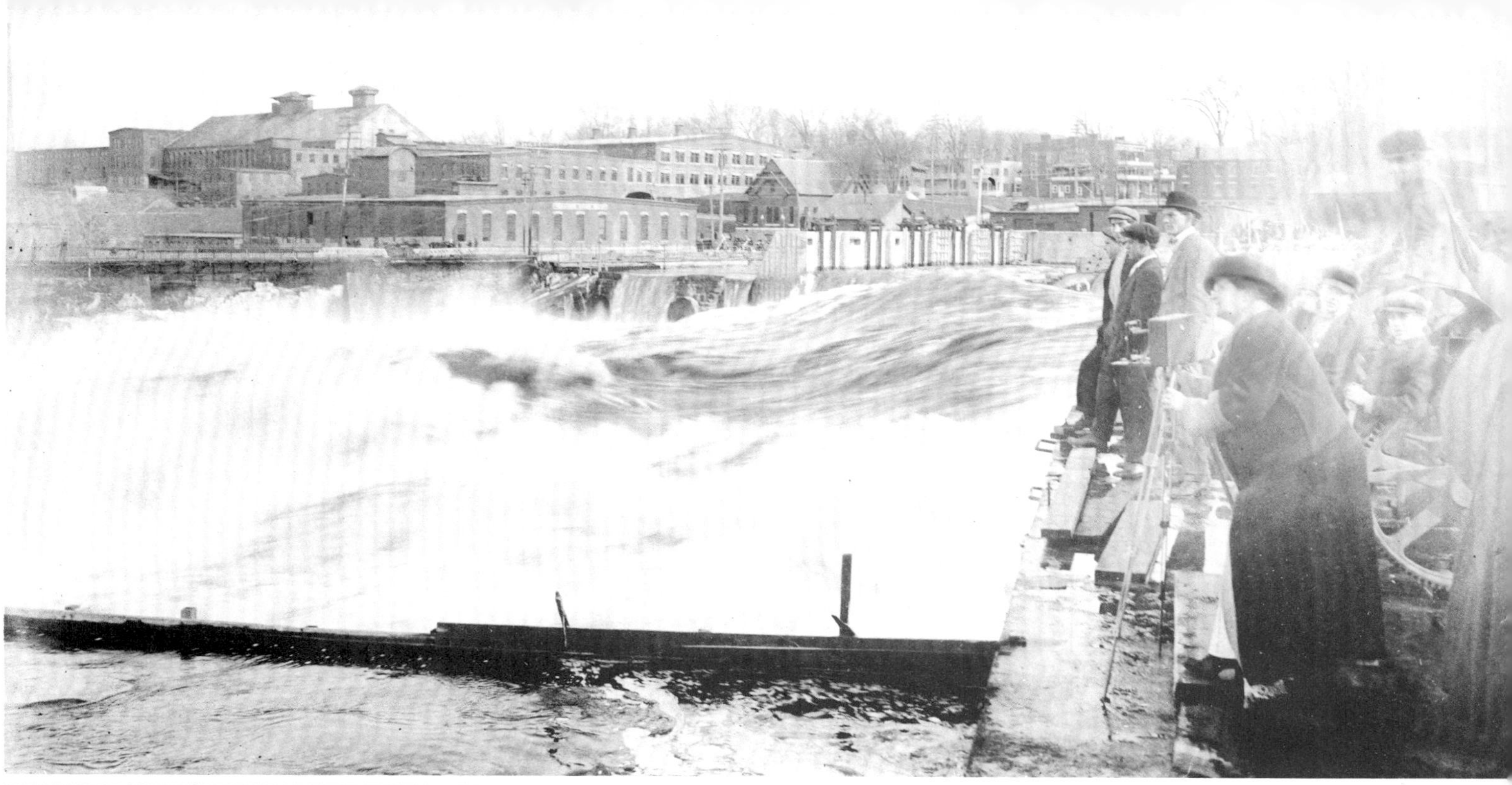

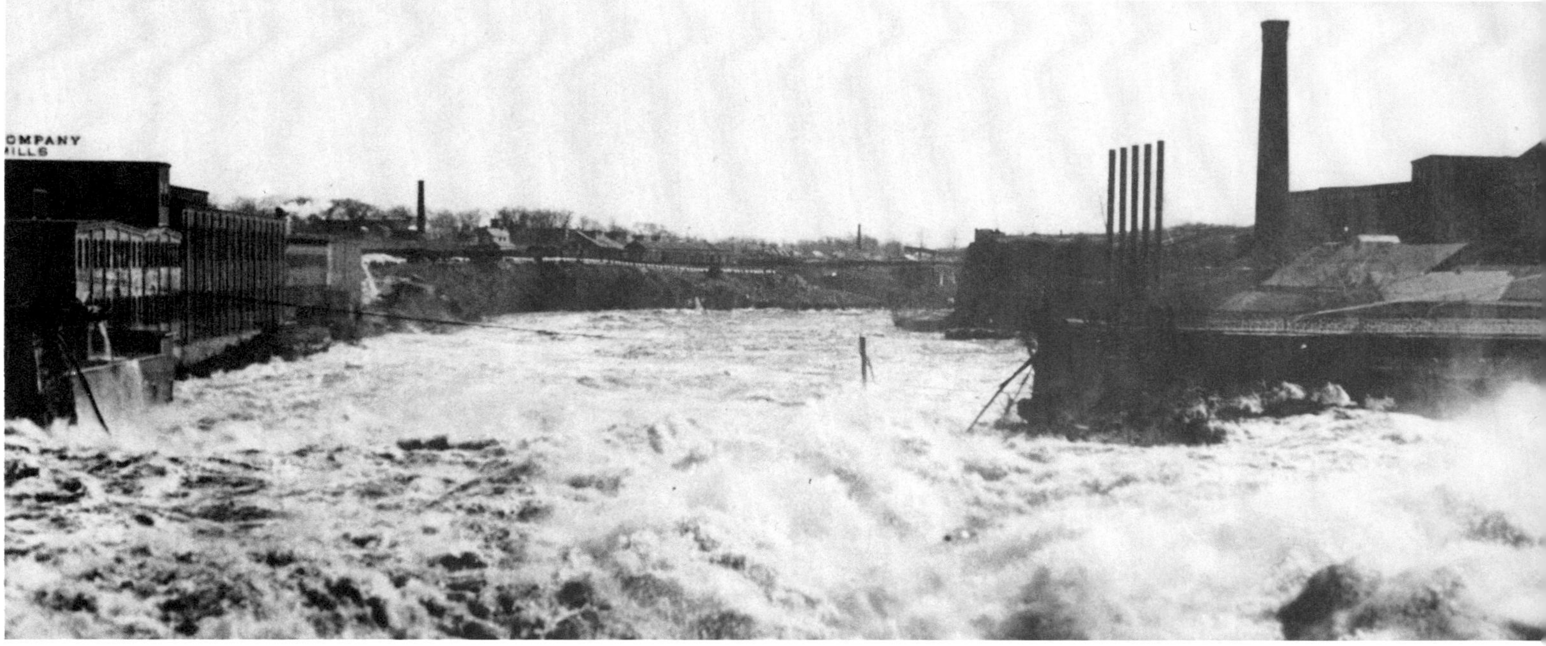
OMPANY
ILLS

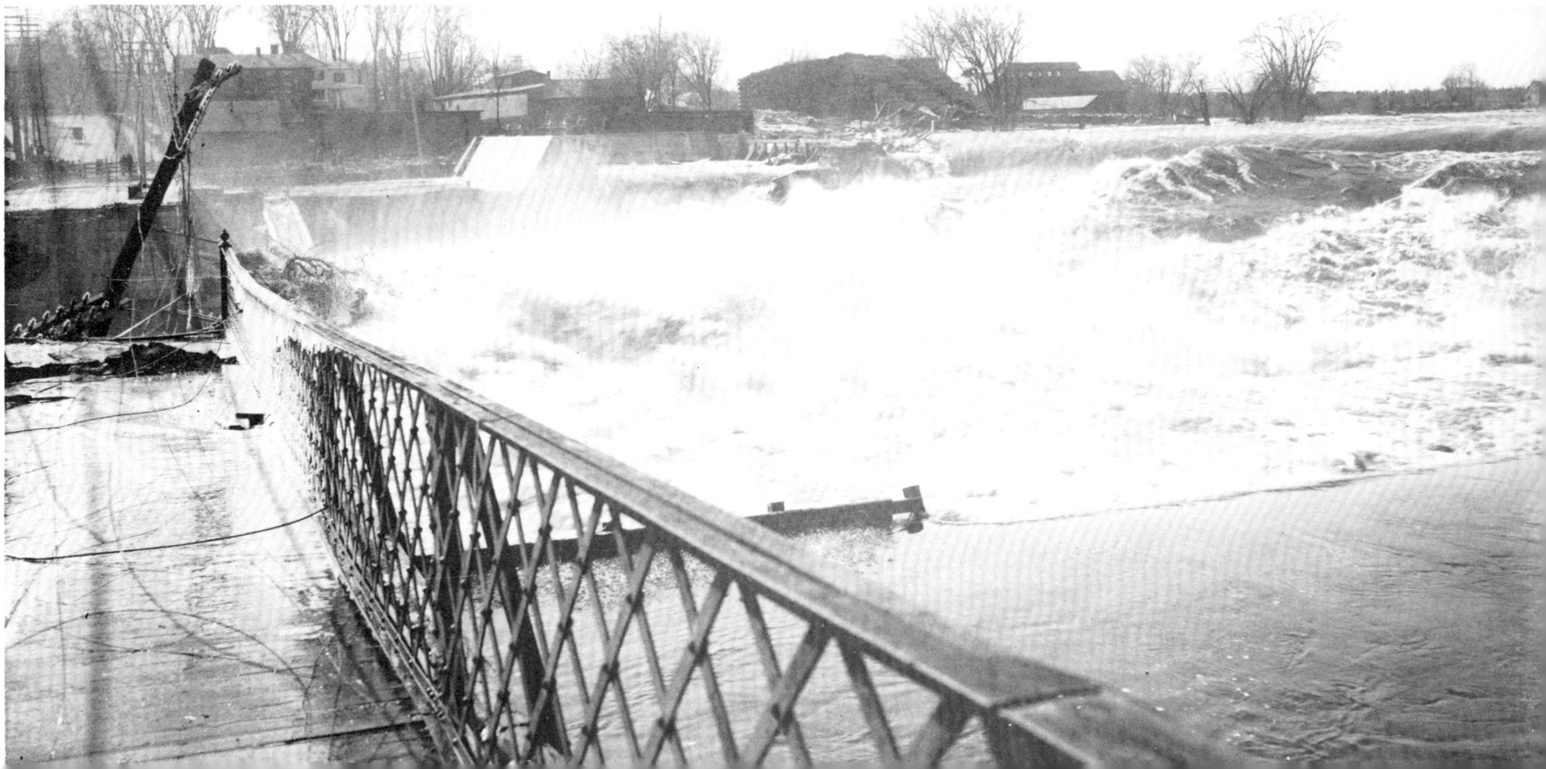

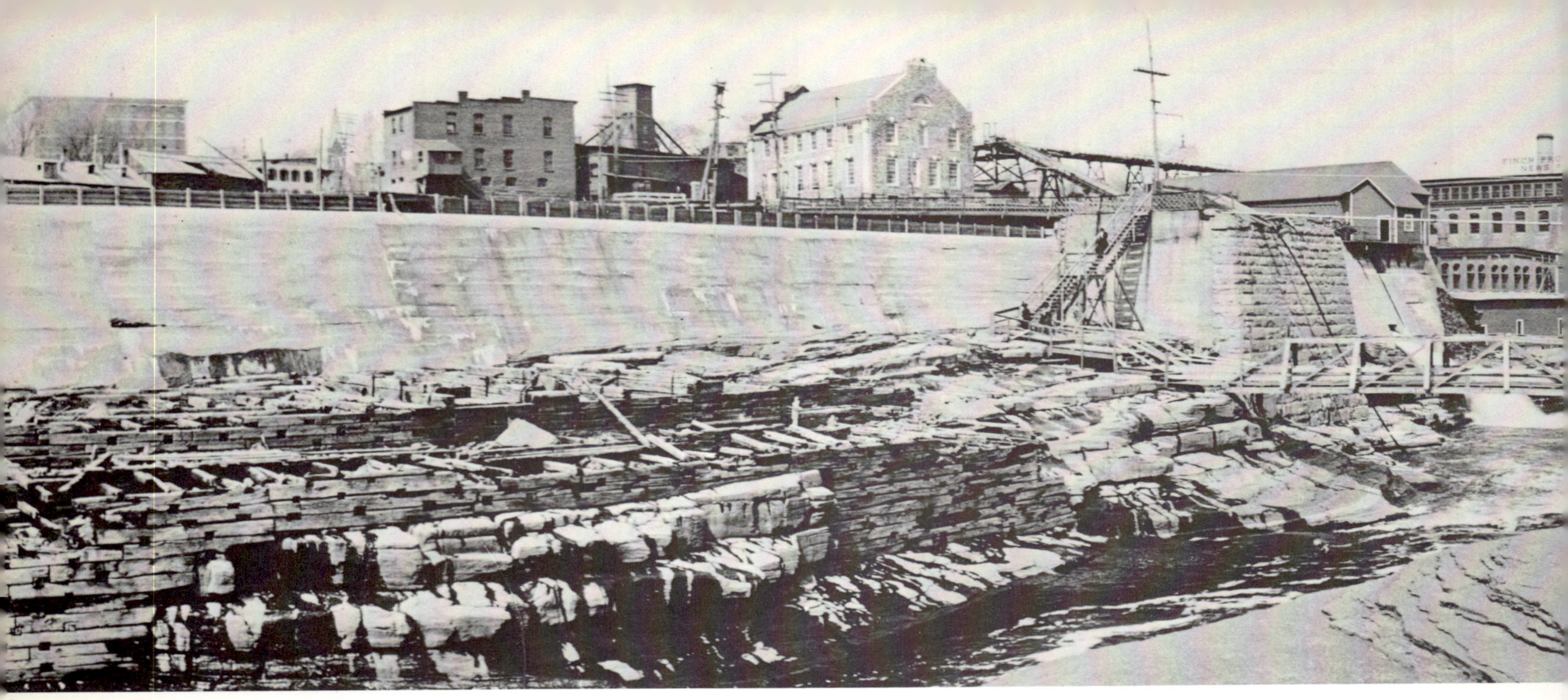

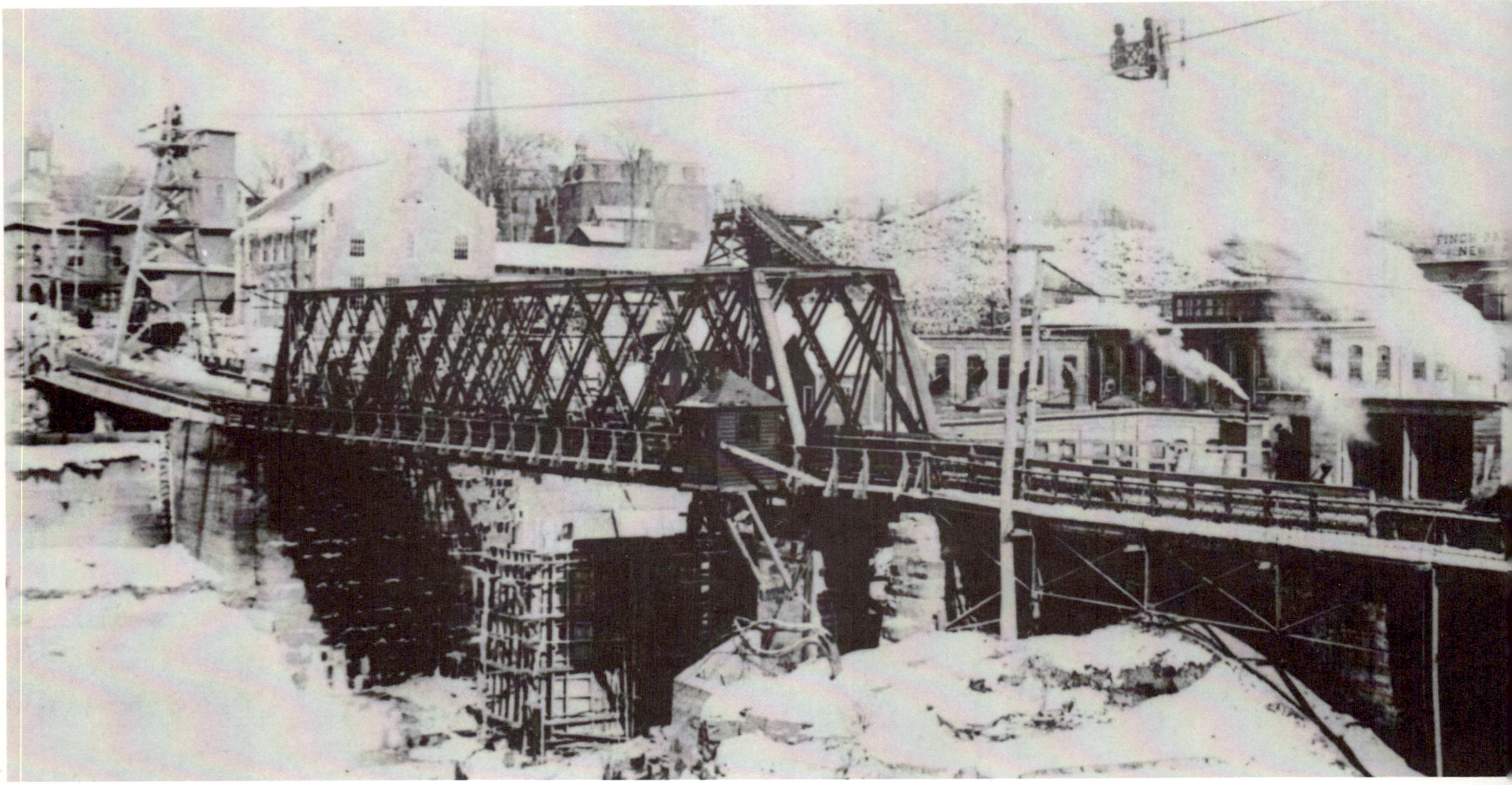

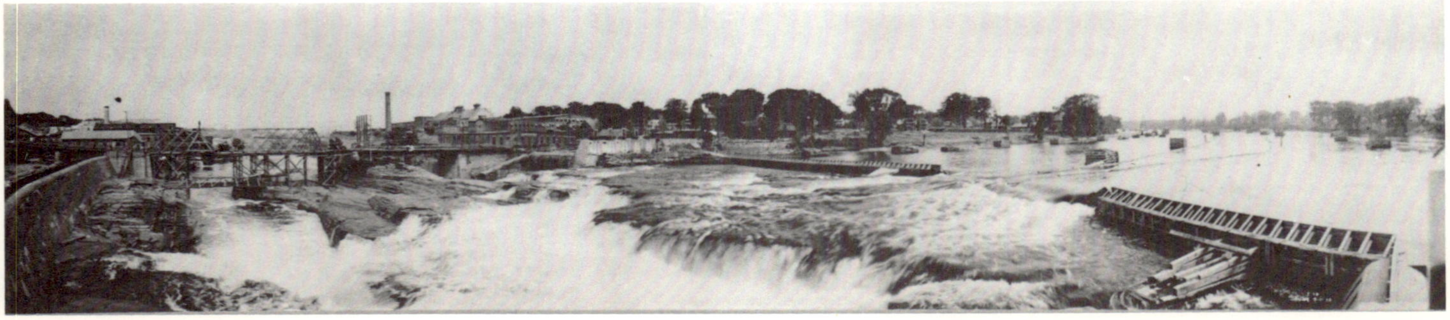

Having no bridge did create problems, but the LOANED BRIDGE (1913-1915) solved them.

Our Loaned Bridge, though an important span, has become almost the Forgotten Bridge. Most accounts give adequate coverage to the footbridge or "catwalk" promptly constructed for pedestrian crossing, but fail to picture the bridge which carried traffic across the river during the two busy years of construction and improvement following the flood.

A railroad bridge, being dismantled at Port Kent, was loaned by the Delaware & Hudson Railroad. It was too narrow to permit trolley cars and other vehicles to pass at the same time so the Hudson Valley Railway maintained watchmen at both ends of the structure to prevent vehicles from entering the bridge while a trolley was crossing. While this bridge was serving as best it could, the old dam of interlocked timbers was used as a coffer and a new concrete dam was built. The dream of many area residents for a beautiful new viaduct was taking shape.

For many years a viaduct had been talked of, and this seeming to be the opportune time, the official boards of the city of Glens Falls and town of Moreau and the counties of Warren and Saratoga decided to build a structure that would be a permanent as well as an attractive approach to the communities on either side. At a special election July 15, the taxpayers of Glens Falls adopted a bond issue of $160,000 by a vote of 322 to 105, one half of the bonds to be paid by the city, the other half by the town of Moreau. On November 19, 1913, the contract for construction of the present concrete bridge was awarded to Callahan and Prescott of Albany for $126,336.50. When finished the final cost was about $150,000.

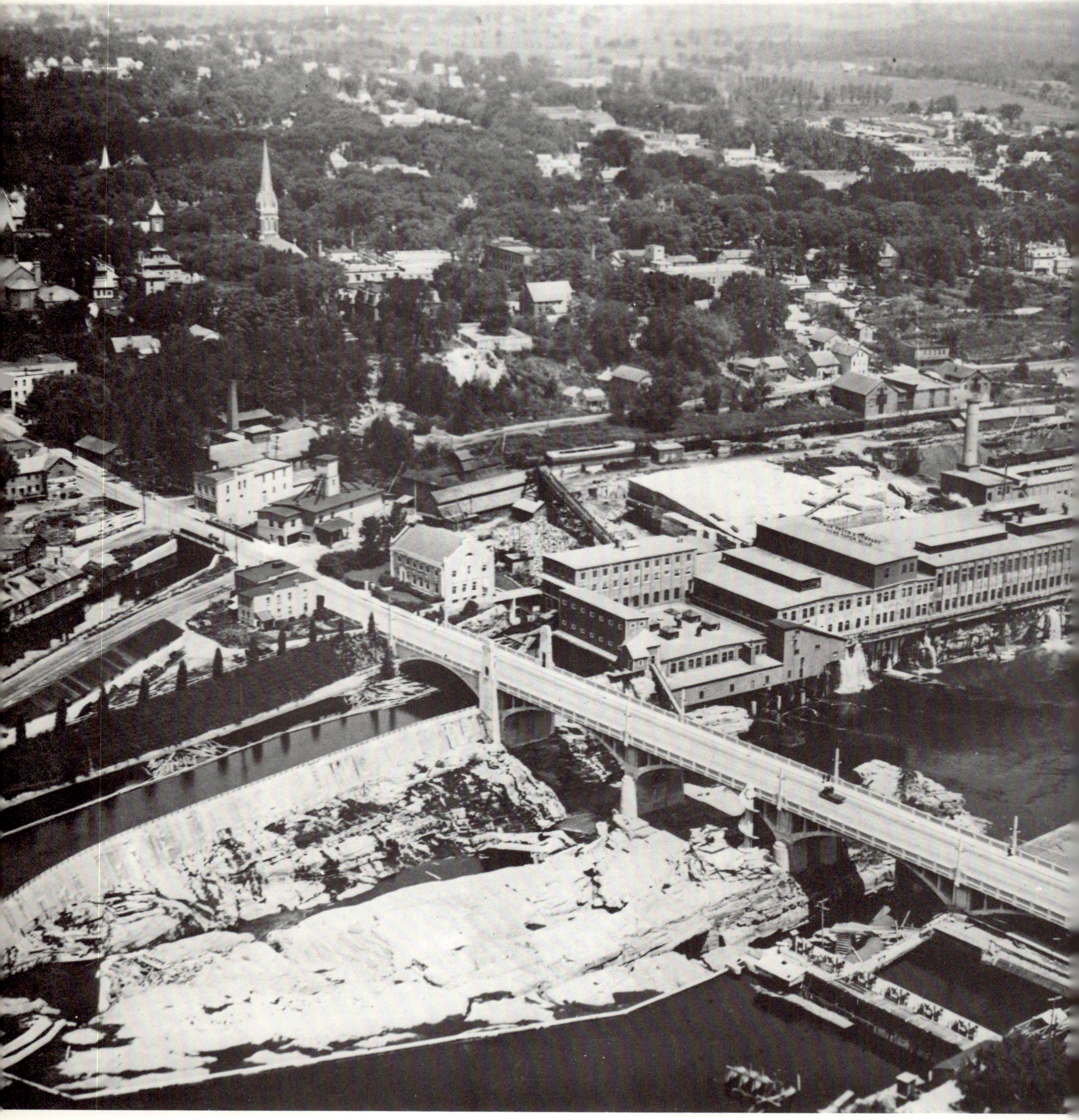

The Queensbury-Moreau VIADUCT (1915-present)... a dream come true...

James A. Holden, writing in 1917, expressed his view: "The entire surroundings of the bridge are now so changed from the writer's boyhood days, that a stranger returning after many years would not know the place.... The greatest change of all, however, is the imposing stone viaduct and bridge now spanning the river and the disappearance on each side of the steep hills which for a century made teaming on both sides difficult and pedestrianism a burden."

From first visions of a viaduct to realization of the dream, many heads and many hands were involved. Accomplishment must have been sweet victory.

... And all the while

The old bridge rested quietly in the river where the flood had carried it. For many years it was plainly visible when the river was low. The main part of the steelwork was retrieved, cut up and sold for scrap. Perhaps our bridge served again, somehow doing its bit in World War II.

This raised-level bridge afforded a changed view looking south. Finch, Pruyn and Company's main office on the east, and housing which replaced old taverns on the west, previously at the approach to the hill, now appeared to be part of the bridge. By 1953 a landscaped parking area for Finch, Pruyn employees, controlled by one of two traffic lights at the foot of the hill, had replaced the dwellings and occupied the old Wing sawmill area.

In 1915 "the most unique concrete spiral stairway in America."

Completed with the Viaduct in 1915, a specially designed stairway near the center pier provided access to the island rocks and Cooper's Cave. Said to be "the most unique concrete spiral stairway in America," it permitted visitors to see the hiding place known around the world from James Fenimore Cooper's *The Last of the Mohicans*. The cave was listed in guide books for many years as a tourist attraction. Mention of Glens Falls on a London street may still elicit the response, "That's where Cooper's Cave is!"

39

Recreating the drama of the cave, this mural by noted American artist Griffith Bailey Coale hangs over the fireplace in the Queensbury Hotel lobby. Hawkeye is portrayed lighting the entrance for Cora, Alice and Major Heyward, for his Mohican friends, Chingachgook and son Uncas, and for the Connecticut singing master, David Gamut, whose habit of breaking into song was helpful in making the enemy believe he was harmlessly demented.

The cave, located in the rocks at the east end of the island under the bridge, has no visitors today. When the bridge was rebuilt in 1961, the crumbling spiral stairway was not replaced, possibly because of liability for dangers of the site. Only a cleft in the surface of the rocks now indicates the cave's position from the bridge.

Upon seeing initials and names inscribed in the rocks by the cave, English traveler, lecturer and voluminous writer J. S. Buckingham was moved to exclaim: "I scarcely remember visiting any place at all remarkable in this country, without finding every accessible space of wall or surface covered with names, initials and dates of visitors . . . as if the parties thought it a wonderful achievement to have journeyed so far from home!"

The legend of Cooper's Cave lives on.

When James Fenimore Cooper stood on the old toll bridge about 1824 and observed the cave in the island rocks below, he visualized an episode for his forthcoming novel, *The Last of the Mohicans*. This book, with its Leatherstocking hero, Hawkeye, became a favorite in this country, was translated into many languages and is today recognized as a cornerstone of American fiction. Glens Falls and its cave became known as the site of this frontier adventure. Thousands have come to see what the cave is really like. In 1961, however, public access to the island rocks was terminated, yet Cooper's Cave remains a legendary landmark, both locally and in literature.

May 1955 – Two traffic lights and an incline at the south end of the canal bridge created an awkward spot at the foot of Glen Street hill which north-south bound traffic could not avoid. Drivers recall that in winter it was almost impossible to get a running start up the slippery hill because of these obstacles.

August 1962 – Only two buildings, from this Glen Street hill scene during rebuilding of the canal bridge, remain standing today: the limestone main office of Finch, Pruyn and Company, far right, and the old brick Finch, Pruyn appliance store between Oakland Avenue and the canal, third building from right.

Our Bridge . . . With A Past . . . A Present . . . And A Future

The dream bridge of 1915 was a traffic nightmare by the early 1940's. Its two lanes could not handle the increasing number of cars and heavy interstate carriers traveling Route 9 between New York and Montreal. Two stoplights at the foot of Glen Street hill, one at Oakland Avenue, another between the canal bridge and viaduct, slowed traffic to a standstill. The Glens Falls bridge was notorious as a bottleneck.

This situation was alleviated somewhat when a section of the Adirondack Northway, west of the city, was opened in 1961. Traffic-flow problems remained, however. Furthermore, the bridge was seriously in need of repairs. In September of that year, a contract for more than one-half million dollars was awarded for full renovation of the span. This work, completed in 1964, provided four traffic lanes, each ten feet wide, and a sidewalk, four and one-half feet wide, on each side for pedestrians. The river bridge was raised, and the canal bridge, about two hundred feet north, was lowered to create a smooth approach to the hill. Traffic still backs up during rush hours, but the modernized viaduct, related to bridges of the past only by its location, answers our present needs. We can only guess at the appearance of future bridges perpetuating this traditional crossing of the Hudson River.

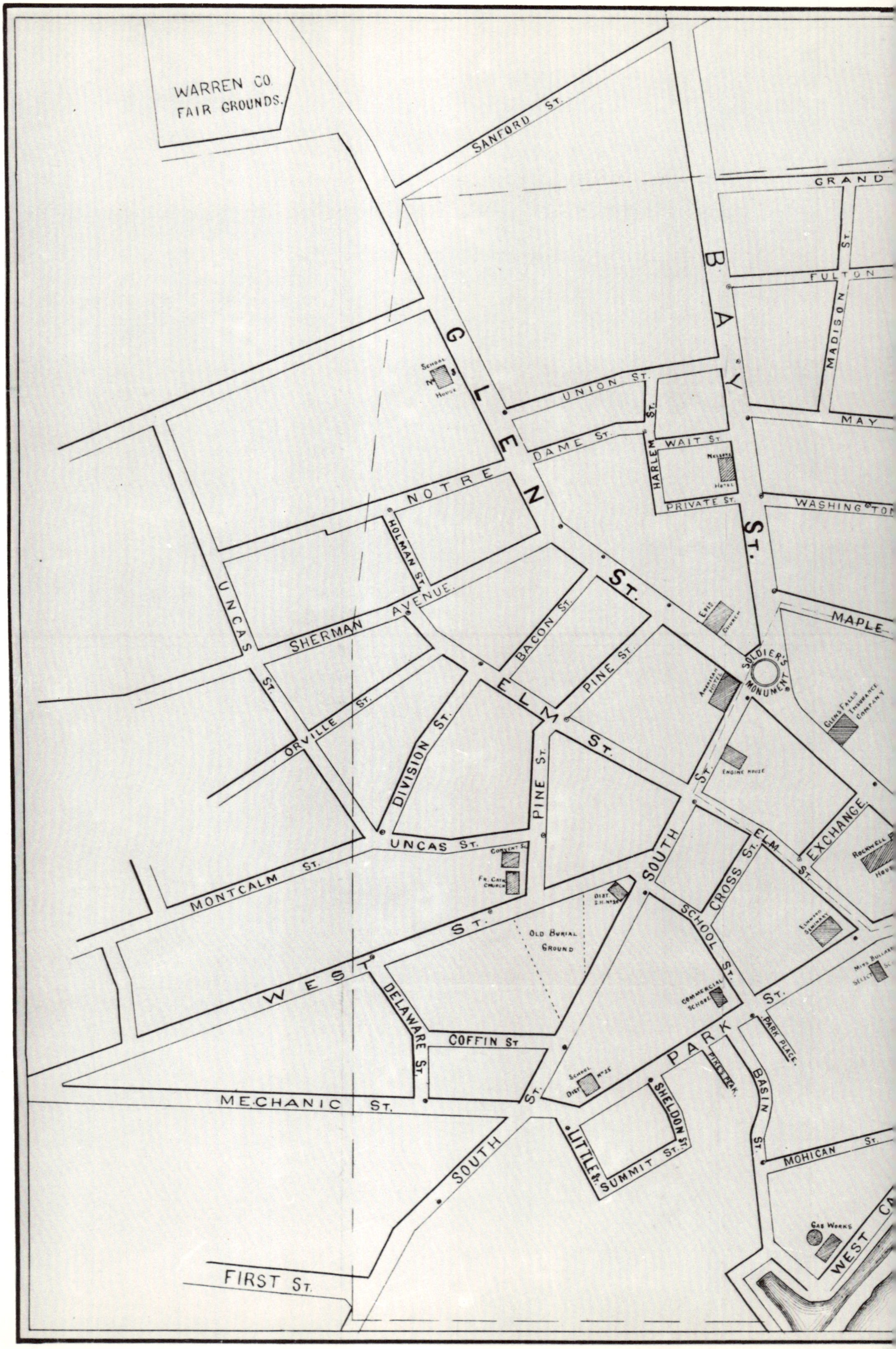
WARREN CO. FAIR GROUNDS.
SANFORD ST.
GRAND
BAY ST.
FULTON
MADISON ST.
UNION ST.
MAY
GLEN ST.
DAME ST.
NOTRE
HARLEM ST.
WAIT ST.
PRIVATE ST.
WASHINGTON
HOLMAN ST.
SHERMAN AVENUE.
UNCAS ST.
BACON ST.
MAPLE
PINE ST.
SOLDIER'S MONUMENT
ELM ST.
ORVILLE ST.
DIVISION ST.
ENGINE HOUSE
EXCHANGE
CROSS ST.
SOUTH ST.
UNCAS ST.
MONTCALM ST.
SCHOOL ST.
OLD BURIAL GROUND
WEST ST.
DELAWARE ST.
COFFIN ST
PARK ST.
PARK PLACE.
BASIN ST.
MECHANIC ST.
SHELDON ST.
LITTLE ST.
SUMMIT ST.
SOUTH ST.
MOHICAN ST.
GAS WORKS
WEST
FIRST ST.

STODDARD & SPENCER'S
MAP OF
GLEN'S FALLS,
N.Y.

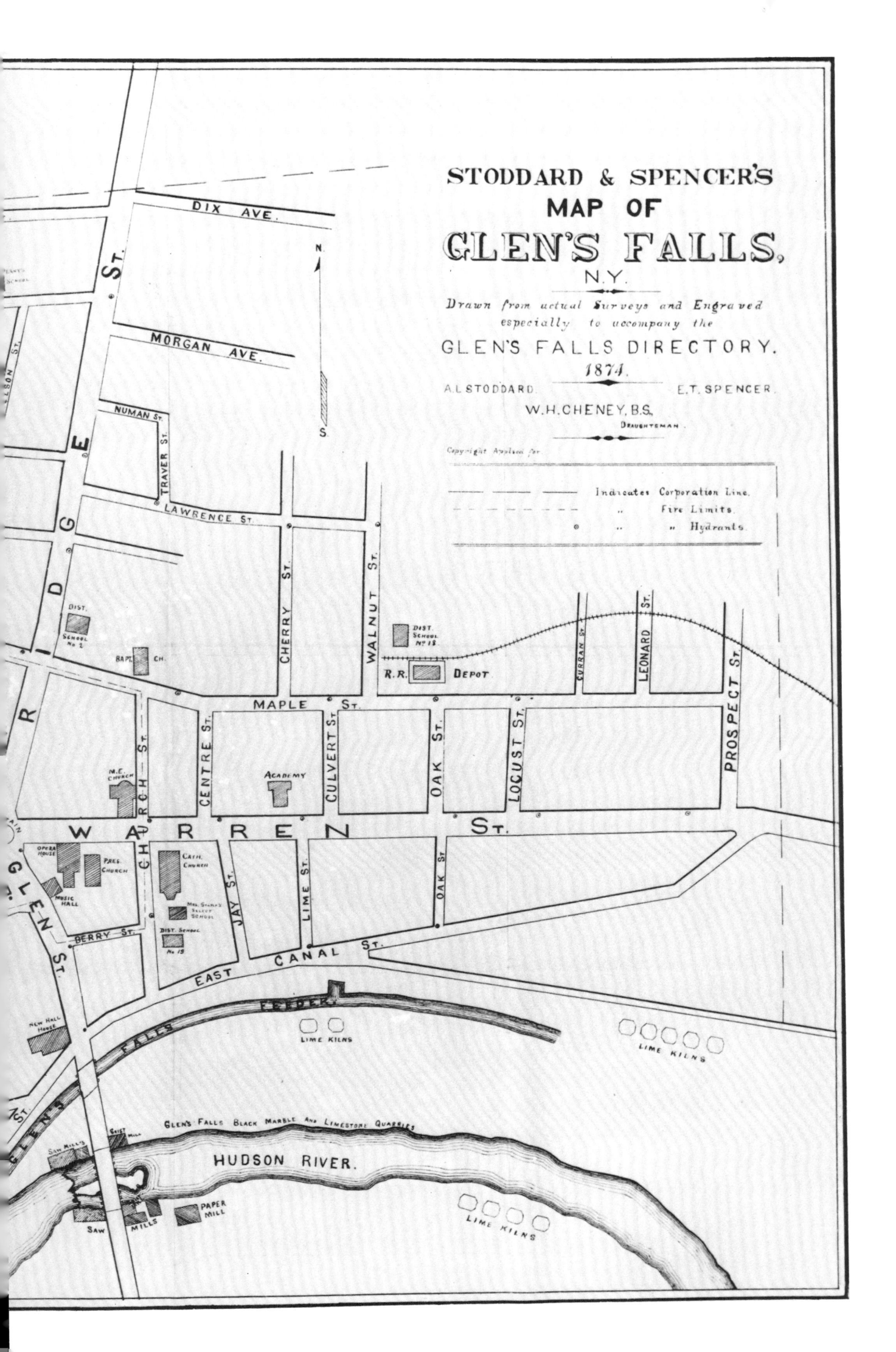

Drawn from actual Surveys and Engraved especially to accompany the

GLEN'S FALLS DIRECTORY.
1874.

A.L. STODDARD. E.T. SPENCER.

W.H. CHENEY, B.S,
Draughtsman.

Copyright Applied for

—————— Indicates Corporation Line.
— — — — " Fire Limits.
∘ " Hydrants.

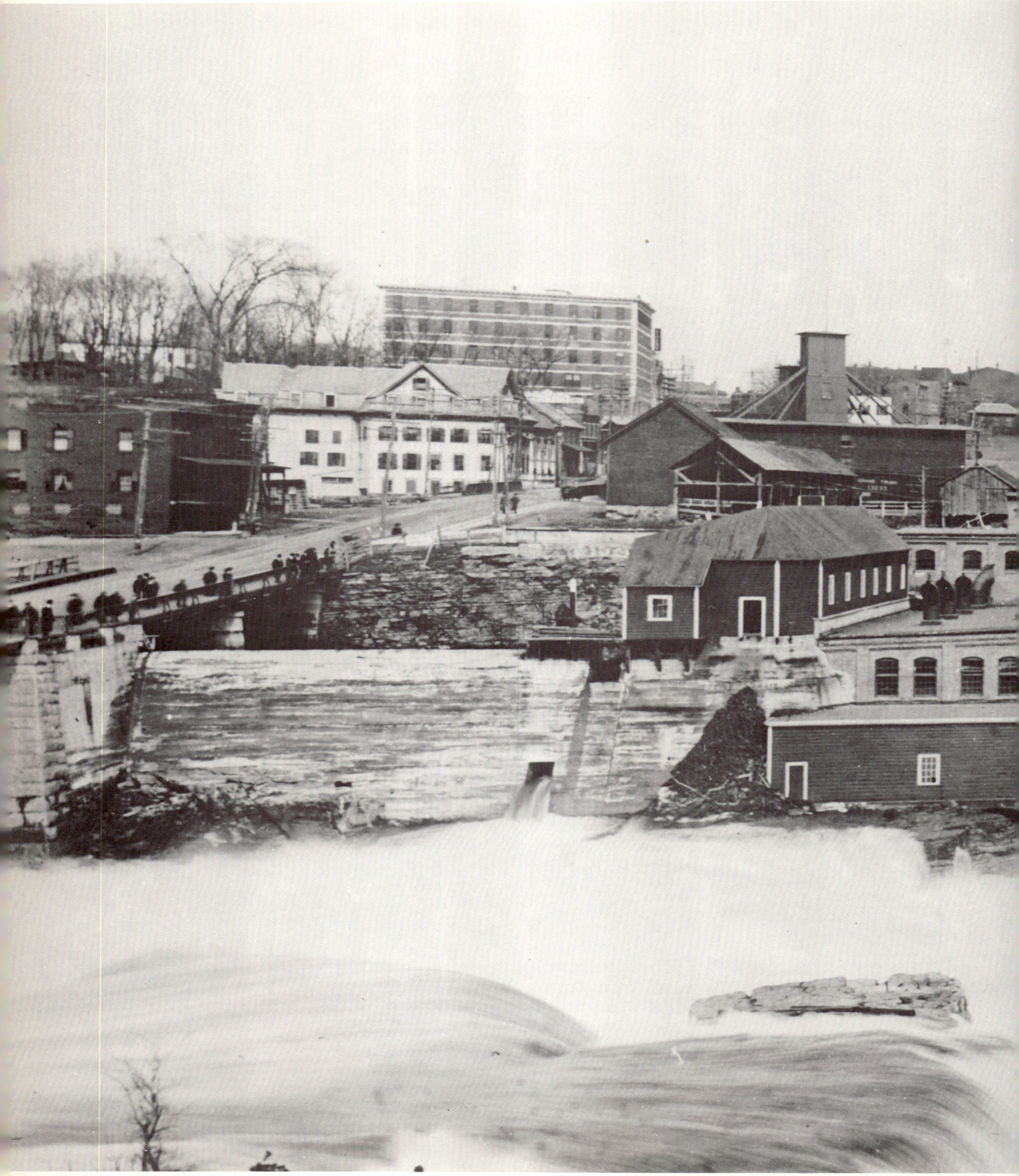

Under the Hill

As our bridges have changed through the years, so, too, has our doorstep "under the hill."

In his later years, the Rev. O. C. Auringer remembered that the portion of Glens Falls "under the hill," from the canal bridge to the river, was the busy part of the village in the 1860's.

Completion of the Feeder Canal for navigation in 1832 transformed Glens Falls from a struggling hamlet to a thriving village. Canal Street, now Oakland Avenue, was a vital thoroughfare. On Glen Street, commercial establishments sprang up between the canal and river bridges.

On the northwest corner of Canal and Glen Streets stood the New Hall House. A large Queen Anne style building with many dormers, it was built in 1861 and later became George Sands' Arlington Hotel. In the 1850's and 1860's several businesses occupied the area now landscaped for Finch, Pruyn parking on the west side of Glen Street south of the canal: the Glen House, a tavern and hotel operated by Ira Green; John Benack's saloon, later Peter La Pointe's; D. J. Linehan's saloon; then the Glens Falls Company sawmill on the bank of the river and, west of it, the Wing mill.

Samuel G. Boyd recalled that on the east side the first building south of the canal was a storehouse owned by the Glens Falls Company. A narrow lane leading to the quarries was next and then the old stone store. A wagon shed, James Hurley's store, a large stone building with a blacksmith shop on the first floor, and the Glens Falls Company's grist mill on the bank of the river all stood in the area now occupied by the main office of Finch, Pruyn and Company, Inc. successor to the Glens Falls Company.

A general store, opened in 1795 by Micajah Pettit, stood in the rear of the site of the old stone store, close by his comfortable home. When the home was torn down in 1874, *The Glens Falls Messenger* noted its demise: "In latter days it has felt the decay of reputation, and has appreciated the lowering and debasing influences which attended a too close proximity to the canal." The article suggested that ". . . the drill-bar and blasting powder will soon commence developing the splendid quarrying ground which lies just under the surface at this spot."

The Pettit home disappeared, and quarrying of choice black marble did, indeed, envelop the site. The Quarries, a term generally applied to the ledges of limestone on the north bank of the river, ran east from the bridge.

Sawmill activity flourished west of the bridge. Upriver at Feeder Dam were the extensive operations founded in 1853 by Col. Zenas Van Dusen, acquired by George W. Freeman in 1884. From the Morgan mills on the south side, a long conveyor crossed the river carrying lumber to the upper side of the canal where it was piled in great square stacks. By 1876 the Finch, Pruyn mill, a combination of the Wing and Glens Falls Company sawmills, extended from the falls to the bridge.

Lumber and lime executives, skilled journeymen in many trades, shopkeepers, tavern owners, canal boat captains and steersmen, rivermen and lumberjacks all participated in making "under the hill" a busy part of town.

French artist Jacques-Gerard Milbert, after spending seven years in America, published in Paris 1828-29 an atlas of fifty-three lithographed plates of Hudson River scenes. Saw Mill at the Village of Glenns *was number twenty-three.*

There was no way to save the Wing Mill in the flood of 1869. As the river's roaring volume increased, photographers recorded its last two days, April 21, next page top, and April 22, bottom, when crowds watched its destruction.

Abraham Wing, according to Holden, in the allotment of the Queensbury Patent "was subsequently granted by the proprietors, as a free gift, a lot of ten acres containing the valuable water privileges on the left bank of the river, in consideration of his erecting a grist mill and saw mill at that point." He carried out his part of this consideration and the Wing Saw Mill and a grist mill were in operation that first year of settlement. Thus the lumber industry, upon which the community would grow, was born "under the hill" by the falls.

Details of the great flood of 1869 which destroyed the Wing mill are found in *The Glens Falls Messenger* April 23 of that year: ". . . the floods came raising the river higher than has ever been known within the memory of the oldest inhabitant . . . Some of the side booms broke and thousands of logs were swept over the falls, and fears were entertained for the safety of the 'big boom.' On Wednesday the middle support of the bridge was carried away and a portion of the stone abutment on this side fell out, endangering the bridge. Timbers were immediately hauled to the place and chained to the bridge, one end resting upon the bank, supported by props, and braces, to save if possible, the main bridge, in case the abutment was carried out. During the day the huge piers above the dam were removed, and yesterday morning the 'bulk-head' above the mills on this side gave way, letting the flood through the mills and street this side, making a deep channel in front of the old stone mill. . . Soon part of the Wing saw-mill went down, and on rushed the mad tide . . . bearing upon its surface the wrecks of buildings and bridges, with logs, lumber, and broken booms, making a grand and awful scene, which was witnessed by large crowds of people."

From *The Glens Falls Messenger*, of October 8, 1869: "Wing's saw mill (destroyed by the April freshet) is rapidly approaching completion, and when finished is intended to be the most perfect of any on the river. A large force of workmen are employed on the inside works and gearing all of which are the latest improvement and the mill is intended to be in running order in about a week."

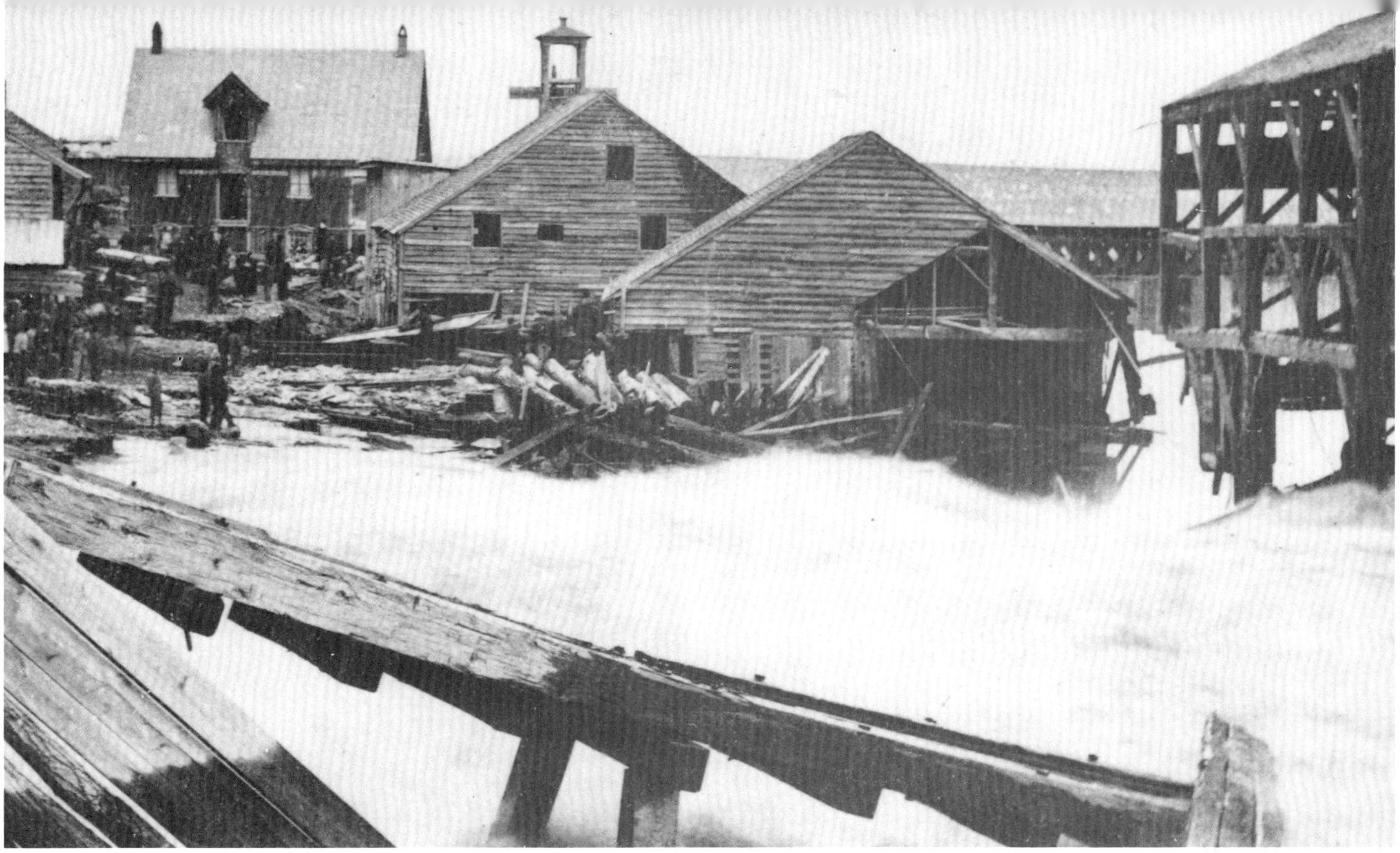

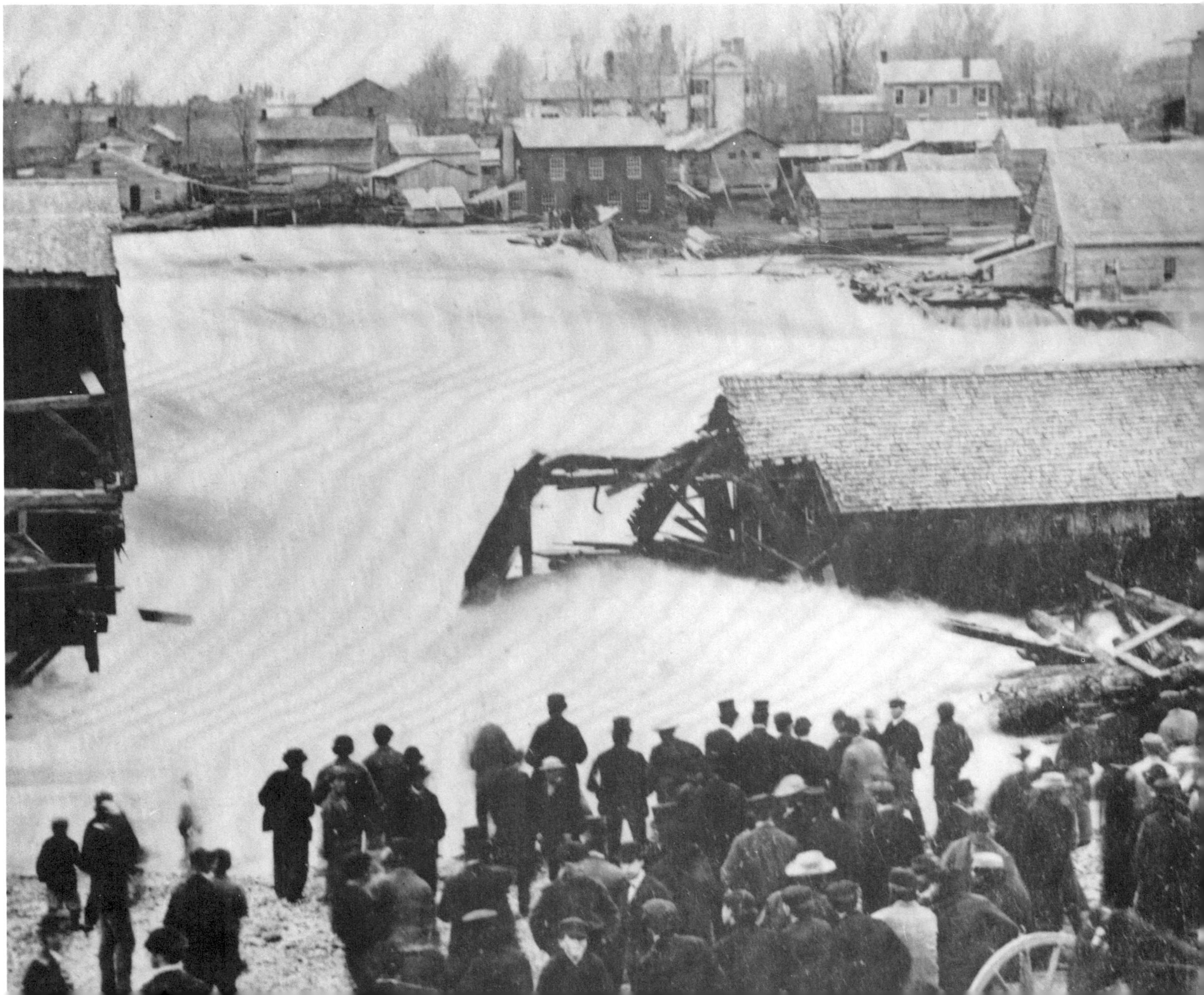

This was drama at the falls sometime after 1911, possibly during the week preceding destruction of the Iron Bridge in the flood of March, 1913.

High water in the mid-1800's boiled under the Covered Bridge. A late 1890's torrent, gushing over the Cooper's Cave rocks, attracted spectators.

Many high waters rushed under our bridges before construction of upriver storage dams. River flow in the flood of '69 may have run as high as 100,000 cubic feet per second, higher than the recorded 84,200 in the flood of 1913. Damage along the banks was not so generally feared as loss of the millions of board feet of prime stock saw-logs held at the Big Boom. Their heaving and rolling against support sections could break the boom and wipe out a year's supply of raw material for sawmills from Feeder Dam to Fort Edward, bringing economic disaster to many. The reverse situation, low water, could cause mill closings and unsanitary conditions in the river.

Flood control problems finally received adequate attention, and the Hudson River Regulating District was created in 1922. Completion of Conklingville Dam in 1930 formed the Sacandaga Reservoir which now regulates the river's flow, preventing floods and assuring year-round power operations.

When water is "jumping the cave," as shown below in 1969, the river is high but nothing compared to previous high waters which, at times, submerged the island rocks. A record flow past Glens Falls since Sacandaga was 42,700 cubic feet per second on January 1, 1949. Manufacturing problems with muddy, debris-laden water are still present, but the threat of flood disaster is all but eliminated.

Broken flashboards on the dam, visible evidence of high-water damage in recent years, result in an untidy appearance of the falls.

51

Feeder Dam, two miles upriver from Glens Falls, was constructed by the state when the Feeder Canal was first dug through as a big ditch in 1824. Carrying water from the Hudson to the Champlain Canal near Sandy Hill (Hudson Falls), the canal's seven miles and thirteen locks were first navigated by a boat in 1830 and were opened to traffic in 1832. Today an improved dam not only holds water for the Feeder but also powers a Niagara Mohawk hydroelectric station where the old Sherman mill operated on the south side. The Van Dusen mills were located at the north end of the dam where the Feeder Canal begins.

Boats tying up for the winter must have vied for this position within a few steps of the Arlington Hotel. Occupants of other boats probably followed the towpath to the nearest part of town for refreshment and stores. Quarters on some of the boats were "fixed up real homey" and wintering aboard was part of canal life. From The Glens Falls Messenger *of April 23, 1858: "The long line of boats that navigate the 'raging canawl' which have tied up by the canal bridge since the close of navigation, have taken up their line of march for the south, loaded with lumber."*

Where the Feeder Canal begins, a community known as Feeder Dam flourished for many years. As the Van Dusen mill grew to extensive proportions, activities there increased. Katharine Cunningham, however, in the delightful book about her grandfather, *William McEchron, 1831-1906, Homely Recollections,* pictures a quiet scene: "The Feeder Dam, a few miles above Glens Falls, had something of the quality of an old-world hamlet. The mill, at the canal's edge, was painted dark red with white trim and wore a substantial, orderly look. The Van Dusen house on the knoll, under its old chestnuts and its one great butternut tree, was homelike and hospitable. Around the turn of the road, in the direction of the sandy, long hill leading towards Goodspeedville [West Glens Falls], were the millhands' cottages . . . From the white porch of the little office, one could often see, on the opposite side of the river, a lighter being loaded with lumber at the mill owned by the Shermans — 'Big Bill and Gus,' as they were called — or, just across the road, in the canal, there might be a canal boat with children at the rail, fishing for 'punkin seeds'."

The Feeder Canal made Glens Falls a part of the great American canal era. Linked with the Champlain Canal, opened in 1823, and the Erie in 1825, this busy waterway "under the hill" started local products on their way to world markets.

The Glens Falls Feeder still delivers water to the Champlain Canal, but canal boats no longer ply its course. An inclined conveyor still crosses the canal at the Glens Falls Portland Cement Company plant, but many years have passed since the John E. Parry *and* W. H. Robbins *loaded cement in its shadow. Railroad and truck competition, offering faster delivery, terminated the Feeder's canal boat traffic.*

The last shipment to be boated from Glens Falls was a load of paper on the Finch, Pruyn boat W. E. Boise, *October 25, 1928. Almost 100 locally owned canal boats have quietly disappeared. Skeletons of several of these worthy vessels lie in the old dry dock west of the Murray Street bridge and may be seen before water fills the Feeder in spring.*

From *The Glens Falls Messenger,* January 28, 1876: "Messrs. Finch, Pruyn & Co. have bought the Wing saw-mill for $40,000. That company now owns all the mills on this side of the river at this place."

Founded in 1865, Finch, Pruyn first purchased the Glens Falls Company's sawmill and lumber business, black marble quarry and mill, grist mill and grain elevator, and an extensive limestone quarrying and marketing operation. A fleet of canal boats was soon added to the enterprises.

The partners, Samuel Pruyn and the Finch brothers, Jeremiah W. and Daniel J., acquired the Wing Mill under precarious circumstances since they had borrowed 75 per cent of the purchase price. Local skeptics regarded them as "young America," over-confident of their ability. After the purchase of this mill, however, additional Finch, Pruyn river drivers joined the growing ranks of lumbermen running the river, and in 1886 the company began buying extensive Adirondack timberlands.

By 1892 Finch, Pruyn and Company was the largest producer of lumber in Glens Falls. Abraham Wing's site by the falls continued to be a major base of area industry.

Samuel Boyd's recollection of the "storehouse owned by the Glens Falls Company" undoubtedly was the old elevator, shown in the background at left, with its radiating grain chutes and tall square cupola prominent in many early photographs. The landmark was vacated by Finch Pruyn Sales in 1973 and restoration possibilities were fully reviewed. Plans were abandoned, however, as estimates for renovation proved too costly to be feasible. In December of 1975 a bulldozer demolished this last vestige of early business between the canal and the river bridges.

54

Black marble was a distinctive product of Glens Falls for many years. The only known commercial source of this product in the country was in quarries "under the hill" east of the bridge.

In a letter from Dr. Holden to his son at school, we have information about these limestone deposits "... of which there are two strata, the upper or gray, which is highly fossiliferous, and averages about from two to four feet in thickness, and the lower or black which ranges about 11 feet in thickness . . . There are two marble saw mills, one on either side of the river, their products forming a very considerable item of our industries and export . . . varying according to commercial demand from $100,000 to $300,000 per annum."

Demand included "huge sawed and squared blocks, for canal locks, foundation walls, etc.; squared slabs polished for ornamental inside work for dwellings and public buildings," such as fireplace mantels, flooring and tile; and "cut stones, for various architectural purposes, such as capitals, friezes, pilasters, plinths, curbing-coping, horse blocks, door steps, window sills, etc."

Glens Falls black marble was internationally recognized for its beauty and workability. A block from the Finch, Pruyn quarry inscribed "New York - Excelsior" may be seen at the 160-foot landing of the stairs leading to the top of the Washington Monument.

Importation of lower priced Belgian and Italian marbles finally terminated local production in 1923. During World War I, however, Finch, Pruyn had again produced large quantities when imports were not available. Black marble is still there but, without a market, quarrying has been eliminated by the company's expanding pulp and paper manufacturing facilities.

Finch, Pruyn's black marble quarry in the late 1800's is shown, top, looking down river from the bridge, and, bottom, north and west toward the bridge and Glen Street. The black marble, a limestone crystalized through eons of heat and pressure, was probably deposited as a muddy sediment in the vast Precambrian ocean, most ancient of the geologic seas that spread over this region. Sediment rich in organic content gave the formation its black color.

The old Jointa Lime Company quarry has been worked for limestone for well over a century and is still supplying marketable material. Today's product is processed in a stone crusher by the canal. This part of the canal is listed in A. W. Holden's names of localities as the "Black Snake: A crooked reach in the Glens Falls Feeder, about one mile from the village, near the Jointa Lime Company's kilns." The canal does indeed follow a sinuous course on its way to Hudson Falls.

The Glens Falls Portland Cement Company occupies both sides of today's quiet canal just a curve or two below the Jointa quarry. An infant industry spawned from Jointa in 1893, the cement company has for many years been quarrying large limestone deposits on the south side of the river. A far cry from the hand labor and wood smoke of lime manufacture is the highly mechanized, pollutant controlled processing of today's product, Glens Falls Portland Cement.

The Glens Falls Lime Co. from 1864 to 1880 operated kilns near Monty's Bridge, about half a mile down the canal from the Jointa quarry. Limestone in chunks was carted to the kilns in heavy wagons and thrown in by hand. Burned bulk lime, taken from the bottom of the kiln, was barreled for shipment. Stoddard & Spencer's 1874 Glen's Falls Directory *notes: "The barreling of the lime is also a large business, as there were required for the 483,000 barrels of last year eight million staves, four million hoops and three million pieces of heading." A cooper was seldom unemployed.*

The lime industry in Glens Falls, second in importance only to that of lumber, flourished for almost a hundred years. As Pittsburgh became the steel foundry of America because of its iron and coal side by side, Glens Falls was in an almost unrivalled economic position with its extremely pure limestone deposits next to huge supplies of waste from the lumber mills to provide abundant and cheap fuel. Glens Falls lime was wood-burned and its producers built their reputation on its superiority over coal-burned lime. Thus when the lumber industry declined and sawmills vanished from the river, the lime industry lost its low-cost character and the burning of lime rapidly declined. Today both industries are legends of the past.

Records show a tantalizing complex of names and partnerships. One partner would sell his holdings and join with others in forming a new company to work new quarries, sometimes only a few hundred yards away. Notes on the subject prepared by J. Thacher Sears, at one time director of Crandall Library, portray one of these personalities: "John Keenan was born in Ireland; in 1809 had migrated to Smiths Basin by way of Canada and had taken work as a farm hand on land not far from the ruins of the old kilns on the Smiths Basin-Adamsville road. On the farm was an old tub kiln used for burning of lime for agricultural and local purposes. Mr. Keenan getting the use of this kiln, with one man as a helper, set to work cutting and drawing wood then quarried the rock and burned it. Then he raised a little money, bought a pair of horses, a wagon and a small canal boat. When he had burned a boat load he took horse, wagon and boat down the canal to Troy and peddled the lime thru the streets. With the money he bought groceries and merchandise and peddled it on the way home. This he continued for several years until in 1841 he had gathered enough resources so that he moved to Glens Falls and with Judge Rosekrans and Eleazar Vaughn as partners started a lime business here. Keenan and Rosekrans soon disagreed however and got into a lawsuit which Mr. Halsey Wing conducted successfully for him. The two men then, John Keenan and Halsey Wing formed a partnership in the lime business. . . ."

From this partnership, in 1851, developed the Jointa Lime Co., by 1880 one of four firms operating 30 kilns with a total capacity of 600,000 barrels of lime a year. The company today produces crushed stone and is one of the oldest names in the Glens Falls business directory.

These may have been kilns of the Sherman Lime Co. which established workings a little further down the river on the south side of the canal near what came to be known as Shermantown.

Adirondack logs, decked on the ice of a winter landing, were cut 13 feet 4 inches or 13 feet 6 inches because much of the prime lumber shipped to the New York market was used for scaffolding which required 6-foot centers with a 6-inch overlap at either end. The 4-inch or 6-inch additional length allowed for trimming, not only the axe kerf, but also bruised and splintered ends damaged in the 60 to 100 mile drive downriver. After winter months of hauling to storage areas, spring breakup signaled starting the run, peak of the year's activity. These dangerous river drives took a daring breed of men to loosen inevitable jams and keep the logs rolling. Many are the stories of tough bull work, tough living conditions and the tough men who did the job.

Some still remember when the Hudson was a working river with its legendary log drives, when that roar coming from the other side of Kettle Mountain meant that spring had come, the ice was going out of the river and the wood had begun to move. Pieter Fosburgh, in his book, *The Natural Thing, The Land and Its Citizens*, wrote of those colorful days:

". . . with thirteen-foot logs, there was always trouble somewhere. The Boreas was bad all the way down. The Hudson was bad at Ord's Falls below Newcomb, bad again just above the mouth of the Indian, and very bad on the big bend below Blue Ledge near Deer Den. Even if the drive got through those spots, it could always hang up on the Moulton Bars at Warrensburg... Every day the work was different. It was an easy day going down Blackwell's because the Hudson there was slow and deep, and each man used to pick a good log and ride it for two or three miles, smoking his pipe. Sometimes he would 'run the wood' from log to log, just to pass the time of day with another driver across the river... Getting logs down to the Big Boom was wild, rip-roaring work from start to finish. The trees were cut in the summer and fall, and then hauled during the winter down to 'rolling banks' on the edge of the river. The teamsters who did this hauling were mighty men. Their reputation depended on the size of the load they could carry and the speed they could make through the woods, and it was common practice for them to go out at night and pour water on the tote road. The next day their sleds, piled ten or twelve feet high, and with the teamster standing on top, would careen through the woods on a bed of ice."

Logs driven under water by the current and then forced back up at a pressure point formed tangled piles of wood to be cleared by Big Boom rivermen with pickaroons, driving Peaveys and cant hooks.

For more than a hundred years, skilled rivermen drove logs from Adirondack timberlands down the Hudson to the Glens Falls Big Boom for delivery to sawmills on or near the Feeder Canal. Before the river drive, as area forests were depleted, sawmills were moved northward to be near new logging operations. As early as 1813, however, the Fox brothers, pioneer lumbermen of Warren County, conceived the plan of driving logs to the mill instead of moving the mill to the logs. After a system of utilizing upper Hudson waterways with dams, sluice-ways, river drives and booms was devised by Abraham Wing III in the late 1820's, the increased number of logs coming down the river necessitated a massive holding area. The Glens Falls Big Boom was built in 1849 to control the flow of logs into sorting gaps for distribution to mills according to the owner's logmark. As soon as these owners were assured an annual supply of raw material, the sawmills expanded rapidly. With the Feeder Canal providing profitable transport, Glens Falls became a lumber capital and significantly helped New York State's lumber production to lead the nation from 1852 to 1860. A wall-to-wall carpeting of prime saw logs around the Big Bend was not an unusual sight in those days.

Rivermen met at the Big Boom shanty to pick up tools for their day's work of moving logs down to the boom for controlled release. Every log was identified by its owner's log mark, stamped with a marking hammer on the ends of his logs while piled in the woods. Some lumbermen stamped their logs several times so one mark could always be seen as it floated past a sorter.

The Big Boom was a floating barricade composed of sections built with heavy timbers bolted together and joined with four-inch-link chains. Control chains stretched from shore piers to the boom, which was anchored with heavier chains to huge piers placed diagonally and at frequent intervals across the river at the Big Bend of the Hudson above Glens Falls. Large breakers upriver protected the boom from pressure of the masses of logs being held.

A floating sawmill and a floating bridge were part of river drive days. Finch, Pruyn's first steam sawmill was a floating mill which was horse drawn up the Feeder Canal from the Murray Street dry dock, locked through at Feeder Dam and anchored off the east end of the big island above the dam. Two piers, to which the mill was attached, also provided a corral boom which held damaged wood sent down from the trash boom for salvage. A channel formed by the piers was used for loading lighters, or barges. Anything good enough for a 2-foot pulpwood stick was sawed and loaded for canal delivery to the paper mill wood yard. Other lighters were loaded with odds and ends good only for burning in the lime kilns or in the old steam boiler at the paper mill. This discard wood was also used to "keep up steam" on the floating sawmill.

The floating bridge provided means of guiding lighters, carrying wood to be used in making lath, to Feeder Dam sawmill on the south shore. Men with pike poles kept the lighters on course crossing the river. This walkway on floats formed a rough triangle extending upriver from Feeder Dam lock to a suspension bridge in the center and then back downriver to the mill at the south end of the dam. The suspension section was high enough to permit passage of logs which went over the dam into booms for company owners. Quite a bit of water separated the walkway from the island so the floating sawmill could not be reached by the floating bridge. Pedestrians crossing from the north to south shores could barely pass on the narrow plank walk which became very slippery when wet.

Sorters were responsible for poling called-out logs into the proper channel for the owners. Rivermen had their own names for log marks such as crow's foot, double O, wine cup or deer's foot according to some fancied resemblance. The calling of these names must have been a familiar river chant. Broken wood in the foreground was channeled to the trash boom for salvage.

A full river at the Big Boom is now folklore but in 1872, when some 60 companies were driving the river, over 200 million separate logs or "pieces" rode the waters around the Big Bend. The colorful river drive ended in 1950 when it became more economical and dependable to transport pulpwood with trucks. Finch, Pruyn was the last company to drive the Hudson and ran alone from 1924 to 1950. The last log drive in the continental United States was on Maine's Kennebec River in 1976. Environmentalists declared that bark settling on the bottom of the river caused pollution and fish kills and that massed logs interfered with navigation rights of boaters and canoeists. Canoes, not logs, now run the Hudson every May in the White Water Derby at North Creek.

Downriver between the Big Boom and Feeder Dam was the junction boom where logs were channeled into sorting gaps and held until needed by the owner.

Glens Falls has reminders of its lusty early days when lumberjacks and rivermen came to town and fortunes were made in lumber. Old log marks commemorate this heritage: the Crandall "Star" atop the obelisk in Crandall Park is visible to visitors from the north, and entrance from the south is greeted by the Finch, Pruyn pound sterling "Dot L" weathervane. The creaking of chains and the crunching of wood at the Big Boom are sounds of yesterday. Today we have only the tales that are told.

Few river drive landmarks remain. Upriver, old piers show when the water is low. Downriver, in back of the Hercules plant on Lower Warren Street, little square islands have grown from piers of the guide boom for logs going to Union Bag near Fenimore Bridge in Hudson Falls.

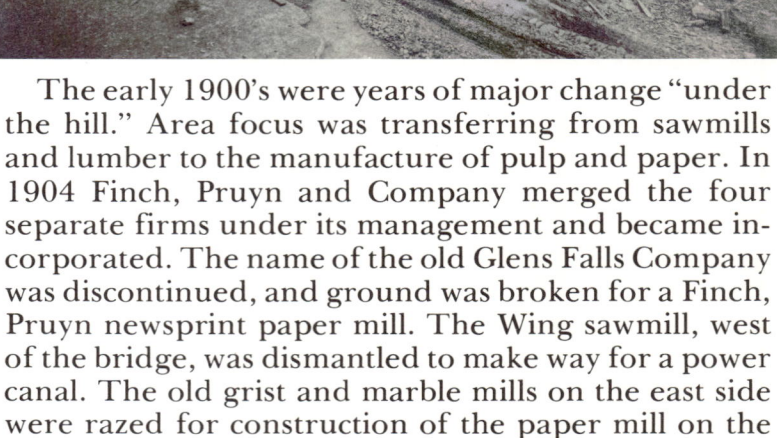

Between 1915 and 1923 canal boats still loaded lumber at the Henry Street sawmill and company houses with their gardens stood on Pruyn's Island. Booms continued to hold 13-foot logs, those for the Finch, Pruyn paper mill, upper right, in the north channel, to be jacked in from the forebay and cut into two-foot wood for the pulp mill grinders.

The early 1900's were years of major change "under the hill." Area focus was transferring from sawmills and lumber to the manufacture of pulp and paper. In 1904 Finch, Pruyn and Company merged the four separate firms under its management and became incorporated. The name of the old Glens Falls Company was discontinued, and ground was broken for a Finch, Pruyn newsprint paper mill. The Wing sawmill, west of the bridge, was dismantled to make way for a power canal. The old grist and marble mills on the east side were razed for construction of the paper mill on the site of quarries. By the 1920's canal boat cargo was mainly newsprint for New York City.

Offices of Finch, Pruyn and Company, Inc., were moved from the old grain elevator when a new building, beautifully designed to utilize limestone from the company quarry, was completed in 1911. The old building was then fully occupied by the firm's retail division with lines of building materials and fuels, along with stone and grain.

The Feeder Canal, now a tranquil ribbon of water, crosses this 1978 view of Finch, Pruyn and Company, Inc., which since 1964 has spent over $50 million to comply with changing requirements of state and federal environmental control agencies. From landscaped parking area and power canal, bottom center, to main office centered between the river and the canal, through acres of pulp and paper manufacturing facilities and pollution control installations, the scene has changed from Wing sawmill, old stone store, grist mill and grain elevator, and once abundant black marble and limestone quarries.

65

In early days, the "long, steep hill" up Glen Street from the river bridge reputedly was a "dread to teamsters and horses." Pedestrians apparently made the best of its dust in summer and wash-outs when it rained, since we have no report of their complaints. These two pictures show only that portion of the hill between the canal and river bridges, looking north, top, and south to the Glens Falls Co. Mill by the covered bridge. This was only the starting grade. The steep part was from the canal bridge to the top of the hill.

One of the oldest buildings in the city, Calvin Robbins' blacksmith shop, restored for the Square Nail gift shop, brightens the west side of the hill today. On the east side, a gas lamp still stood in the 1890's after electric light and telephone poles appeared on the steep hill. By 1956 the street was wide enough to permit parallel parking, and the grade between the canal and river bridges was lessened when the viaduct was built in 1915. None of these buildings remains. This entire section of the hill is being occupied by a new Civic Center designed to seat 4,000 to 7,000 patrons for a variety of sporting, entertainment and convention events.

The home of Duncan McGregor, built about 1836 by Capt. Sidney W. Berry for whom Berry Street was named, was for many years an admired landmark near the top of Glen Street hill. Its retaining wall, which dipped sharply with the roadway, is still a part of the hill, supporting the entrance driveway to J. E. Sawyer & Co., Inc. The Sawyer building was originally occupied by Griffing and Leland's livery stable and sales establishment which offered four floors of carriages, buckboards, harnesses and the best in driving equipment.

In 1835 a visionary scheme for the improvement of the village of Glens Falls was conceived for "under the hill" by the Rev. Dr. Ephraim H. Newton, minister of the Presbyterian Church of Glens Falls and a noted geologist. His design called for land near the river to be "a sidewalk, street, wharfs and lumber yards." From the corner of Canal and Glen Streets up to the Glens Falls Hotel, the plan was to "erect a line of elegant stores, shops, offices, etc., with a finish of stone-pillared fronts, of three or more stories high . . . This street will be spacious, the centre of business and wealth, accessible to every species of trade and art. The Glen House to be rebuilt, finished and furnished with special accommodations for travelers and visitors . . ."

He knew the scheme was grand in theory, "but will be grander if carried into effect."

Today's transformation of the east side of Glen Street hill is not so grand as Newton's 1835 scheme, but with completion of the community's $6 million Civic Center, the goal of attracting "every species of trade and art" can be realized. The hill is the same route up from the bridge that S. R. Stoddard photographed in the 1890's, but its horizon is widening. "Under the hill" may again become a busy part of town.

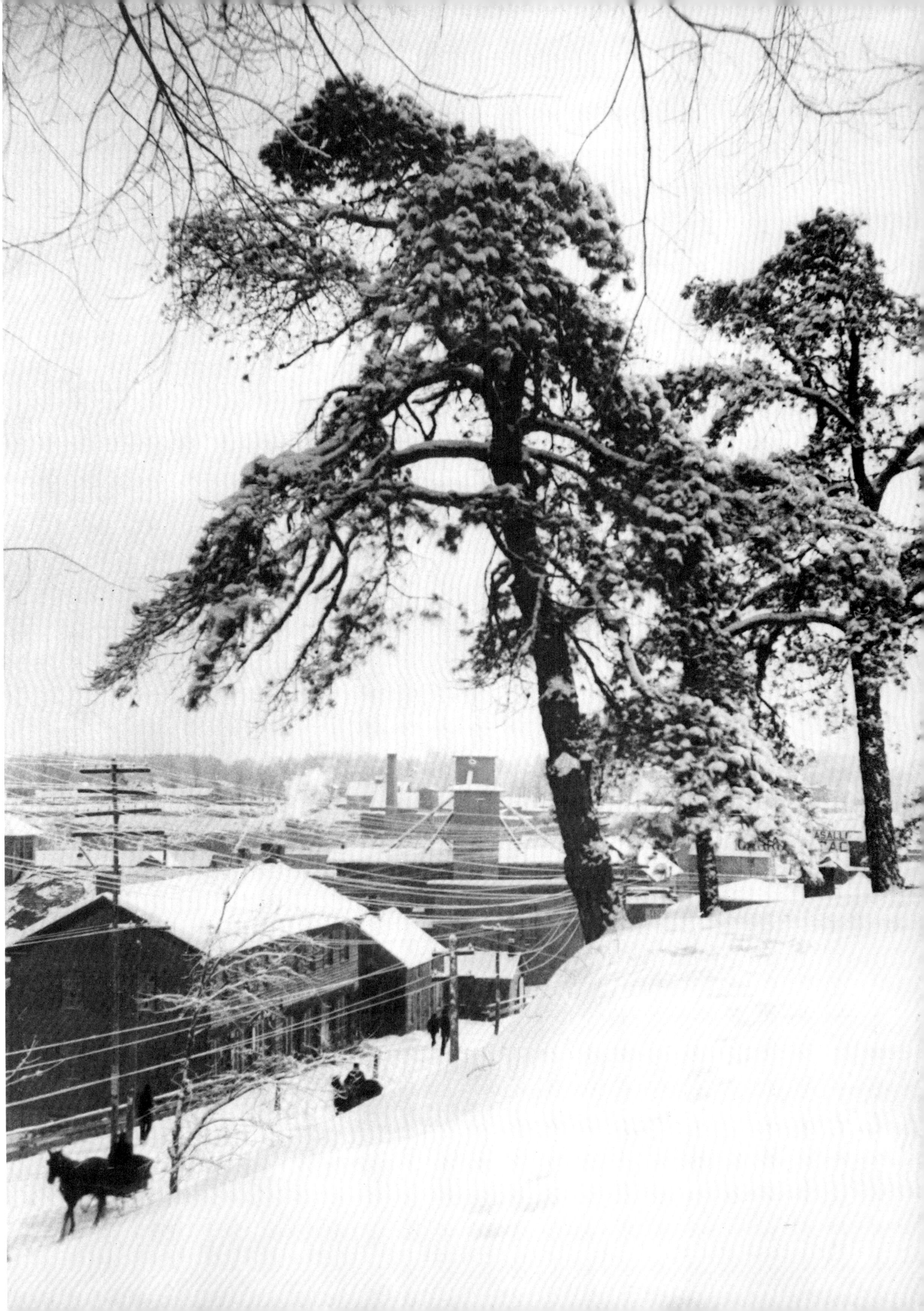

Looking up Glen Street from Park Street at ruins left by the great fire of May 31, 1864

Downtown

Fires of the Revolutionary War destroyed a decade of progress made by the pioneers, but they returned and rebuilt their settlement into a growing community.

The great fire of 1864 ravaged more than three-quarters of a century of development in the business section of Glens Falls. Destroyed in that disaster were 112 buildings, including 60 stores, three churches, two banks and many homes. Stunned but not dismayed, citizens set about rebuilding downtown. Temporary business quarters were set up in shacks built by owners to house their wares until new stores could be erected.

Location of the downtown section of Glens Falls was determined around 1765 when Abraham Wing established the first business enterprise on what is now the corner of Warren and Ridge Streets at Bank Square. The old military road from Fort Edward, Warren Street, turned north to Lake George, becoming Glen Street, and a road to "the Ridge," Ridge Street, came in to form the triangle upon which he built a large log building combining tavern, inn and store.

In his tavern at The Corners, Wing was host not only to the local people who legend says ran up bills of "lusty proportions" for food and drink, but also to the few travelers who came this way. Among these latter in 1776 were Benjamin Franklin and a party en route to Canada to seek support for the colonies in the Revolution.

Bank Square has not always been known by that name. For many years it was simply "The Corners," or "Wing's Corners." Then in 1873 the Village Board of Trustees, enthused by the success of a new gravity water system, authorized the spending of $1,900 to construct an ornate fountain in front of the Rockwell House to make use of some of the plentiful supply from West Mountain. The Corners became, logically enough, "Fountain Square."

This was fine until 1898 when progress, in the form of brick paving for Glen Street and extension of the trolley line to South Glens Falls, dictated removal of the fountain. The name "Fountain Square" no longer appropriate, a new one was sought by the village board. They did not have far to look. At that time all three banks in the village either faced directly on the square or were only a few steps from it. It became Bank Square and by that name has been known ever since, even though today the banks have all moved elsewhere.

In Bank Square before the days of telephone, telegraph, radio and television, we received by stagecoach news of our victories and defeats on the battlefields of war, and welcomed home returning veterans. Here also we listened to some of the most eloquent political candidates of the day speaking to crowds from the porch of the Rockwell House. Rival political factions built bonfires in the square, sometimes stealing each other's wood.

In November of 1856, the village's first gas lamps cast their flickering shadows through the darkness at Bank Square, to be replaced many years later by the first electric lights. Here we also watched parades, tightrope performers, "human flies" and many other forms of entertainment, not the least of which were volunteer firemen's tournaments featuring water fights and other contests. Unhampered by traffic, they carried on their activities in an area where today even crossing the street is an adventure.

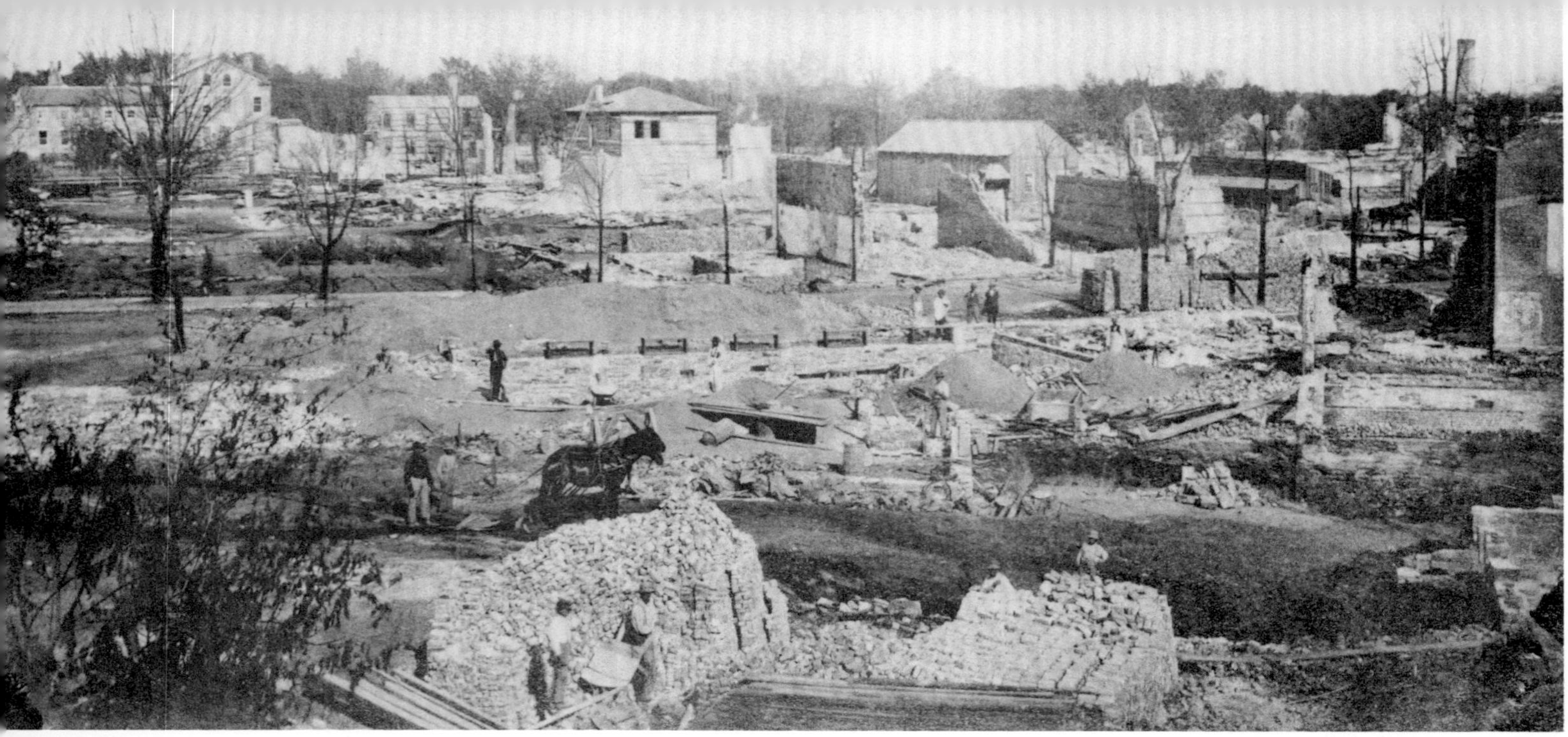
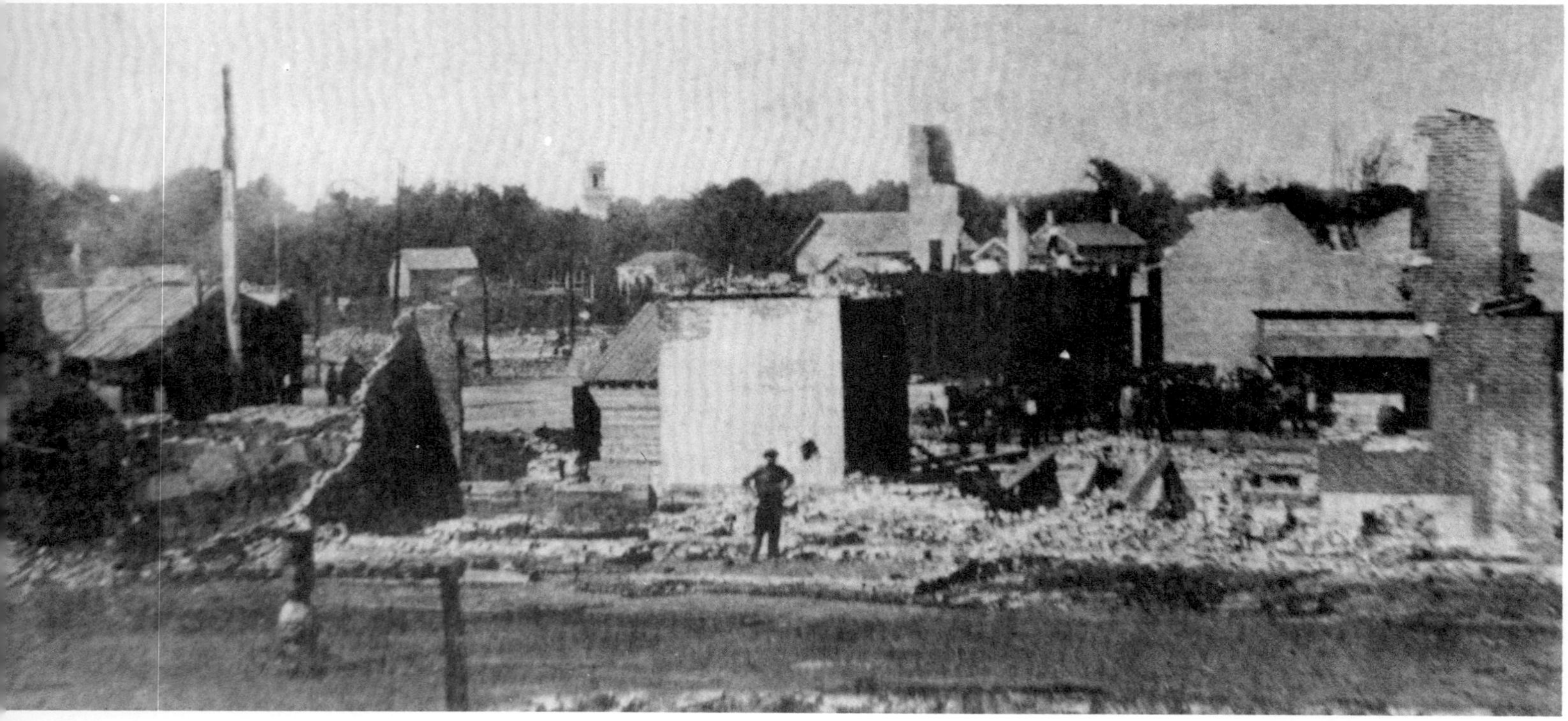
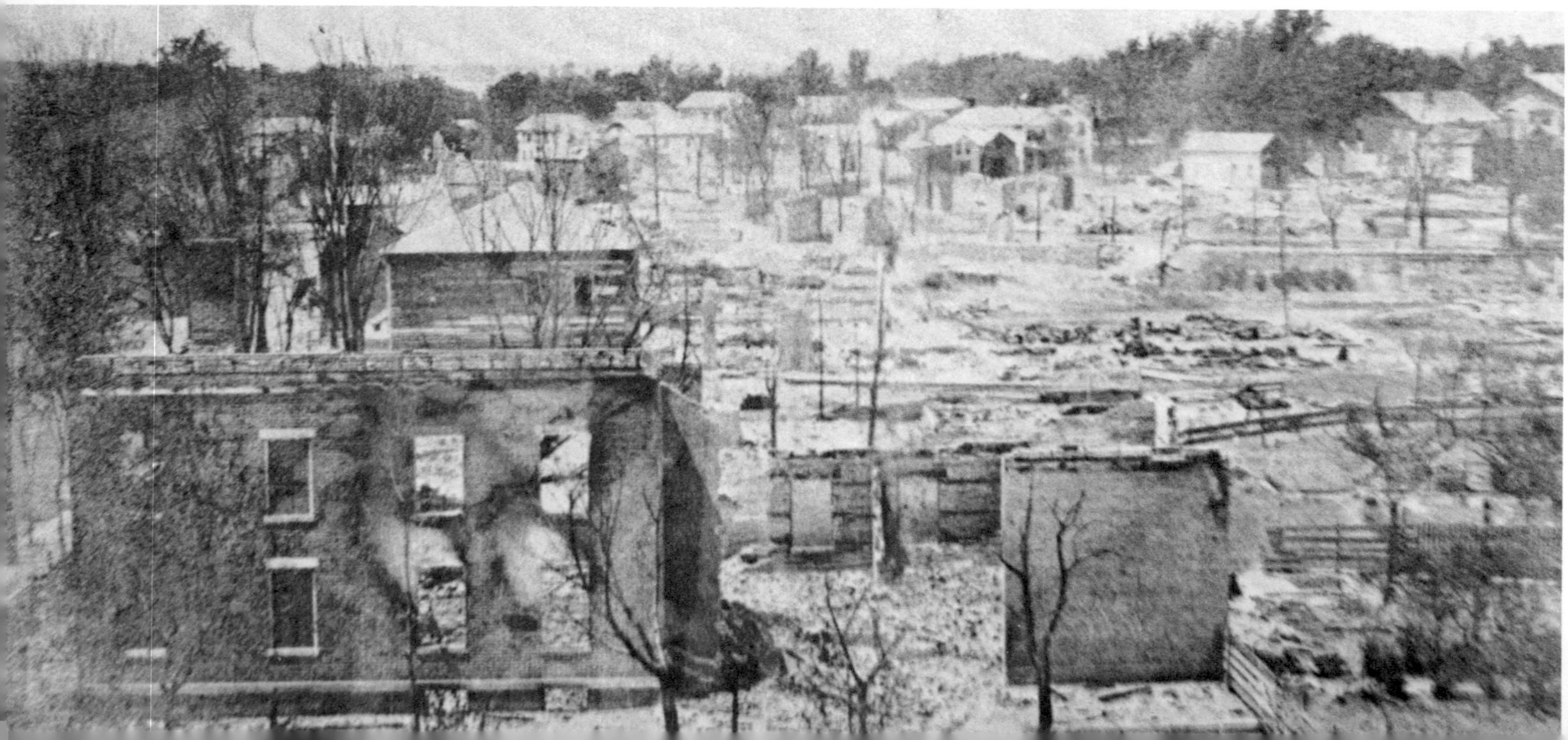

On June 6, 1863, Defiance Engine Company #1 gathered along Warren Street at Bank Square to welcome home local Civil War veterans whose enlistments had expired. Within a year the site of these festivities had been ravaged by a great fire which began in Wait Carpenter's Glens Falls Hotel, seen here to the left beyond the arch, and swept through the village center. Photos on opposite page show ruins left by the fire of 1864.

Writing about the Fire of 1864 in *Homely Recollections*, a biography of her grandfather, William McEchron, Katharine Cunningham tells us:

"The dooryard of Grandfather's house on Elm Street adjoined the garden of the new Glens Falls Hotel which Wait Carpenter had recently completed . . .

"Mr. Carpenter had built a very nice hotel. He was ambitious for it; and in his kitchen equipment he was trying to outdo the previous landlord, a Canadian named Threehouse . . . whose stoves were so small that on gala occasions he had to take his roasts and turkeys to the neighbors to be cooked . . . Wait Carpenter had gone so far as to switch from wood to coal; and he had bought a fine generous, big stove. Its only drawback was a tendency to get very hot.

"On the last day of May, 1864, in the early afternoon, Grandmother was sitting near the window while the children, Maggie and Bertha, played outside . . . Drawn to the window by their voices, Grandmother realized that a brisk wind was blowing, and to her horror saw smoke and flame pouring from the windows of the hotel kitchen. She went out to fetch the children who were reluctant to stop their play; and the three stood for a few moments, watching the fire beyond the trees of the garden. Poor Mr. Carpenter! It was too, too bad! But probably not serious. They must have sent a messenger to the Firehouse, and the two splendid fire-engines, Defiance I and Cataract II, would shortly be along with the volunteers of the Fire Department. What a mercy that there was that nice big cistern, right in the middle of Bank Square! Meanwhile, the children must come in, out of the wind. Grandmother did not guess that they were seeing the start of a disaster that would wipe out the whole center of the village.

"Fanned by the lively breeze, flames travelled quickly in all directions. A woodyard in Exchange Street, to the north of the hotel, added fuel to the blaze. The frame buildings on both sides of Glen Street were soon burning brightly, beyond any help the Fire Department could possibly give. To the south of the hotel, in the direction of the river, small wooden shops and markets spread the fire to the Mansion House, an old wooden structure with a verandah across the front and a second-floor gallery above. This was gone in no time. In Warren Street, a section below the Square caught fire, and several buildings, among them the Presbyterian and Methodist churches, were completely destroyed . . . As the afternoon wore on, the fire was held to the east side of the long hill, and danger to Elm and Park Streets seemed to be past. William, coming in from time to time, reported that at the upper end of Glen Street, below the Ranger's house on one side, and the Finch's on the other, the fire had been slowed down by wider gaps between the buildings; gradually it was being brought under control. Engines had come from Sandy Hill and Fort Edward, the local fire-fighters were not alone in the battle; but the lack of an adequate water supply had made the situation hopeless, so far as the middle of the village was concerned. After all, there were only wells and cisterns.

"After sundown, when they had done what they could in the center of town, some of Grandfather's old neighbors from Fort Edward, with their fire engine, suddenly appeared before the house. They had come, they said, to wet down his walls and roof, just in case flying sparks should make trouble later. It had been a losing fight in Glen Street; but they could at least do a good turn for an old friend."

A crude attempt at rebuilding the business section after the fire of 1864 is shown in this picture looking east across Glen Street toward Warren, where the gaunt ruins of the First Presbyterian Church stand out in the center of the photo. At right, on Glen Street, Anson Staples, one of the merchants burned out in the fire, has put up a temporary building housing his Glens Falls Market, and the vault of the Glens Falls Bank stands in the center foreground. Much of this burned section is included in the present Urban Renewal area bounded by Glen, Warren and Church Streets, a small part of which is shown at lower right in aerial view.

From ruins of the fire of 1864 has emerged today's city of Glens Falls. Its spirit, many times tried by disaster, depression or apathy, has risen to meet the challenge of change. Efforts of people with initiative and determination, who wanted this community to be a comfortable hometown, have made it so.

A 1975 aerial view shows downtown's pattern: Glen Street up the hill from the Hudson River bridge to Bank Square, center foreground, and continuing northerly. Warren Street, the old Military Road, coming in from the east at lower right, and Ridge Street, the "road to the Ridge" in early days, veering northeast from the same intersection, and with Warren Street forming the old Wing's Tavern corner. New to the scene is Hudson Avenue Extension, lower left, completed in 1975 on the site of the old Rockwell House and expediting five lanes of traffic into and out of Bank Square. Two blocks up Glen Street is what in olden days was called "the upper part of the village," the present day Monument Square, with Bay Street, top center, extending to the northeast and South Street to the southwest. This picture was taken after completion of the 11-story Continental Insurance Companies Northeast Headquarters building on Glen Street and before razing of the five-story Glens Falls Insurance Company building at Glen and Bay Streets, facing Monument Square.

Commercial buildings abounded on both sides of Glen Street at the brow of the hill as the community grew. There has been virtually no change in the architecture on the west side north from the Park Street intersection from the days of Fountain Square to the present, as the top photos, taken from the same spot, witness. The fire of 1884 destroyed almost everything on the east side, and the bottom photo shows what was built thereafter. Urban Renewal was the next mass destroyer, and the block was cleared by razing in 1970.

By 1889, ruins of the 1864 fire had been replaced by buildings shown in this photo, looking north on Glen Street toward Fountain Square. When the fountain was removed in 1898, the hub logically became Bank Square because of the three banks located there: Merchants National, center right, at Ridge and Glen Streets, in what was the old D. Peck grocery store location when this picture was taken; First National, adjoining the Rockwell House, center left; and, separated from the First National only by the Dolan building, Glens Falls National, left.

The regeneration of the east side of Glen Street south of Warren was rapid. The fire of April 28, 1884, started in Union Hall, which occupied the right hand portion of the site in above foreground, destroying that structure and the Cosgrove Opera House next door. Jumping to the rear of buildings on Warren Street, it consumed the Glens Falls Opera House and the First Presbyterian Church, the belfry of which shows through the smoke. The view below, taken from nearly the same vantage point as the fire shot, demonstrates the substantial rebuilding of the block in short order.

The east side of Glen Street at the brow of the hill was a thriving commercial strip on July 4, 1946, when Fitzgerald's Hotel and Restaurant burned. David J. Fitzgerald's establishment had a national reputation for good food and was frequented by luminaries, particularly from the world of politics. Below is a bird's-eye view, taken from the Stichman Towers apartment building, of the open area left between Glen and Warren Streets by Urban Renewal in 1970. Every building was demolished in the block bounded by Glen, Warren, Church and Berry Streets. In fact, all buildings on the south side of Berry were razed as well and the street eliminated. The Civic Center is now under construction on the site.

The intersection of Glen, Warren and Ridge Streets has always been a focal point of the community. It was called Fountain Square in 1892 or 1893 when Gov. Roswell P. Flower made a speech from the front of the Rockwell House. "People" events were frequent here in the days before television and shopping malls. Today, a new street, Hudson Avenue Extension, has poked through the former Rockwell House site from the west, further complicating pedestrians' lives. Vehicular traffic at the square was completely halted above, however, when the Governor spoke to a largely male, largely hatted assemblage. The hotel porch made a fine dais from which those of distinction could beam upon the throngs.

Not quite so many folks were on hand for Circus Day in 1905 when the elephants lumbered up through Bank Square, behind a band wagon. The trolley cars wait on Ridge Street. Seneca Ray Stoddard produced this fine panorama.

80

Bank Square had three banks when this photo was taken about 1900. The Merchants National Bank, shown above, occupied the ground floor of the Moynehan Building at the intersection of Glen and Ridge Streets. This bank, organized in 1893, was acquired by the National Bank of Glens Falls in 1922 and is now the Glens Falls National Bank and Trust Company. Burns' Newsroom occupied the corner space for many years after the bank moved. Just up Glen Street in 1900 were the Western Union telegraph office, the Pearsall and Gray cigar store, Greek-American Fruit Company, and Brown's Hotel. The First National Bank and the National Bank of Glens Falls were on the opposite side of Glen Street.

Bank Square was still called "The Corners" when a different kind of activity was staged on the night of January 6, 1870. A bank burglary, accomplished with Civil War horseblankets and dynamite, provided an exciting episode in the history of downtown.

Burglars broke into the "Old Brownstone" of the Glens Falls National Bank and well-planned thievery was successful. First soaking the blankets in a watering trough at the rear of the building, they somehow entered through the back of the bank and strung the wet blankets across all doors and windows to deaden the sound and to avoid detection. The safe was blown open and the rascals escaped with their loot, mostly greenbacks of large denomination.

At a special board meeting next day, it was resolved that a reward of $7,500 be paid for the recovery and return of the money and bonds stolen, and for the apprehension and conviction of the criminals. To date that reward has never been claimed.

Glens Falls National lost no time, however, in taking steps to prevent such occurrences in the future. According to a recap of the incident in *The Post-Star* of September 17, 1953, an arrangement

Glens Falls National Bank and Trust Company, the oldest bank in Warren County, began in 1851 as the Glens Falls Bank. After the 1864 fire which destroyed its Glen Street location, it reorganized as the Glens Falls National Bank and built the familiar brownstone building, top, on the old site, which it occupied until 1950. In 1905 it became the National Bank of Glens Falls and in 1922 acquired the Merchants National Bank, organized in 1893, and in 1932, the Glens Falls Trust Company, left, founded in 1898. The bank's present name was adopted at that time and the move to its present building, below, was made in 1950.

Almost side by side in Fountain and Bank Square days, the two banks ... today's Glens Falls National Bank and Trust Company and the First National Bank of Glens Falls ... now face each other across Glen Street at Monument Square, their beautiful buildings adding much to the attractiveness of downtown.

was made "whereby every night a horse drawn lunch wagon drew up before the bank and opened for business for the night, remaining in front of the bank until dawn the following day. The bank furnished light for the restaurant on wheels, and the proprietor served as watchman for the bank."

The First National Bank, only a few steps up Glen Street from the "Old Brownstone," promptly held a board meeting following the crime and a resolution was made to offer any plausible assistance to their victimized neighbor.

The board, evidently impressed with the fact that its own quarters were scarcely less vulnerable, held a second meeting on January 12, 1870. As reported in the 1939 centennial issue of *The Glens Falls Times*, "they voted to buy beds and bedding and have the teller and clerk sleep in the bank, while the cashier was instructed to procure a watchdog." In consideration of their sleeping in the bank, the teller's and clerk's annual salaries were increased to $1,200 and $500, respectively. No further information has been discovered about the watchdog. Electronic alarm systems and police vigilance have replaced such astute precautions, but the practice of watchfulness was effective. No further burglaries occurred in downtown banks.

The First National Bank of Glens Falls opened August 1, 1853, as the Commercial Bank of Glens Falls, under a state charter, and was reorganized as a national bank in 1865. Its first home, on the west side of Glen Street facing "The Corners," was destroyed in the fire of 1864. The bank was rebuilt at the same location and that building, right, was occupied by the institution until July 15, 1915, when the present Vermont marble structure, below, was completed and opened.

The distinctive Italianate architecture of the old First National Bank building, above, was changed when the bank moved to its new quarters up Glen Street. A third floor was added and a neoclassical facade became familiar as the Braydon and Chapman music store. The building, which originally adjoined the Rockwell House, now stands on the southwest corner of Hudson Avenue's entrance to Glen Street.

The Neptune fountain at the square was erected atop the village water cistern in front of the Rockwell House in 1873. Workmen above begin the job of dismantling on October 21, 1898. The paving of Glen Street and extension of the trolley system to South Glens Falls necessitated removal of the fountain to Crandall Park, below, where it remained until World War II, when it went on the victory scrap pile at City Park.

Bank Square has been the scene of such novelties as a miniature church pealing forth carols during the Christmas season, an automatic traffic whistle, and a midget policeman. The church, hit by several cars, was removed and never used after the 1949 holiday. The traffic whistle, which blew when lights changed, caused unsuspecting motorists to stop in the middle of the intersection and was short-lived. The midget was on loan from a vaudeville troupe as a publicity stunt by the Rialto Theatre in the early 1920's.

The Fourth of July in 1870 brought a big crowd of spectators to Warren Street, looking east from Glen, for a Firemen's Muster, held frequently in the old volunteer days. Even the rooftops are lined as a water fight shapes up. The church spires, from left, are those of the Methodist, St. Mary's and Presbyterian churches. A quieter day on Warren in 1889 is seen from behind the fountain, top of opposite page. The first three buildings at left are the same ones shown in 1977 photo below. At right, however, all of the buildings to St. Mary's Church have been torn down.

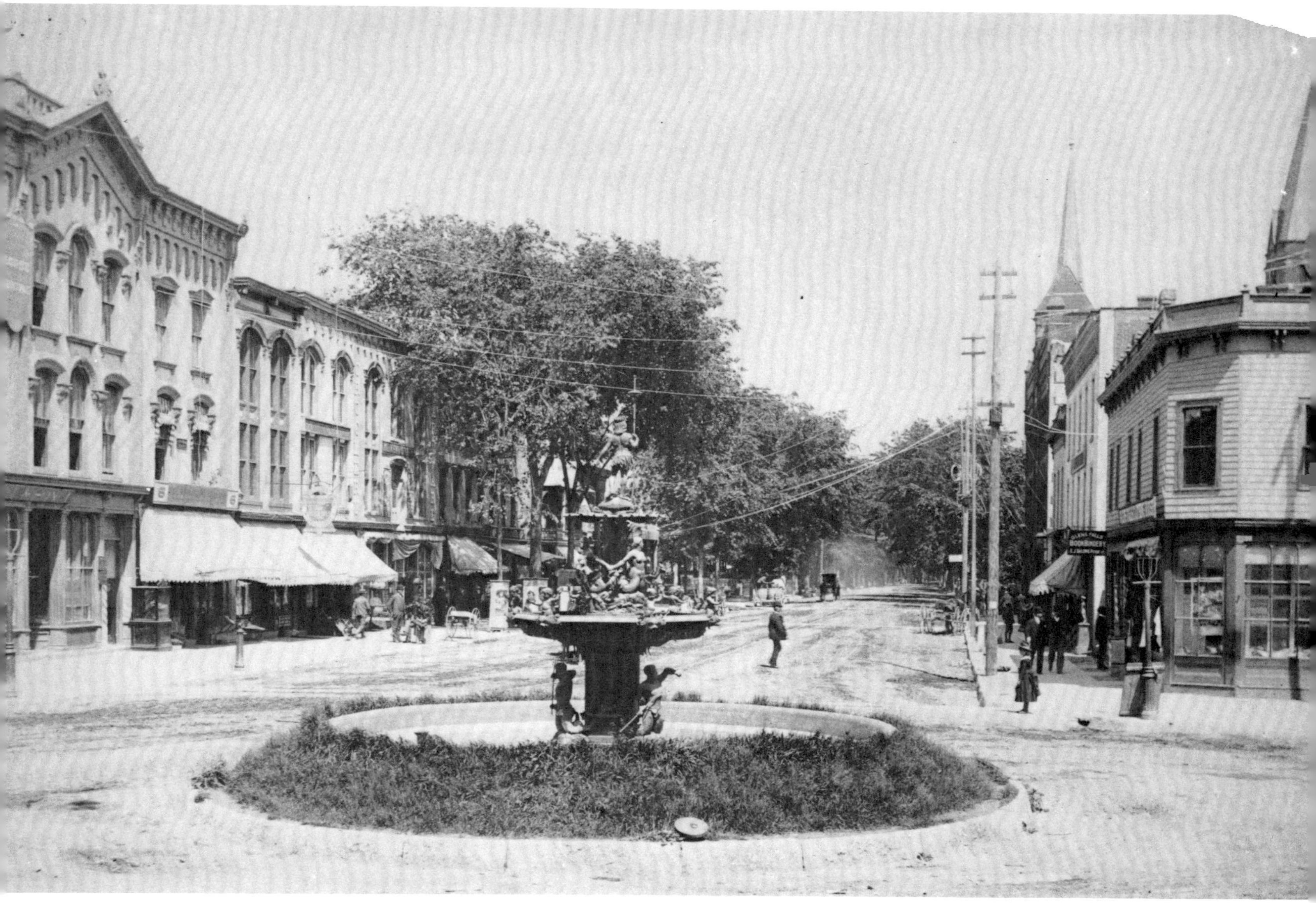

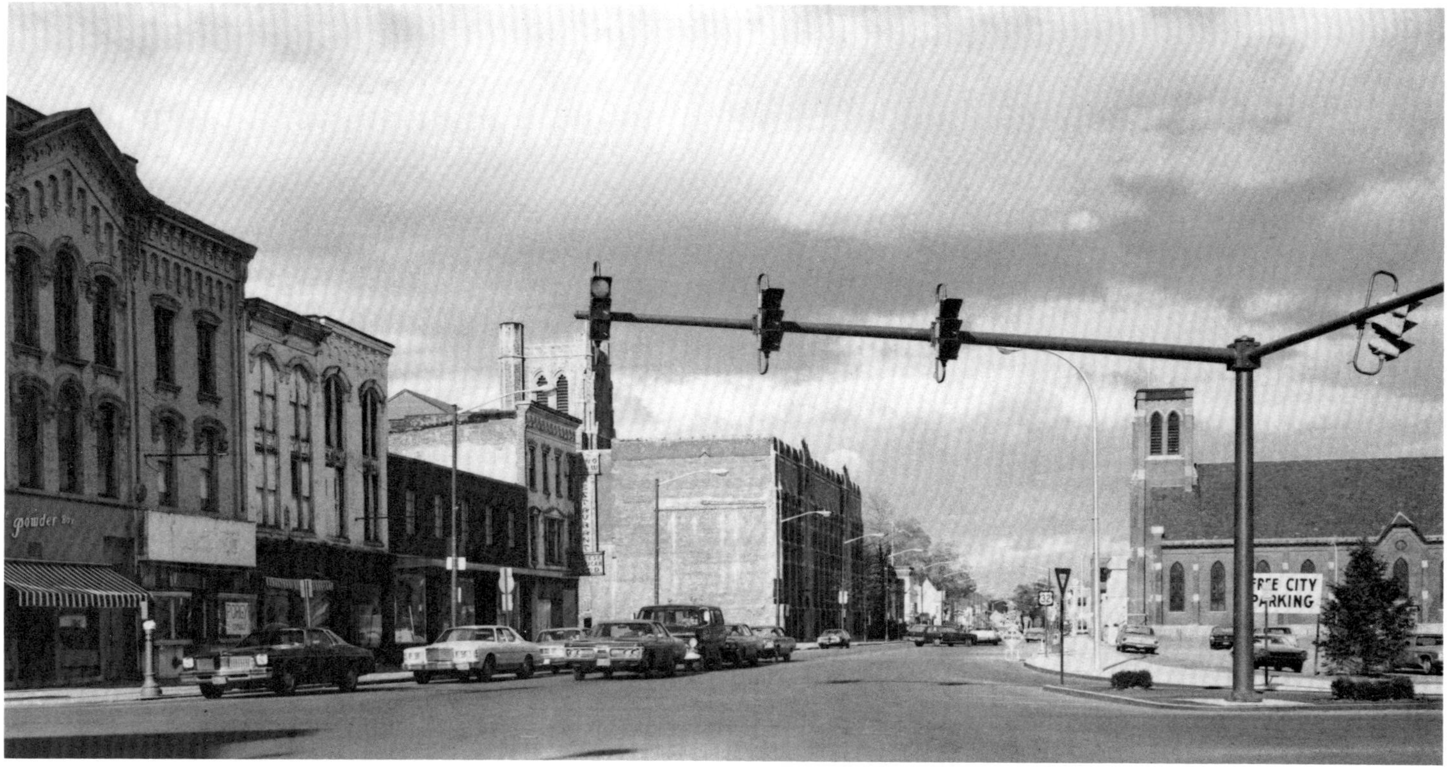
CITY
PARKING

"Busy Ridge Street" wasn't busy as usual when these two photos were taken, more than half a century apart. A trolley car and horse-drawn wagons and carriages provided most of the traffic in 1920, above, while parked automobiles line the street in 1977. The brick pavement and trolley tracks are removed or beneath the asphalt.

Abraham Wing, founder of the community, chose this site, corner of Ridge and Warren Streets, for his log tavern before the Revolution. The tavern lasted until after 1816, when it was replaced by a business building, which, in turn, was burned in the fire of 1864. The present Cowles building, constructed after the fire, is seen as it appeared from behind the Fountain in the 1890's. It looks not much different today, and is the object of a restoration project.

The Rockwell House, before and after the fountain, which was removed in 1898. Notice the hotel's own horse-drawn jitney bus, which met all trains.

90

The bed of Hudson Avenue, where it intersects Glen Street at Bank Square, was for nearly one and one-half centuries the location of Glens Falls hotels.

Way back in 1802, a hostelry was operated there by John Akin Ferris, foremost among the early promoters of the village. One of Ferris' successors was Peter D. Threehouse, a Frenchman who called himself "Pierre de Trois Maisons" in Warren County Surrogate's records.

The substantial brick Glens Falls Hotel was built there by Wait S. Carpenter in 1852 but was destroyed in the fire of 1864, which started in its kitchen. The ground lay idle for several years thereafter.

A proposal to erect a row of stores was not greeted with public enthusiasm, and a citizens' committee raised $15,400 to buy the lot and offer it to a responsible person for hotel operation.

The Rockwells of Luzerne took up the offer and opened the Rockwell House on February 22, 1872. Festivities that evening were capped with a community ball at the Opera House.

Modernization eliminated the huge front porch in the 1920's, and the place became known as the Hotel Rockwell, which lost its prominence with the opening of the Queensbury Hotel. The Rockwell became the Hotel Towers in 1949 and burned on February 22, 1950.

Here are two approaches to the Rockwell House, before the turn of the century. The winter scene is from Warren Street, with the Presbyterian Church at left. The summer view is from muddy, tree-shaded Ridge Street, with the Moynehan building and a corner of the old engine house at right.

The three Swiss towers for which the later Hotel Towers was named are evident in the 1920's photo of the Rockwell House, above. Scaffolding covers the face of the hotel, left, during extensive remodeling operations in 1949. The later history of the location is recorded on the opposite page with, successively, destruction of the Hotel Towers on February 22, 1950, by fire; occupancy of the site by a new one-story W. T. Grant Company department store, and elimination of buildings altogether with construction of Hudson Avenue Extension in 1975.

93

94

Glen Street, between Bank Square and Monument Square, has been the heart of community retail life from early days. Trees have disappeared from the view up the street, and today the end of the block is dominated by the Church of the Messiah and the Continental Insurance headquarters instead of the old brick Glens Falls Insurance Company office or private homes. A close examination will show that the buildings on the west side of the street have stood from the days of the fountain and trolley cars to those of one-way traffic and plastic holiday wreaths.

Alterations over the years notwithstanding, you'll find enough distinguishing characteristics in the buildings shown in these two pictures to recognize them as the same ones on the west side of Glen Street between Bank Square and Exchange Street. The older photo was taken about 1865, soon after the business structures rose from the ashes of the great fire of 1864, while the later one is contemporary. The residence on the right in the older picture was later replaced by the B. B. Fowler store, which burned in 1902. Fowler rebuilt, and the site is today occupied by the Outlet store.

Glen Street was paved with brick by the Troy Public Works Company in 1898, the first thoroughfare in the village so improved. In 1909, the street is being torn up again to permit the laying of a double track trolley line.

Why are there so many people on Glen Street and why are they all hurrying toward Fountain Square? The occasion was probably Gov. Roswell P. Flower's visit here in 1892 or 1893. Don't miss two little girls with their tricycle near the utility poles or the people atop the Liberty Building at Glen and Warren Streets and in the second-floor windows of the B. B. Fowler store. The 1949 view from the same vantage point, opposite page, shows a typical busy day from the post-war era. Things are quieter today, and all of the buildings shown in center background have been torn down under an Urban Renewal program.

It's truly great
BEVERWYCK
BEER IRISH CREAM ALE
ECONOMY
STORE
HOTEL
TOWERS
BEAUTY
ABSOLUTELY THE BEST EVER BREWED
ALES Stanton BEER
NBC
BREAD
LIQUOR
STORE
A. SCHULTE CIGARS SCHULTE
PIPES
EXECUTIVE OFFICES

Can you imagine the howls of protest if Glen Street were to go unplowed after a snowstorm today the way it was when the above photo was taken in the 1890's? Still in all, it looks like business as usual with cutters and sleighs on the move. At left is a contemporary shot from the same point.

Sidewalk displays of merchandise were a matter of course in 1892. Thomas C. Stilwell and James M. Allen sold hardware, and B. B. Fowler had been in the dry goods business since 1869. These buildings were destroyed in the fire of 1902. Long-time occupants of the successor structures, still standing, were Fowler's department store and the Englander men's wear store, both now out of business.

'Tis the Season to Be Jolly. Looking down Glen Street toward Bank Square in a snowstorm in 1971.

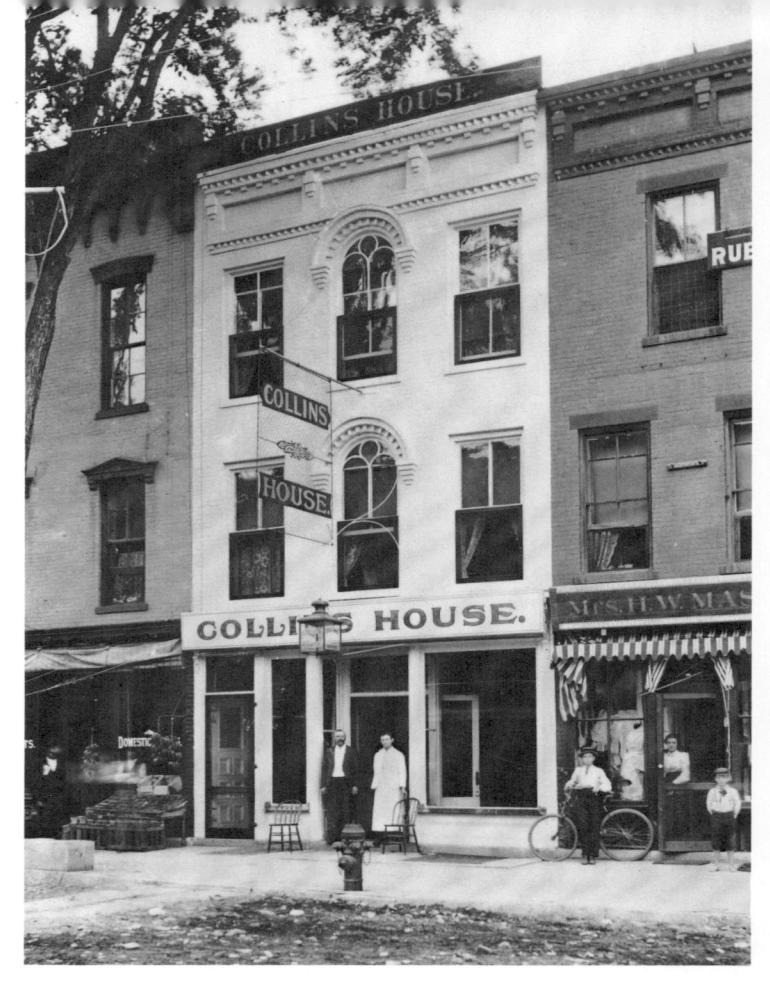

The east side of Glen Street between Bank Square and Monument Square has featured a variety of businesses through the years. The Collins House (1895-1903) later became Brown's Hotel and advertised rooms for 50 cents a day and meals for 35 cents each. Later it was Peabody's Hotel. In the scene of the Greek-American Fruit Market, don't miss the cigar store Indian, shoeshine stands and telegraph delivery boy. A woman in "widow's weeds" approaches from the north.

More business blocks on the east side of Glen Street. The building at top right is the same as the one second from the left at bottom, where men are working on Glen Street paving in 1898.

103

Glen Street on a pre-Northway summer day in 1953 and with one-way traffic on a quiet spring morning in 1976.

After World War II, there were four five-and-dime stores in downtown Glens Falls: Kresge's, Woolworth's, Grant's and Newberry's. All are gone today except Woolworth's because of relocation or changes in merchandising. The three-story F. W. Woolworth Company and Lerner Store buildings on the east side of Glen Street were destroyed by a St. Patrick's Night fire on March 17, 1956. Woolworth's today occupies the ground floor of a two-story commercial building on the site.

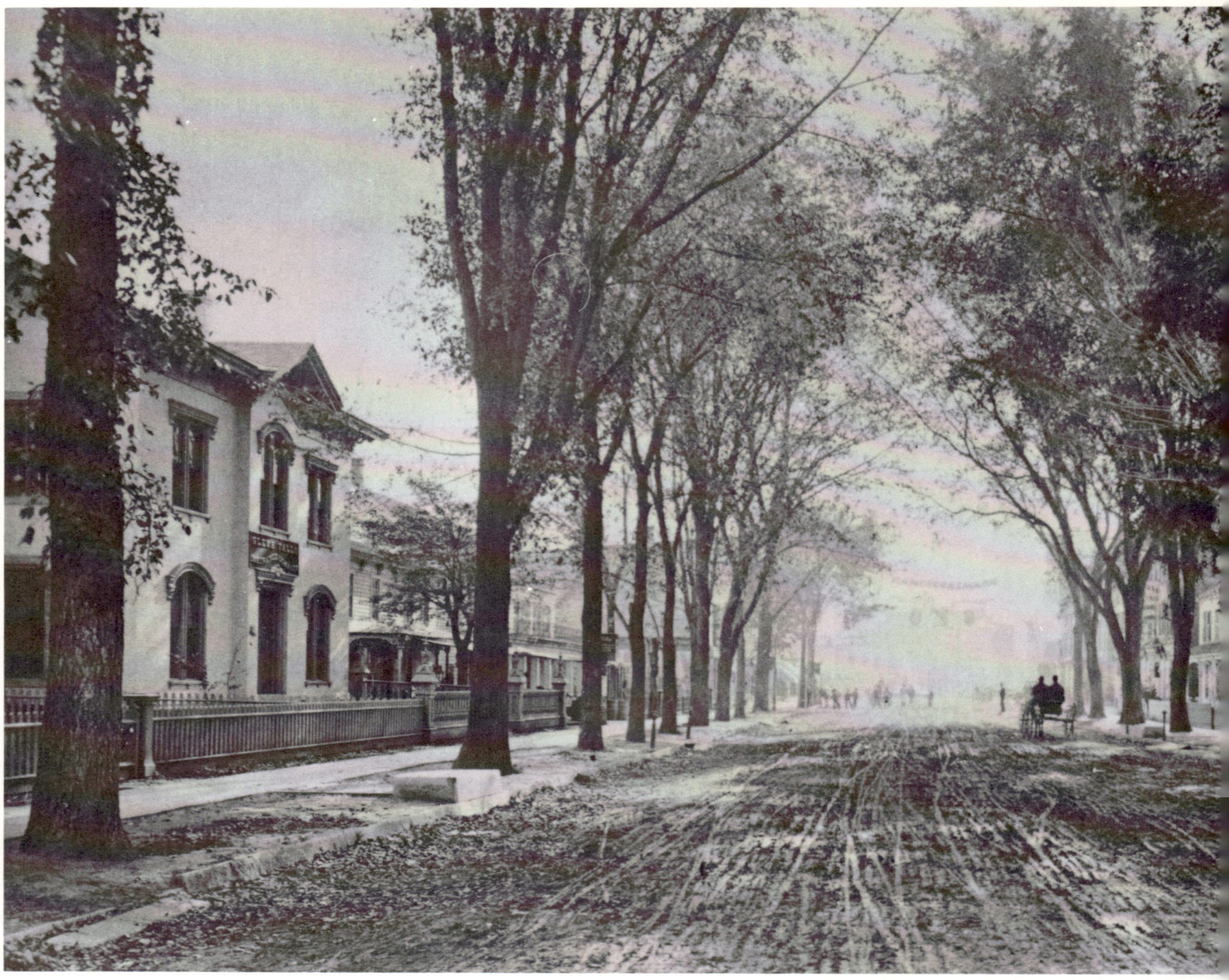

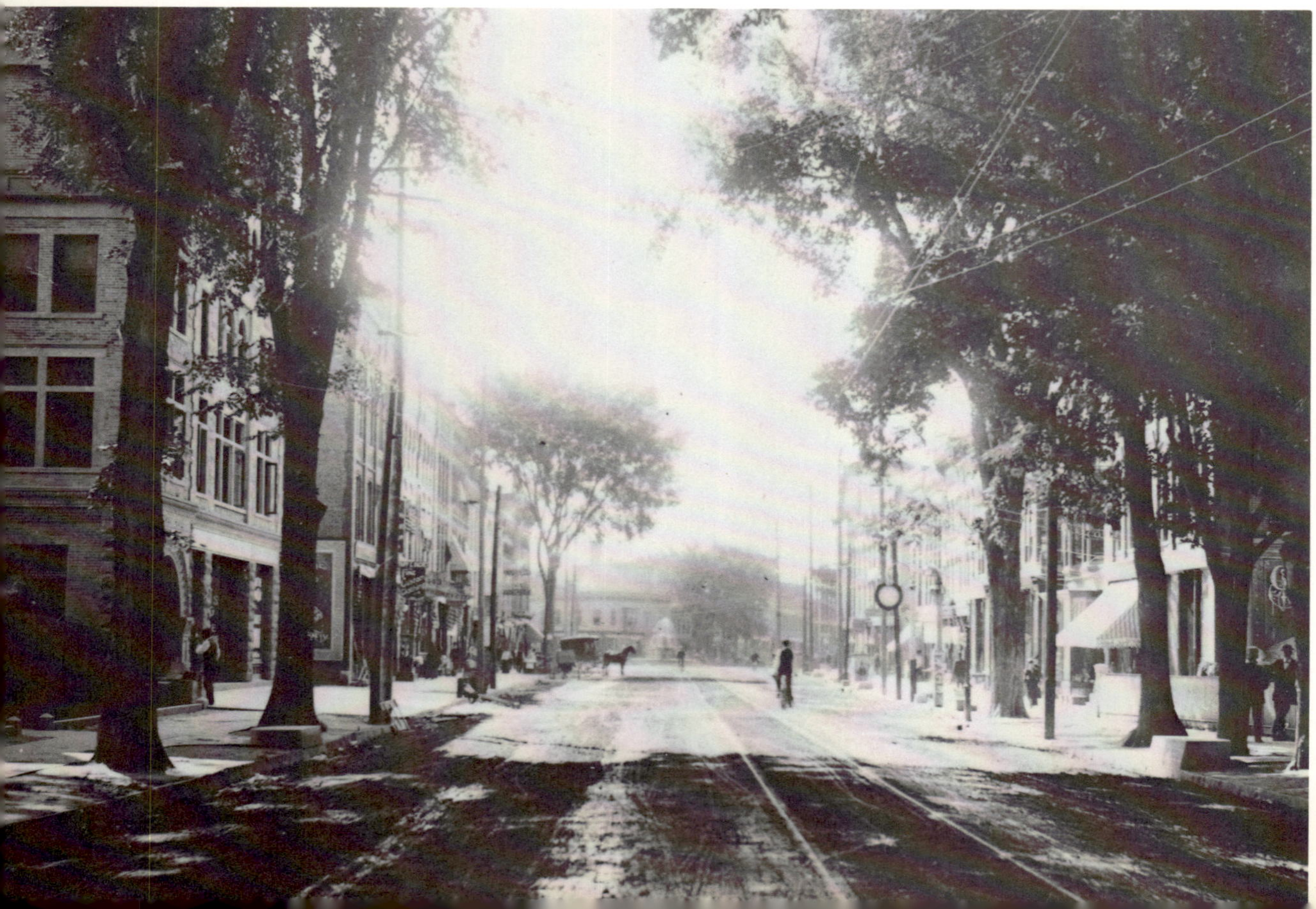

The year was 1880 and James A. Garfield was running for President of the United States against Winfield S. Hancock when the picture at the left of muddy Glen Street was taken. Note the Democratic campaign banner for Hancock and his running-mate, William H. English, hanging over the street near Bank Square. Garfield was elected but was assassinated the next year and his vice president, Chester A. Arthur, became President. The first office building of the Glens Falls Insurance Company is at the extreme left and the home of Joseph Fowler at the extreme right. Glen Street was still unpaved when the photo at the lower left was taken in the 1890's, but streetcars had arrived and several new buildings erected, including the YMCA on the former Insurance Company site at the left. The picture below shows the same area on the east side of Glen Street in the 1940's, with the First National Bank at the left and the "Y" beyond.

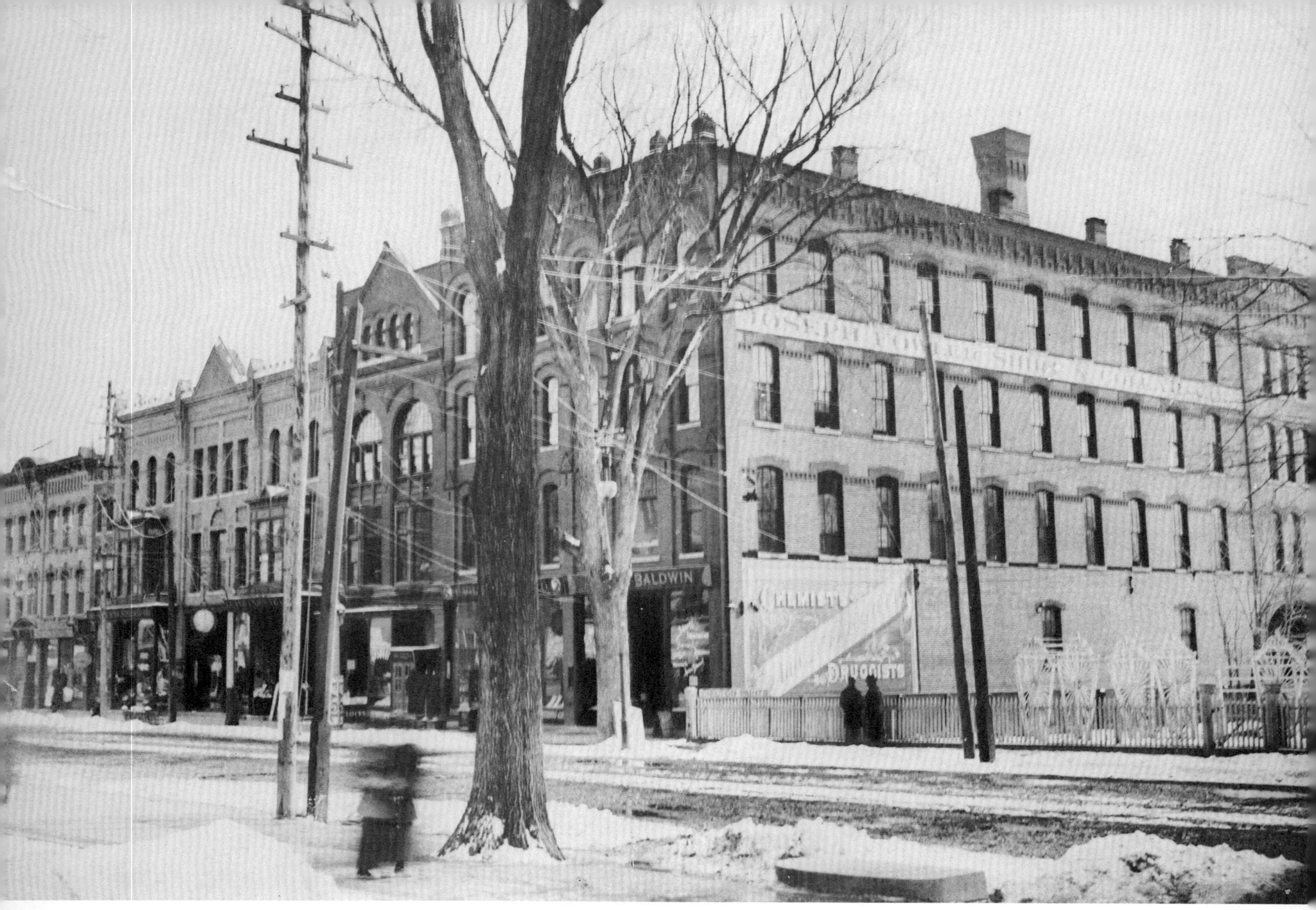
BALDWIN

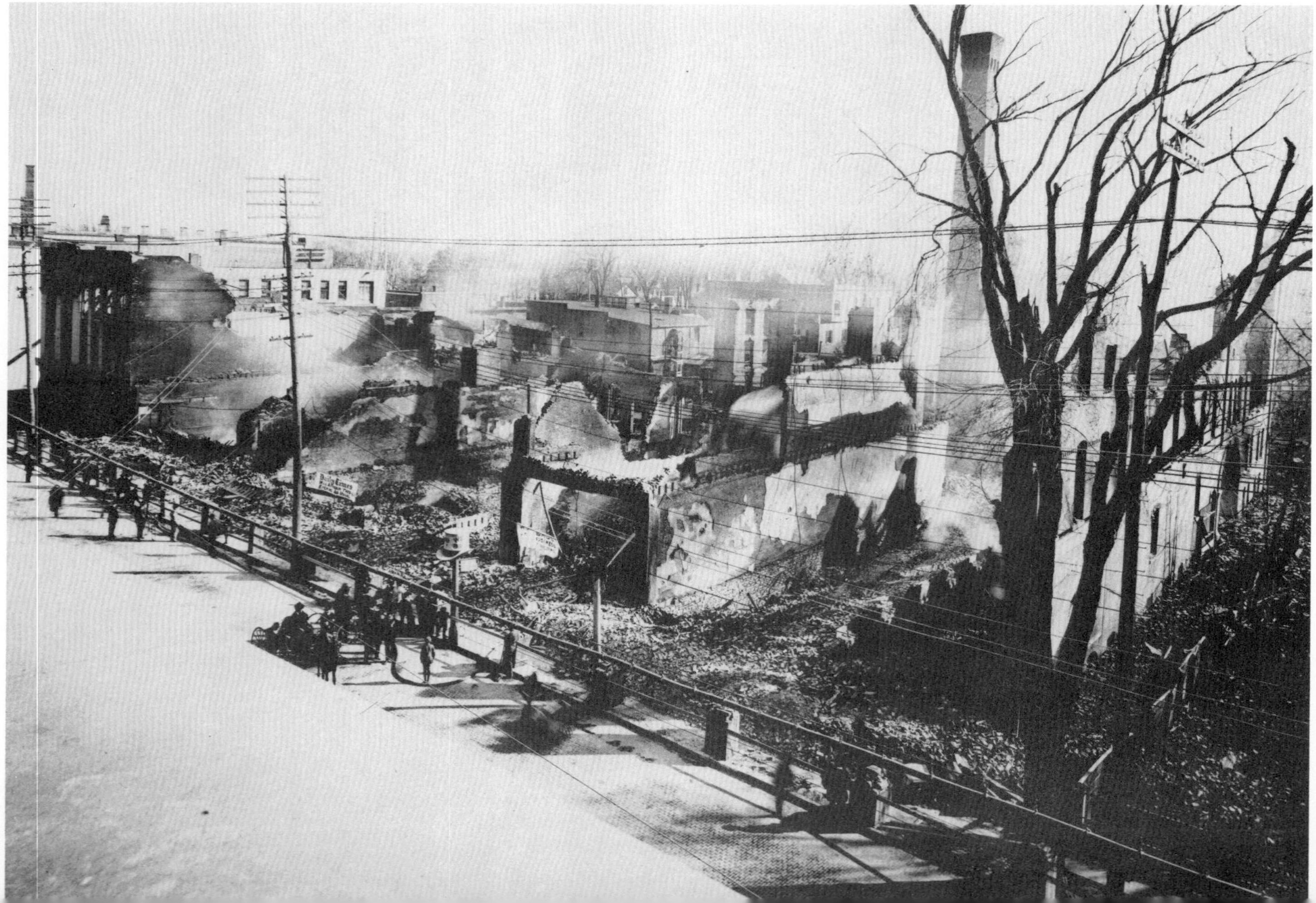

By the 1890's the Jeremiah W. Finch house, extreme right in the photo above, was one of only a few homes still standing in "downtown" Glens Falls. The remainder of that block on the west side of Glen Street was occupied by business buildings, and in that block on April 26, 1902, Glens Falls' third big fire started in Webb Brothers' clothing store. All of the buildings from the Finch house south to Exchange Street were destroyed with a loss estimated at half a million dollars. Photos on the opposite page show the area before and after the fire. The conflagration was a severe economic blow to Glens Falls, not only from the loss by fire but also from the fact that the Joseph Fowler Shirt and Collar Company, one of the burned-out tenants, decided to discontinue business, throwing 800 people of work.

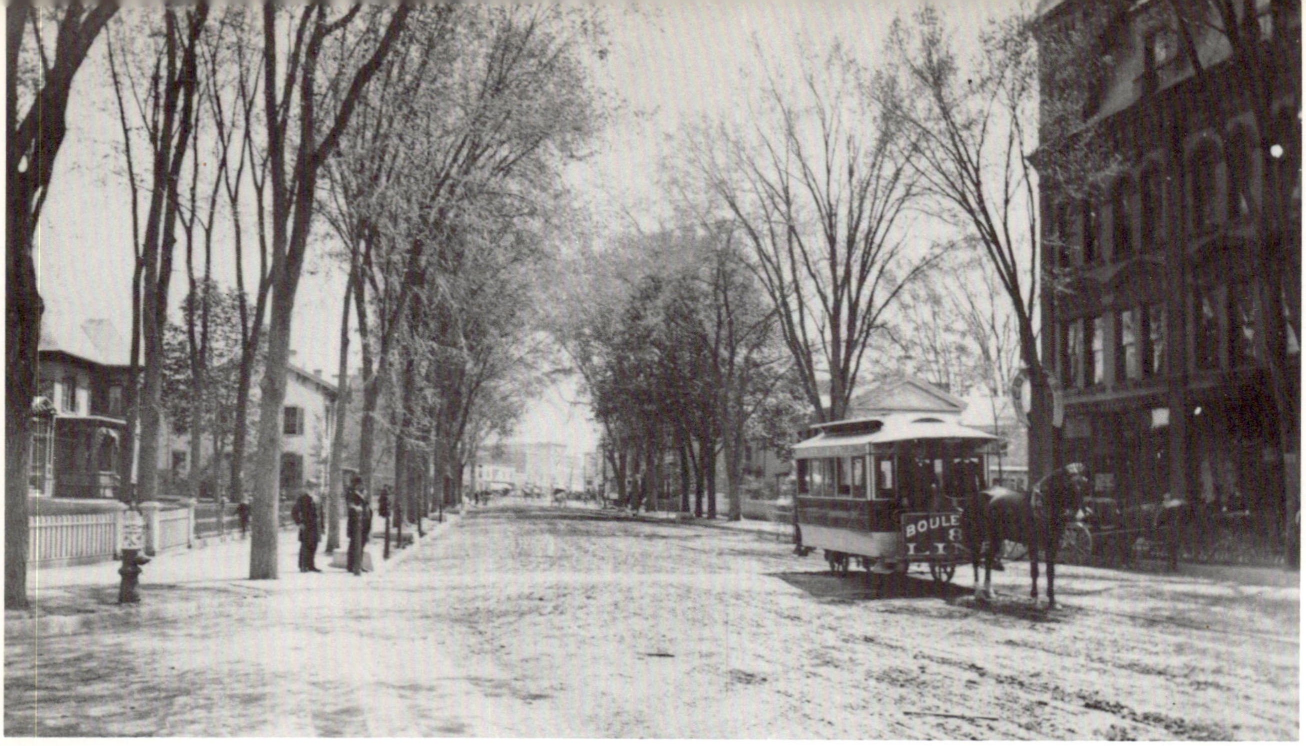
BOULE

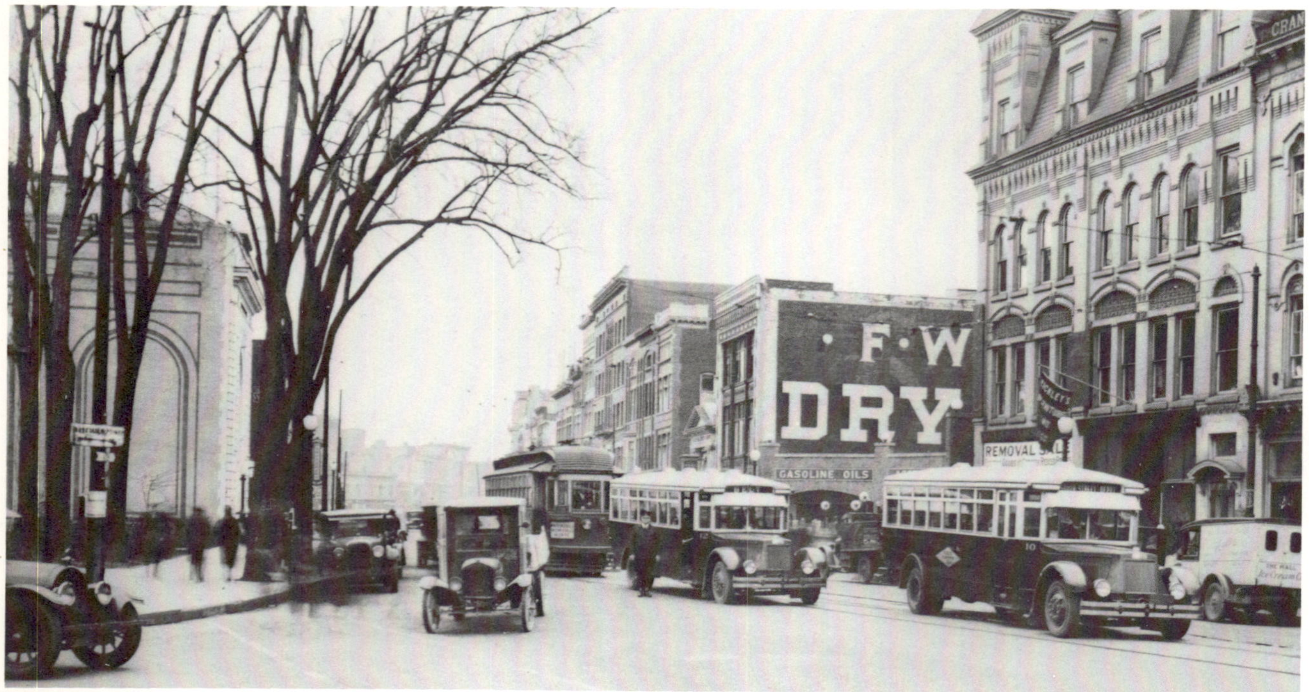
F·W
DRY
GASOLINE OILS

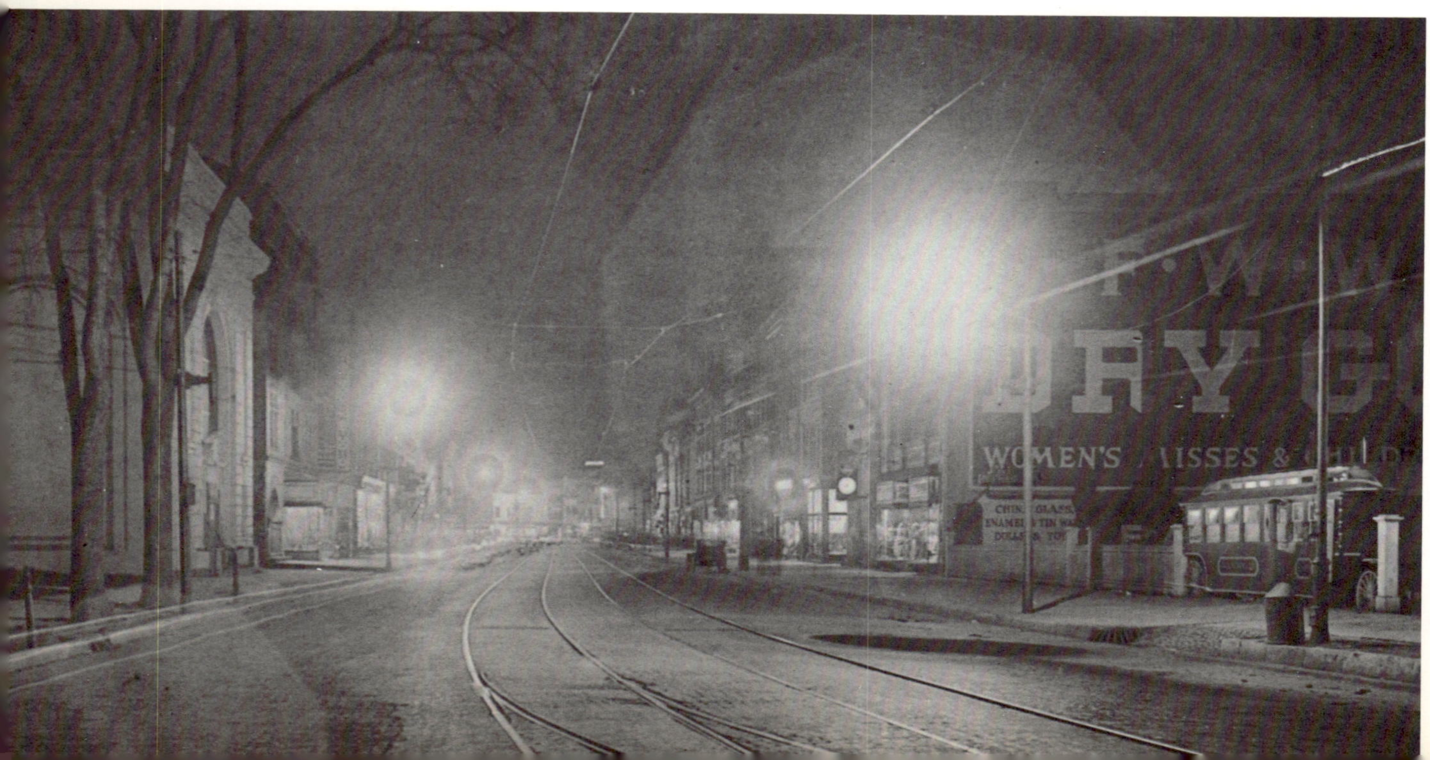
DRY

Horsecars made their appearance in Glens Falls in 1885, continuing until the line between Monument Square in Glens Falls and the Bradley Opera House in Broadway in Fort Edward was electrified in 1891. At top left, car No. 8 stops in front of the Crandall Block, near the end of the line. Busses replaced electric cars in 1928, with both forms of transportation operating for a time as shown at center left. Bottom view shows a virtually deserted Glen Street on a World War I night. Greeno's lunch wagon, a downtown landmark for many years, stood at the right on the site of the Jeremiah W. Finch house. This property beginning in 1922 was occupied by the Empire Auto Co. filling station, above, the south half of which was torn down in 1937 for the Montgomery Ward building, now National Auto Stores, and the north half, right, in 1949 for the Glens Falls National Bank and Trust Company. Below is a contemporary view of the west side of Glen Street beginning at the bank.

112

Three stages in the history of the Crandall Block, a Glens Falls landmark for many years until it was swept by fire May 27, 1963, are pictured on these pages. At left, the interconnected buildings were fairly new when famous photographer Seneca Ray Stoddard took this view between 1885 and 1890. Note the horsecar tracks in the muddy street. Corey's store, with the horseshoe-shaped sign, occupied the southerly part of the block, and a paper box factory an upper floor. The American House, a leading Glens Falls hotel, later renamed the Hotel Ruliff, was at the farther corner of Glen and South Streets. Below, left, the buildings were mostly vacant about 1962 before their sale to the Glens Falls National Bank and Trust Company. Below, smoke and flames pour from the buildings in a fire that started while they were being razed for an addition to the bank.

Looking down Bay Street toward Glen in the late 1800's, one saw, past the monument, the Crandall Block at the southwest corner of Glen and South Streets. It was on this corner in 1784 that Abraham Haviland, an early settler, erected the first frame house in the "upper part of the village." A blacksmith by trade, he also had his shop on the property. The Crandall Block burned in 1963.

The Glens Falls National Bank and Trust Company now occupies the scene past the monument. The bank's landscaped corner, with fountain and flowers, is the site of the Haviland house, the first building to change the pattern from pioneer log dwellings to frame homes and places of business following the American Revolution.

The northwest corner of Glen and South Streets in Glens Falls has been a hotel site longer than any other location in the city. The American House, shown here in the early 1870's, dated from the mid-1800's, perhaps as early as 1835. The big two-story porch was on the South Street side. The American House was a stopping place for stagecoaches between Glens Falls and Lake George; the horses and coaches, in fact, were kept in barns in the rear of the hotel.

Following a fire which destroyed the venerable old American House on August 5, 1879, George Pardo, proprietor, erected a three-story brick hotel which continued the old name. About 1899 it was changed to the Hotel Ruliff as shown by the photo at top right. About 1924, the big porch, this time on the Glen Street side, was removed, the entrance moved to the South Street side, and the name changed to the Plaza Hotel.

Since then the hotel has passed through a succession of ownerships and changes of name, having been known for a number of years as the Hotel Bennett and later as the Northway Hotel. The building is now known as "Monument Square." A restaurant occupies the corner.

Two views taken from almost the same angle are shown above and below. Top photo shows Monument Square in the 1870's, with the Sisson house beyond the monument and the Church of the Messiah, without its steeple, at the left. The Sisson house, the second framed building in the village, was razed in 1890 to make way for the Glens Falls Insurance Company's second office building. The lower photo shows the third Insurance Company building, erected on the same site in 1912, with the Episcopal church steeple at the left.

The Soldiers' Monument, right, at Glen and Bay Streets is shown decorated for its dedication on May 30, 1872. At a town meeting in 1866, the voters approved an appropriation of $8,000 to erect a suitable monument to commemorate the services and sacrifices of the soldiers of Queensbury who fell in the Civil War. The contract was awarded to R. T. Baxter, a local marble dealer, who started the work in the spring of 1867. The foundation is of Glens Falls marble, the base of Maine granite and the rest of Dorchester freestone brought from New Brunswick. The monument, about 50 feet high, is believed to weigh around 100 tons. The actual cost was $12,000 and Baxter had to absorb the $4,000 difference between his contract price and the actual cost. The monument is surmounted by an eagle carved from a block of stone five feet square and three feet thick.

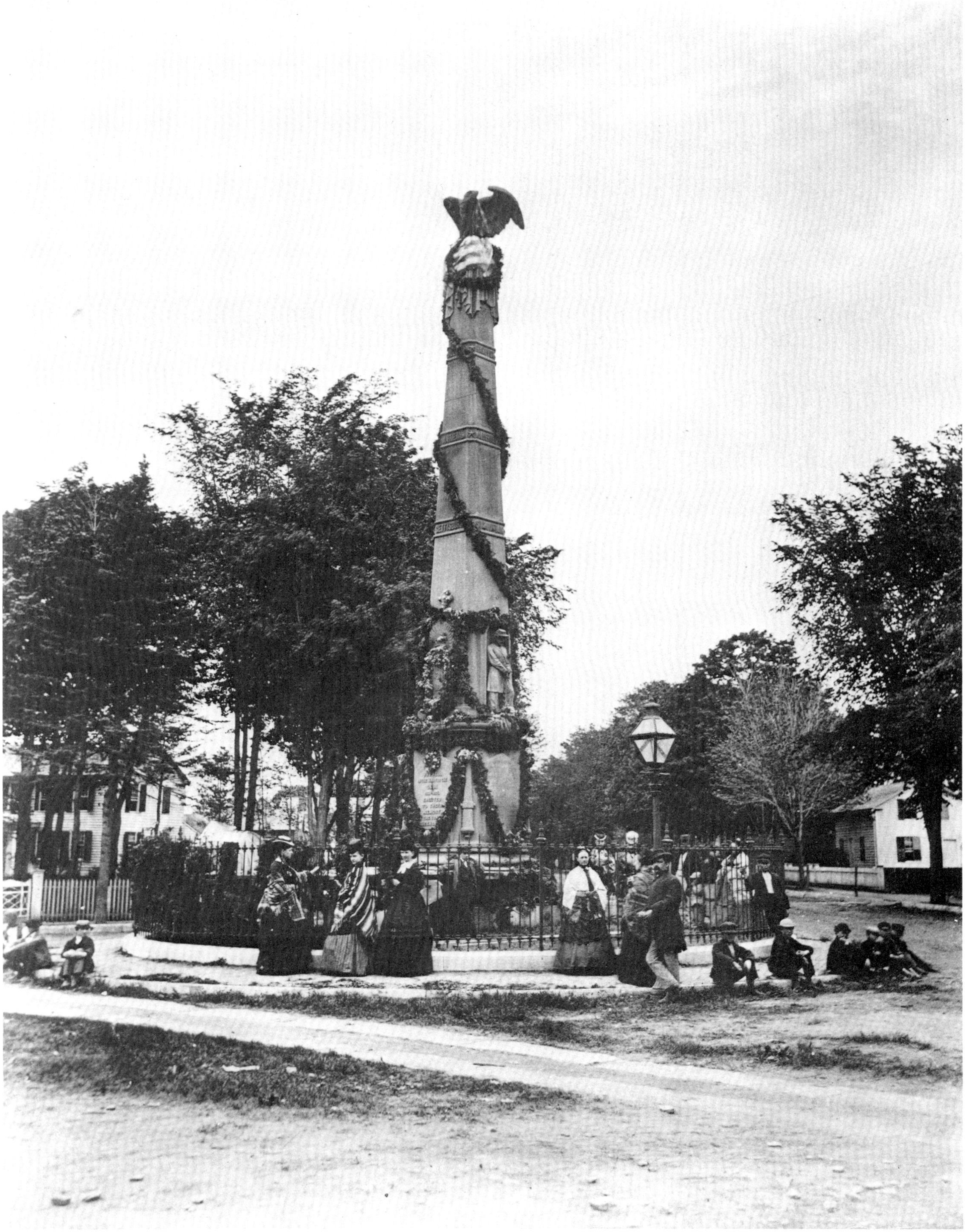

One of Seneca Ray Stoddard's outstanding photographs was this panorama taken about 1872 of the section along Glen and Bay Streets in what is now City Park. The angle of view extended from the old Sisson house at the extreme left to beyond the first Glens Falls Insurance Company building on the right. The Sisson house, constructed soon after the Revolution, stood on the northeast corner of Glen and Bay Streets on the site later occupied by the Insurance Company. Continuing to the right are the Civil War monument with the view looking up Bay Street, and then the home of Gideon F. Mead. The land was vacant between Mead's house and the next building, the home of Henry Crandall, lumberman and

A more detailed view of Bay Street buildings shows an area now occupied by City Park. From left, the home of Joseph Mead at the corner of Bay and Maple Streets; his blacksmith shop, and Gideon F. Mead's home. At extreme left is a portion of the white picket fence around the romantic Sisson home on the corner of Glen and Bay Streets.

philanthropist. Later, Crandall was to erect a three-story business building to the north of his house; the first Crandall Library would be located on the second floor of that structure. South of Crandall's house was the Rufus Lasher place, and next to that the Lawn Cottage. When the park was enlarged about 1918 the latter building was moved to 50 William Street where it still stands. Next was the Locke shop and home, and then the first Glens Falls Insurance Company building, designed to be easily converted into a house should the company fail. "Penny" Wilson's store came next and then the home of Squire Ranger. Beyond that, looking down Glen Street toward Bank Square, the buildings are unrecognizable.

The scene below comes alive with a rain-drenched crowd, military units, a boys' club and other groups participating in a Decoration Day observance in the early 1900's. The building then housing Crandall Library is at the left, with Henry Crandall's home next door, and spacious lawns of other homes lining Glen Street to the south.

The Glens Falls Insurance Company, founded in 1849, did more than any other single factor to spread the name of Glens Falls throughout the world.

Organized only a decade after the village was incorporated, the "Old and Tried" carried the name "Glens Falls" to every part of the globe. Its branch offices dotted the United States from coast to coast. Ships that sailed the seven seas took the protection of the Glens Falls with them to the world's most distant ports. The company boasted that the sun never set on its far-flung operations.

Today the Glens Falls Insurance Company is a part of the Continental Insurance Companies, operating under the latter's flag from an eleven-story office building in downtown Glens Falls. Gone is the beautiful brick and marble five-story office building which graced Monument Square for 64 years, but the business at its new location continues to attract wealth to the community and is one of our largest employers.

In the latter part of 1849 a number of prominent citizens of Glens Falls, led by Russell Mack Little, a former minister turned insurance agent, met to consider the organization of a fire insurance company designed purely for local purposes. In the same year the company was incorporated as the Glens Falls Dividend Mutual Insurance Company.

It began business in a one-room office on the second floor of the old Exchange Building at Glen and Exchange Streets, with Mr. Little as secretary and sole employe. The company soon outgrew its office and moved to the second floor of the D. H. Cowles and Company building at Ridge and Warren Streets, where it remained until 1859 when an increasing volume of business compelled it to erect an office building on Glen Street, above, on the site now occupied by the old YMCA building.

The directors of the company, with characteristic caution, built a two-story brick structure which could easily be converted into a dwelling in case the company failed.

The mutual insurance plan fell into disrepute as one company after another failed under reckless or dishonest management. In 1864 the Glens Falls was almost alone among the mutual companies, and Mr. Little, realizing the difficulty of continuing under that plan, proposed reorganization into a stock company. His proposal was approved, and the name was changed to the Glens Falls Insurance Company.

Steady growth resulted in the construction of a new office building starting in 1890 on the former Sisson property at Glen and Bay Streets, the old one being sold to the YMCA. By 1912 the new building had been outgrown and the company gave it to the Masonic order, which moved it across Glen Street and used it as a Masonic Temple until 1967. Part of it still stands as a portion of the Church of the Messiah Parish House.

The third building, a five-story structure on the same site, was started in 1912 and completed the following year. Despite a large addition on Bay Street, built in 1928, and subsequent "penthouse" additions, the building became insufficient for the company's needs. After merger with Continental Insurance Companies in 1970, the present 11-story building was erected, the old one razed and the land converted into a park.

The Glens Falls Insurance Company's second home, above, completed in 1891 on the site of the century-old Sisson house, was outgrown in 1912. Plans were announced for a new building on the same site and the old one was given to the Masonic fraternity. In a fantastic engineering accomplishment, the three-story brick and stone structure, pulled by horses and winches, was moved intact, except for its tower, across Glen Street and backed into its new location. Many "sidewalk superintendents" watched its passage north of the Ruliff Hotel, below, after trolley and other wires were cut to clear its path. The building served as the local Masonic Temple until 1967 when the Masons built a new home. Part of it was then razed and the rest incorporated into a new Parish House for the Church of the Messiah which still stands on the west side of Glen Street opposite the church.

Old Glory flies from the roof of the third Glens Falls Insurance Company building, photographed shortly after its completion in 1913. Notice the open touring car parked at the curb at the left, and the horses and wagons the automobile was soon to replace. The awning and benches around the Civil War monument in the center of the picture were placed there by Henry Crandall for the benefit of tired passersby and those waiting for trolley cars.

Demolition of the third Insurance Building is almost completed in this picture taken in August, 1976. Continental Insurance created an attractive mini-park on the site, setting out trees, shrubbery and flowers. For the first time since the Insurance Building was erected in 1912, the Church of the Messiah now has southern exposure.

This 11-story steel, marble and glass building, left, at 333 Glen Street is the Glens Falls headquarters of the Continental Insurance Companies, successor to the Glens Falls Insurance Company. Started in October, 1970, the building was completed and opened in 1973.

The aerial photo below shows all three Glen Street locations of home offices of the Glens Falls Insurance Company and its successor, Continental: Lower left, the new building; right center, cleared site of the second and third buildings south of the Church of the Messiah; extreme right, the site of the first building where the old YMCA now stands.

History does not record the occasion for the Monument Square celebration shown in the photograph above, taken about 1910. It may have been the annual observance of Memorial Day, known then as Decoration Day. Almost every form of transportation known at that time was in evidence: the trolley car, a closed hack, a surrey with fringe on the top, a man on horseback, a right-hand drive open automobile, numerous bicycles, and, of course, good old "shank's mare," travel afoot. None of the buildings shown in the photograph exists today, except Christ Church, United Methodist, a corner of which appears next to the old Glens Falls Insurance Company building at the left. City Park occupies the site of all the Bay Street buildings shown at the right except the Chitty house, just to the right of the monument, which was where the Rogers Building now stands at the northeast corner of Bay and Maple Streets.

The Farmers' Market now held every Saturday in season in Exchange Street in Glens Falls had its counterpart in the old days. Farmers drove into town by horse and wagon and automobile and parked along Bay Street at Monument Square, where they offered their produce for sale, as shown in the top photo on the opposite page. Crandall Library occupied the second floor of the first building beyond, owned by Henry Crandall, whose home was just out of camera range at the right. This building and all the others shown along Bay Street to Maple were razed when City Park was expanded about 1918. The center photo on the opposite page, taken within a few minutes of the first, shows some of the market patrons with their baskets and bags. Many years later the LARAC (Lower Adirondack Regional Arts Council) Festival became a popular annual feature in City Park, and the bottom photo shows a typical crowd about 1975.

124

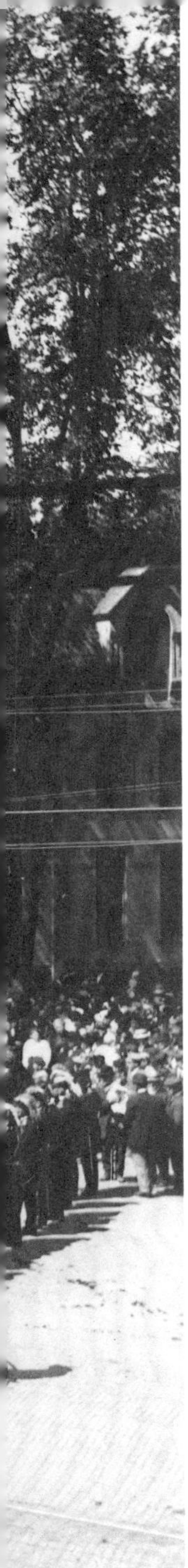

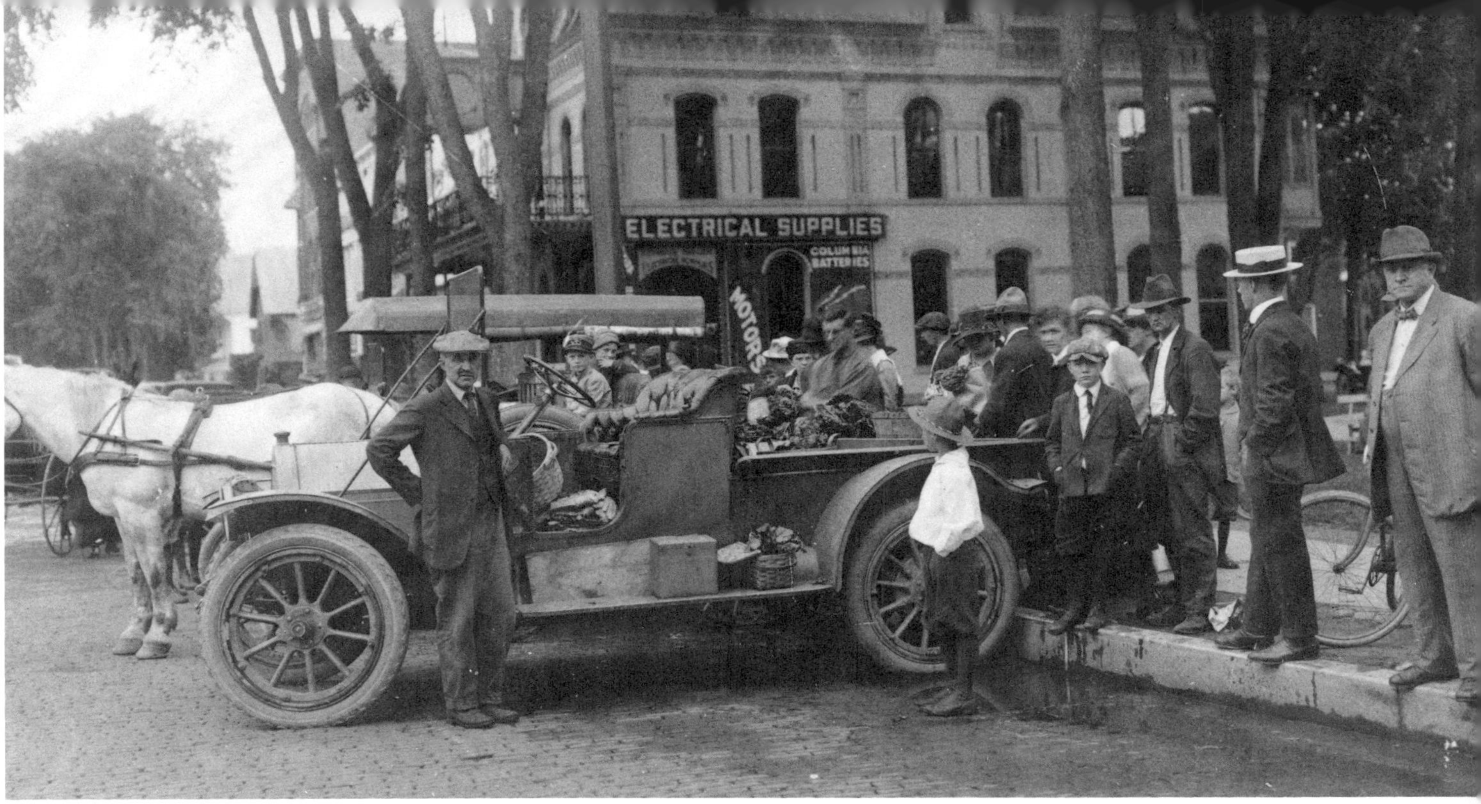
ELECTRICAL SUPPLIES
MOTORS

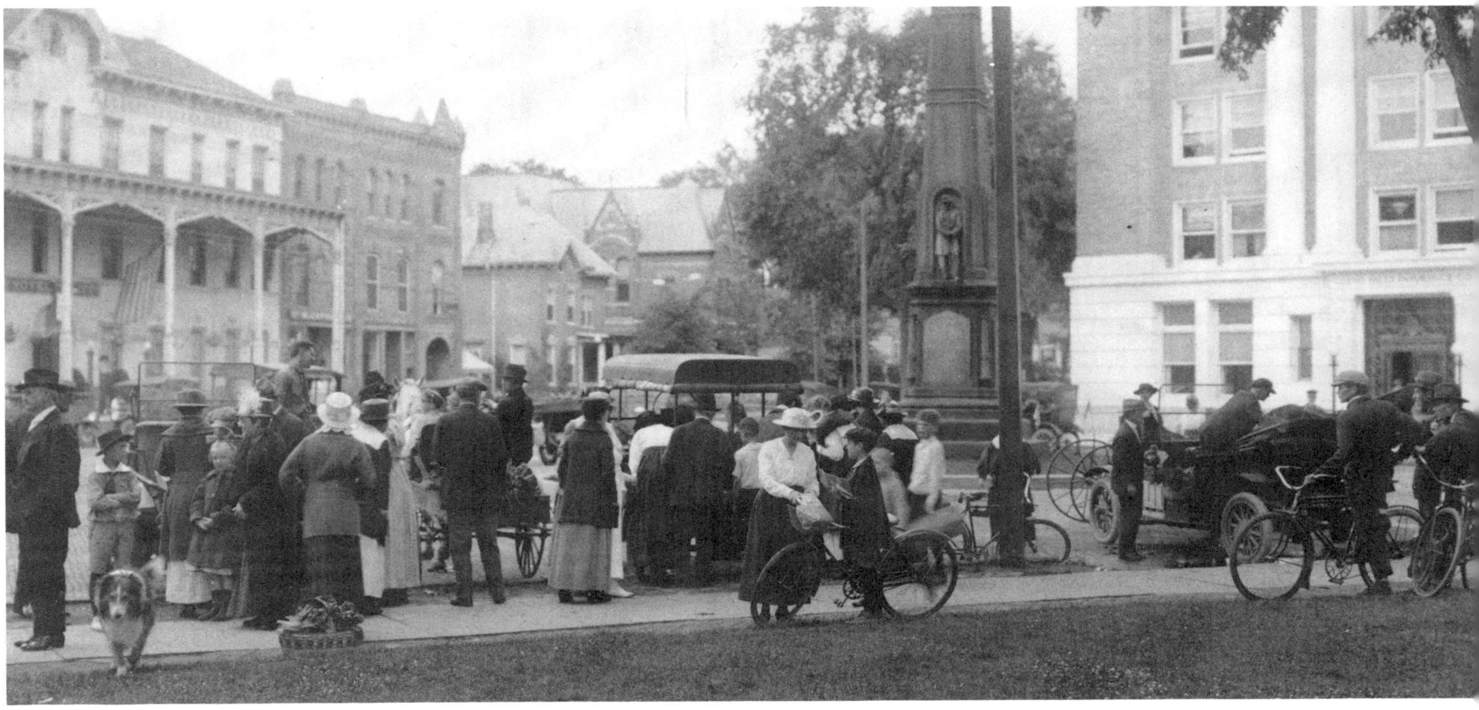

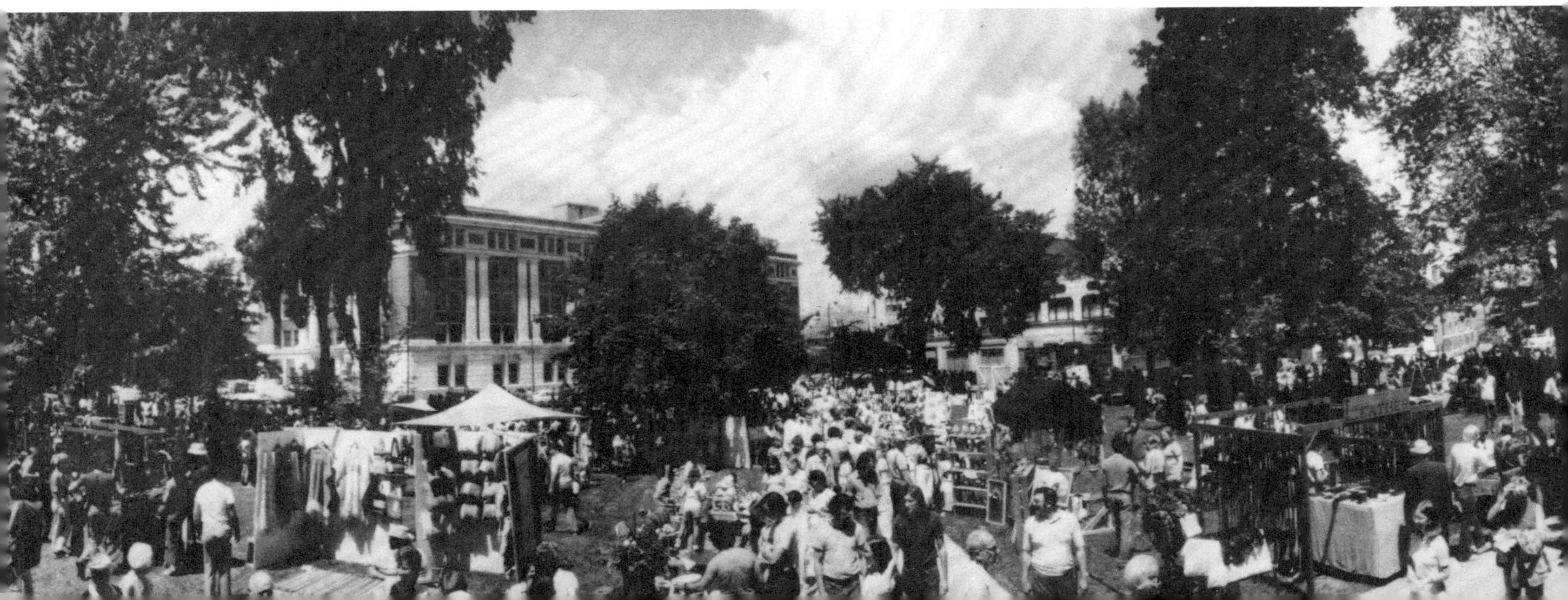

One bicyclist, three pedestrians and a carriage were the extent of traffic in this part of Monument Square when the photographer snapped the picture above prior to 1912. City Park now occupies the sites of the Glen and Bay Street buildings shown, except for the old YMCA building, which is still standing, and the location of the First National Bank. Below, showing a part of the park and Crandall Library, five motor vehicles and two motorcycles have taken the place of the lone cyclist shown in the top photo emerging from Bay Street onto Glen.

The more things change, the more they are the same. There was always a crosswalk on Glen Street across Bay at the monument, as the top photograph on this page shows. For a few years it was eliminated by the city in favor of a shorter and less dangerous walk up Bay Street a bit, but with the realignment of the corner in 1977 the old crosswalk was restored, and in the photo above a young bicyclist makes use of it.

There wasn't any traffic jam to divert his attention, so the white-hatted policeman on duty at Glen and South Streets in the photo above, taken about 1918, had time to give directions to an inquiring bicyclist, obviously a stranger in town. This is the view of Bay Street buildings near the monument as seen from South Street. A similar view, below, taken from farther up South Street after the blizzard of February 14, 1914, shows huge snow drifts, unplowed except for the trolley tracks. "Quo Vadis" was playing at the Empire Theatre. The Empire Hotel and the South-End Livery were at the left, on the present site of a city parking lot, and the Hotel Madden was on the right.

The First Library

It is a refreshing reflection on human nature that Henry Crandall, a man of meagre background who was not a reader himself and had no children, gave a library and two parks to the people of Glens Falls. Crandall, who made a fortune in the lumber business, responded to the urgings of School Superintendent Sherman Williams and donated the second floor of one of his business buildings for a library. It was located next to his home opposite the monument. Crandall also gave $2,500 for the first books, together with the income from the rest of the building for continuing support of the library, which was chartered by New York State in 1893.

Crandall died in 1913 and was buried in Crandall Park beneath a tall granite shaft surmounted by the five-pointed star that was his logger's mark. From 1919 to 1931, while the first library and other buildings were being razed for establishment of City Park, the library operated from the Jerome Lapham house on Ridge Street, just north of City Hall. The present library in City Park was opened in 1931, and a large wing was added to the Glen Street side in 1971, necessitated by designation of the library as central reference site for the four-county Southern Adirondack Library System.

The Jerome Lapham House

Crandall Library

Henry Crandall

Henry Crandall, who gave his community a library and two parks, also organized a Boys' Savings Club at the turn of the century because he remembered his own early struggles. Membership was limited to 100 boys between the ages of 12 and 16, and each received a uniform, brass pin and bankbook with provisional deposit of $25. If a boy earned by his own work and deposited the sum of $37.50 by the time he was 16, he then retired from the club but received from Crandall an additional $62.50 upon reaching the age of 21.

In each boy's bankbook the benefactor had written of his members: "None of them is poorer than I was when a boy," and "All of them have a far better chance to earn money than I did." Joseph Hannan of East Washington Street, a member, recalls that the club had a fife and drum corps, and each meeting ended with a parade from the meeting place on South Street to Mr. Crandall's home on Glen Street. The boys would throw their hats into the air, shout "Three cheers for Uncle Henry," and then be treated to ice cream and doughnuts.

The Boys' Savings Club in 1902, with the fife and drum corps at the left and "Uncle Henry" Crandall seated at the center.

130

A familiar scene on Glen Street toward the end of the last century was Henry Crandall and his team of grays, posing above at the Crandall home. Mrs. Dora Bullock recalls that Mr. Crandall drove his wife by horse and carriage up Glen Street to his park almost every afternoon in their late years. Addison B. Colvin had a similar recollection: "The writer sees the picture today, as though the principal were before him, of the grey carriage team, harnessed to a light wagon loaded with utensils, starting from the Crandall residence for the park. The faithful caretaker [Benjamin] Betty, holding the reins, jogging the team along, both anxious to do as much work as possible at the park in the allotted time." Legend has it that the horses are buried in the park, not far from the resting place of the Crandalls.

On this page: A century in time and several hundred feet in elevation separate these two photographs looking up Bay Street from Monument Square. Above, from ground level in the 1870's, with the historic Sisson house at the left of the monument; left, from an airplane in the 1970's, looking down on the third Insurance Building on the former Sisson site. The Insurance Building was razed in 1976, having been replaced by a new building farther north on Glen Street. Bay Street was one of the first streets laid out in Glens Falls and at one time had more buildings than Glen Street. Originally it was known as "the road by the meeting house," a reference to the first Quaker church at what is now the southwest corner of the Bay and Quaker Roads.

Opposite page: Top left, the oldest house in Glens Falls when it was razed in 1956, this Bay Street building was erected in 1790 by Alfred Ferriss. Top right, the building which now stands on that site, erected in 1956 for the Glens Falls Savings and Loan Association and now the Albany Savings Bank, with which the Savings and Loan was merged in 1970. Center, parking was beginning to be a problem on Maple Street near Bay in 1926 when this picture was taken. The Hall Ice Cream Co. building, still standing, is now Borden's, but many of the rest of those shown are gone. Bottom, the Rogers Building, built in 1927 at Bay and Maple Streets, stands on the corner shown in photo next above.

The Reliance
INSURANCE
AGENCY

ALBANY
SAVINGS
BANK
GLENS FALLS OFFICE
2 TO 5 YEAR
TIME
DEPOSITS

THE HALL ICE CREAM CO.
Williams Tire & Rubber Co.
GENERAL TIRES
STABILATORS
Vulcanizing
WILLIAMS TIRE & RUBBER CO.

GLENS FALLS TRAVEL
TRAVEL AGENCY

Only two of the business buildings shown in this 1922 view of the north side of Maple Street opposite City Park are still standing. From the left, the Glens Falls Electric Installation Co., where the Niagara Mohawk Power Corporation building is now located; Hall Ice Cream Co., still standing, now Borden's; Henry Crandall's old carriage house, still standing, then the Bullard Press and now Loeb Rhoades Hornblower and Co., brokers; Morf and Galusha, automotive electricians, now the Cool Insuring Agency; and the three-story Miller Brothers garage, razed for the First National Bank drive-in and parking lot.

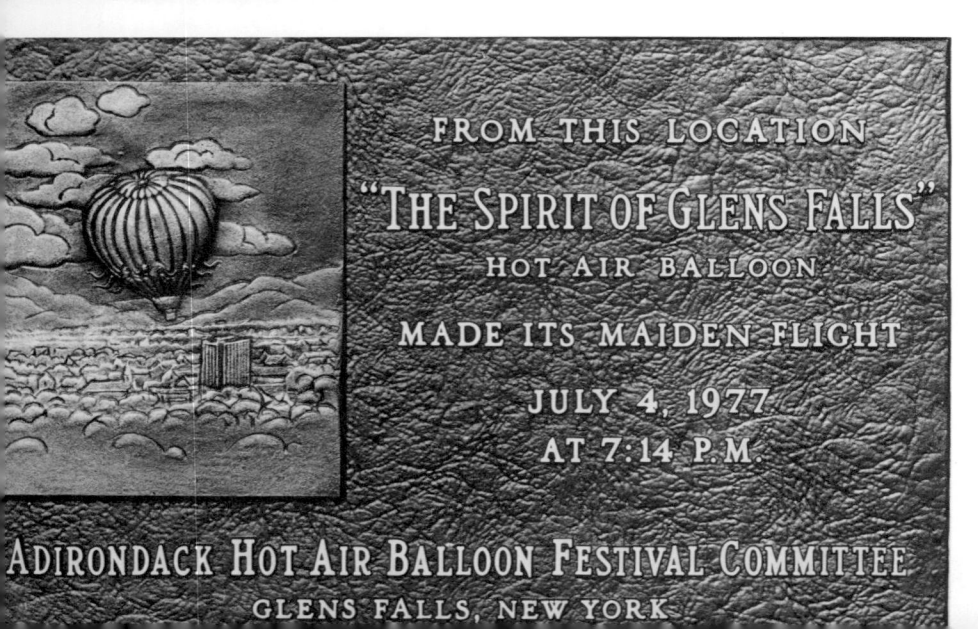

A corner of City Park near the Queensbury Hotel and City Hall and the bandstand was the scene of an event July 4, 1977, which took place 101 years after it was originally scheduled.

The Glens Falls Centennial program for July 4, 1876, listed a balloon ascension at 4 p.m. For some reason the "Jupiter" failed to get off the ground. In the Bicentennial year of 1977, however, the "Spirit of Glens Falls," locally owned flagship of the annual Adirondack Hot Air Balloon Festival, lifted off from City Park on her maiden flight, carrying air mail bearing "Jupiter" stamps issued in 1959 to commemorate the 100th anniversary of ballooning in the United States.

On August 10, 1978, a bronze plaque, atop a small cement capsule containing memorabilia of that flight, was unveiled in the park in ceremonies sponsored by the Balloon Festival Committee and the First National Bank. The capsule is to be opened in 2027 with the hope that the next generation will insure a commemorative flight from the same location.

FROM THIS LOCATION
"THE SPIRIT OF GLENS FALLS"
HOT AIR BALLOON
MADE ITS MAIDEN FLIGHT
JULY 4, 1977
AT 7:14 P.M.

ADIRONDACK HOT AIR BALLOON FESTIVAL COMMITTEE
GLENS FALLS, NEW YORK

Originally the home of District Attorney Isaac Mott and one of the first houses in Glens Falls to be lighted with gas, this home on the north side of Maple Street opposite City Park served a variety of purposes. From 1908 until 1921, it was the home of Glens Falls Council, 194, Knights of Columbus. Later it became the Wellington Hotel and finally was occupied by the Glens Falls Savings and Loan Association and other business places until torn down several years ago to make way, with other property, for the First National Bank drive-in and parking lot. View at left shows the building as it was many years ago; at right, shortly before it was razed.

Glens Falls' Bicentennial Bandstand in City Park, surrounded by lawns, flowers and shrubbery, took the place of an earlier structure which it resembled greatly in size and appearance. The latter was given to the Veterans of Foreign Wars and moved to West Glens Falls, where it was used briefly before being burned to dispose of it in 1978. For a number of years the only bandstand in the city was a platform next to the First National Bank in Glen Street.

The Benjamin Lapham house, above, left, stood on the site of Glens Falls' City Hall on Ridge Street until the municipal building was erected in 1900. Above, right, Lapham Place had not been extended through to Ridge Street when this picture was taken, showing the old Ridge Street engine house next to the city building. At the left, the building, shown before 1908, looked pretty much the same as it does now, except for the words "Village Hall" replaced by "City Hall" at the top. The small white building at the right was Jerome Lapham's carriage house, now Honigsbaum's women's apparel store. The interior of City Hall is being completely renovated in 1978 to accommodate an expanding city government. Below, a photo of the 1942 salvage pile in City Park shows a part of nearly 400 tons of metal contributed to the World War II drive, including an old fire department steamer, 200 tons of trolley tracks, a 1,360-pound fire bell and the old fountain which once stood in Bank Square.

The large and beautiful William McEchron home at Ridge and Maple Streets was given to the city in 1920 to be used as a Health Center. Sharing the quarters now with the Health Department are the Voluntary Action Center, Family Service Association, Big Brother-Big Sister program, Homemakers and other civic and health-related activities.

The Dr. George W. Little home on Ridge Street, with its unique conservatory and aviary, stood next to the William McEchron home, now the Health Center, on a portion of the property presently occupied by a nine-story apartment building. The Little house is shown above, the Robert J. Cronin High-Rise, into which the first tenants moved August 21, 1978, at the right.

Looking up Ridge Street from Bank Square in the 1920's, above, and in 1977, below. The former Cowles Building, at the right, was once doomed to Urban Renewal razing, but that and nearby buildings have been saved and are being restored by New Fountain Square, Ltd. Wing's Tavern, erected by Abraham Wing about 1773, stood on the Cowles site at Ridge and Warren Streets.

The home of Dr. and Mrs. Thomas Hammond Foulds on Ridge Street, at the right, was one of the showplaces of Glens Falls but this city received little benefit from the $5,000,000 estate left by Mrs. Foulds when she died in 1958. Dr. Foulds had died previously. She left $4,500,000 to the Metropolitan Museum of Art in New York and the balance in small amounts to the Church of the Messiah and various relatives, but many local residents and organizations were disappointed that she left nothing to them. The house was torn down for the Kamyr Ridge Center project.

A vital impetus to the city's economic future was initiated when Kamyr Incorporated, a Sweden-based firm, selected Glens Falls for its United States headquarters. Internationally recognized for pulp machinery design, mechanical contracting and the manufacture of valves, the company moved into its impressive downtown business complex in Ridge and Pearl Streets in 1967 and has become notably influential in the city's development and beautification. Its subsidiary, Kamyr Valves, has an attractive new plant under construction on Pruyn's Island, where a Finnish manufacturer of certain components for the pulp and paper industry, the Ahlstrom Company, has also chosen to locate.

Looking west on Warren Street, above, from near Culvert Street in the 1880's and from near the Opera House, below, after the blizzard of 1888. Note the little boy, properly hatted, sitting on the horse block at the right in the upper photo and the horses attempting to pull a sleigh through the snowdrifts in the lower.

Some of the stores which lined the north side of Warren Street around 1890 are shown above. Photo at the left shows the same buildings in 1977, partially vacant and doomed to demolition. Today they are being restored and renovated by New Fountain Square, Ltd. Below, looking east on Warren Street about 1900 after a heavy snow storm. The fountain, foreground, had been turned off for the winter. A sign on a pole at the right said "Electric Cars Stop Here."

The 1874 directory boasted a total of 22 hotels in the city, but 15 were operating as saloons only. City Hotel, opened about 1886 on the south side of Warren Street just east of Glen, was one of 16 hotels, most of them small, in business by 1907. A downtown fixture of longer standing than the hotel was the general store next to it, conducted from Civil War days by William Cronkhite and his son. The site of these buildings, now vacant, is part of the proposed location for a large chain hotel with shops and restaurants. Completion of the Civic Center, below, is expected to swell the need for visitor accommodations.

Modern downtown Glens Falls, from the banks of the Hudson to Monument Square, is an area central to the hopes and aspirations of some 17,000 city residents who want a revitalized and attractive hometown.

Botany students from the Ridge Street School enjoy a field trip at Crandall Park about 1905

All Around the Town

The story of Glens Falls encompasses more than industry and commerce. It extends to all day-to-day activities in our homes, our churches, our schools and our meeting halls . . . all around the town.

A pleasant glimpse of old Glens Falls family activity is perhaps best afforded by Katharine Cunningham's *Homely Recollections*. She tells that the daily round began early: "At six the Angelus from St. Mary's and the Presbyterian town-clock clashed in a pleasant jangle; at seven the whistles blew. Grandfather's family lived by the mill whistle. Breakfast was at seven-thirty, followed by family prayers before it was time to start for the office, or to school, as the case might be. Later came household tasks for everybody."

After supper, her grandmother and grandfather enjoyed "the veranda with its comfortable if somewhat mixed collection of rocking chairs. The neighborhood was still at this hour, save for one clattering interlude when busses from the Rockwell House, the American House, and Dr. Bemis' Sanitarium tore down Maple Street to meet the evening train. When they had returned at a more normal pace - so as not to scare the daylights out of any new arrivals - the grandparents would continue to sit there in the tranquil dusk, watching, as darkness gathered, the chimney swifts who nested in the roofs and chimneys of the Baptist Church, dipping and wheeling against the evening sky."

Of growing up she says: "There was discipline, but there was plenty of fun for the McEchron girls, and it varied with the seasons. Chestnutting parties came in October when the trees were gold and scarlet along Gurney's Lane and on West Mountain; there was skating in winter; and moonlight sleigh-rides up the Ridge Road with hot chocolate and cookies in the Haviland's kitchen; hunting for mayflowers in the spring; trips to Pearl Point in the summer, or even a climb up Prospect Mountain."

Late summer afternoons brought the sprinkling cart on its final tour of the unpaved streets: "The watering cart always made rounds at sundown, badly needed in the village, in spite of many shade trees and busily whirling lawn-sprinklers. It creaked past with heavy wheels and arching tiers of spray; the dust was laid, the green borders of the streets were wet again, and the air was suddenly alive with lovely refreshing coolness. One could feel in the peaceful evening air the serenity of this pleasant, big village with its green dooryards, its well-kept houses, its spreading elm trees."

Most of the elms are gone, but Glens Falls still has beautiful trees, green dooryards and well-kept homes. We still enjoy many simple pleasures of those earlier days. The coming of diverse nationalities and ethnic groups through the years has added new dimensions to the inventiveness and distinction of the community. The "East End" attracted the Irish and Italians, the "West End," the French Canadians, but it is in the meld of all groups that the richness of our heritage is found.

Individual graciousness, civic pride and a commitment to community service abound in Glens Falls, giving rise to a quality of life rarely found today. Glens Falls . . . a good place to call home.

Glens Falls welcomed the automobile age. In 1917 alone, the Empire Automobile Company, 45 Warren Street, sold 840 Model T Fords. Above, two new buses for the Hotel Champlain await delivery. Originally the home of Joubert and White, whose name appears at the top of the building, this is where the famous Joubert and White buckboards were made in the 1880's and '90's. It is now occupied by Armando's candle factory.

The Eden Park Nursing Home, below, stands at Warren and Prospect Streets on the site once occupied by one of Glens Falls' most gracious homes. It was the residence, left, of George R. Finch, banker, lumberman and Democratic leader. By 1967, long gone out of the hands of the Finch family, the house was falling apart. Windows were boarded up, the once-lush lawns had grown high with weeds and the interior had been ravaged by fire. In 1968 the house was razed and the Nursing Home was opened on the site in 1970.

Church Street, looking south from Warren Street, is shown in this Seneca Ray Stoddard winter picture taken before the turn of the century. St. Mary's Academy is at the left, with the bell tower. There are no buildings now in that block of Church Street, except for St. Mary's Church at the corner of Warren and the Stichman Towers apartments, right, which actually face on Jay Street.

The building shown below, erected in 1915 at Warren and Jay Streets, was Glens Falls' post office for 62 years. A new one was opened at Hudson Avenue and Murray Street in 1977 and as of October, 1978, the future of the old building had not been determined.

The home of Mr. and Mrs. Louis Fiske Hyde was built on Warren Street in 1912, not only as a beautiful residence but eventually a museum for their outstanding collection of paintings, sculpture, tapestries, choice furniture and rare books. Mrs. Hyde was the eldest of the three daughters of Samuel Pruyn, co-founder of Finch, Pruyn and Company. Her husband was a vice president of the firm and his posthumously published History of Glens Falls *reflects a wide knowledge of the community. After his death in 1934, Mrs. Hyde continued to live in the home and enjoyed opening it on Sunday afternoons to share her treasures with area art lovers. In 1952 she founded a charitable trust which would assume responsibility for establishing and maintaining the museum. The Hyde Collection was opened in 1964, the year following Mrs. Hyde's death, and is ranked among the twenty-five finest art collections in the country. One of the greatest paintings in this hemisphere, Rembrandt's* Christ with the Folded Arms, *hangs in the library of Hyde House. In the livable surroundings of a home, works by such masters as Renoir, da Vinci, VanGogh, Raphael, Van Dyck and El Greco delight visitors with every turn at The Hyde Collection.*

The year was 1895. The streetcar tracks had been laid, but Warren Street was not yet paved, and workmen were applying the finishing touches to the new State Armory when this picture was taken. Built to house the 18th Separate Company, New York National Guard, the Armory today is headquarters for the 646th Medical Company (Ambulance), Army National Guard, and for a detachment of the 105th Infantry. A unit of the Guard designated as Company K has occupied the Armory for most of its 83 years, but there is no unit by that designation there today. The Hughes Light Guards, organized in 1876 at South Glens Falls, were the original local Guard unit. Two years later the name was changed to the 18th Separate Company and in 1880 it moved to Glens Falls, meeting and drilling in the Opera House Block and Keefe Hall before taking possession of the new Armory on November 11, 1895. The company, under a series of different designations, fought in the Spanish-American War, the Mexican border incident, World War I and World War II.

Once the residence of William McDonald, a former member of Assembly from Warren County and the man credited with bringing prosperity to Glens Falls by opening up the Feeder Canal, the original Glens Falls Home for aged women, at Warren and Prospect Streets, is shown at far left. McDonald bought the former Wing farm in Warren Street about 1823, shortly after moving to Glens Falls from Sanfords Ridge in the Town of Queensbury. He enlarged, rebuilt and completed the half-finished house on the property, the original part of which was built by Abraham Wing, the first settler of Glens Falls. He died in 1870. The Glens Falls Home was incorporated Jan. 6, 1899, and on Feb. 28 of that year Mrs. Mary A. Conkling, the then owner, offered to convey the property to the new corporation for half the appraised value for use as a home for aged women. The offer was accepted and the home opened June 26, 1899. William McEchron later offered to build a new home, the old house on the property was removed, and the present home was opened and dedicated Feb. 9, 1903.

149

Not many of the younger generation realize that at one time a deep ravine bisected Park Street just west of Elm. The slopes on each side were steep enough to provide youngsters with good coasting in wintertime. Samuel B. Goodman and family lived in the big house just west of the ravine, shown above, which is now the Sullivan and Minahan Funeral Home, and they took full advantage of the sloping terrain with terraced and landscaped lawns. The next house beyond, at the left in the photo, was that of W. F. Bentley, still at the corner of Park and School Streets, and this was the first house in Glens Falls lighted with electricity.

Eventually the city constructed stone retaining walls across the ravine and brought the street level up to that on each side, thereby eliminating the dip in the street. Later the ravine was filled in on both sides of the street and several buildings were erected, one of them being a structure which eventually became LeRoy J. Gordon's filling station and welding supply business. This settled a foot or more below the sidewalk level before it was finally torn down in 1976 after being acquired by Glens Falls Hospital.

Photos on the next page show work under way on the retaining walls. The Farmers' Sheds were in the background at the right in the top picture. Leonard Hoag's service station and parking lot were on that site later.

150

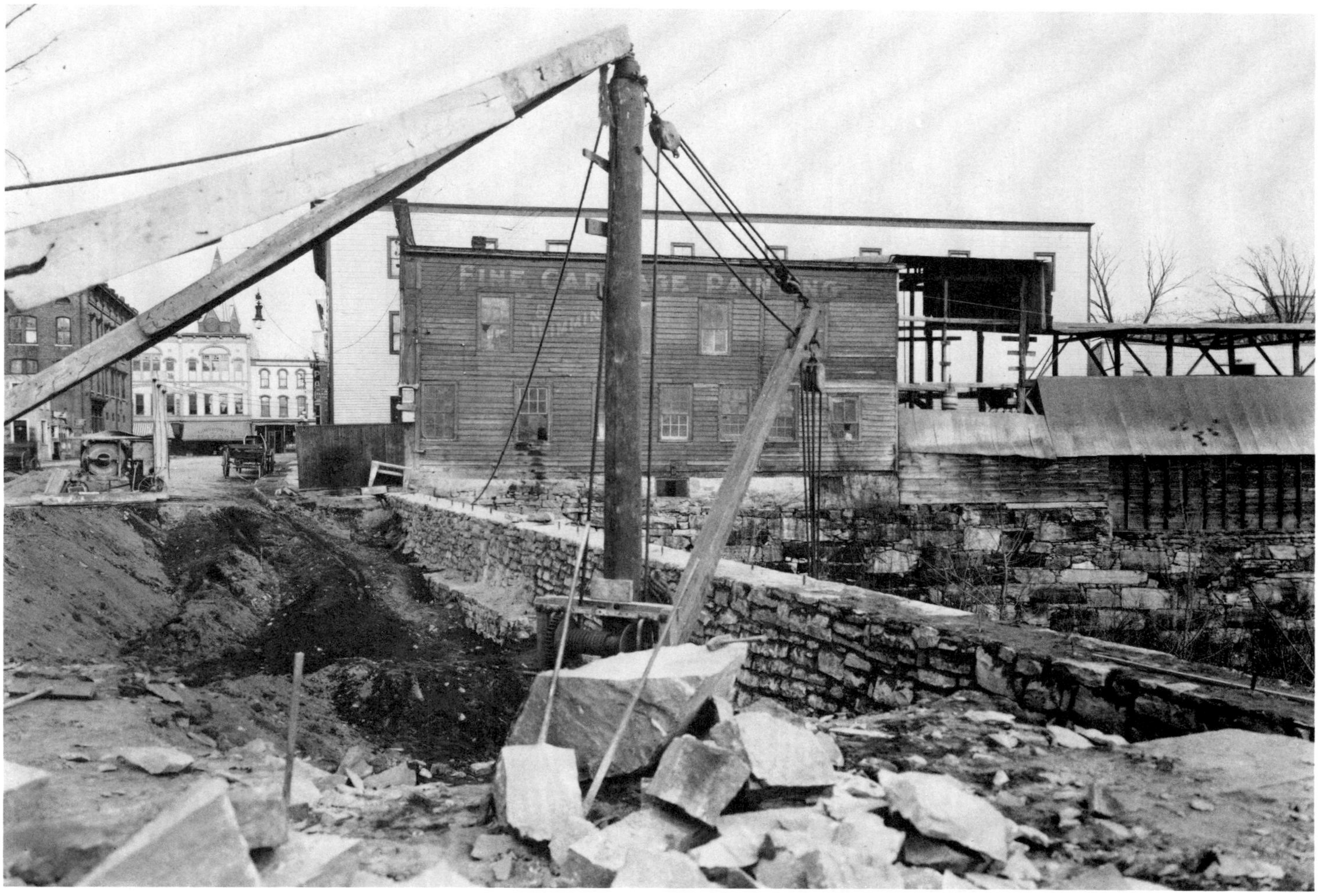

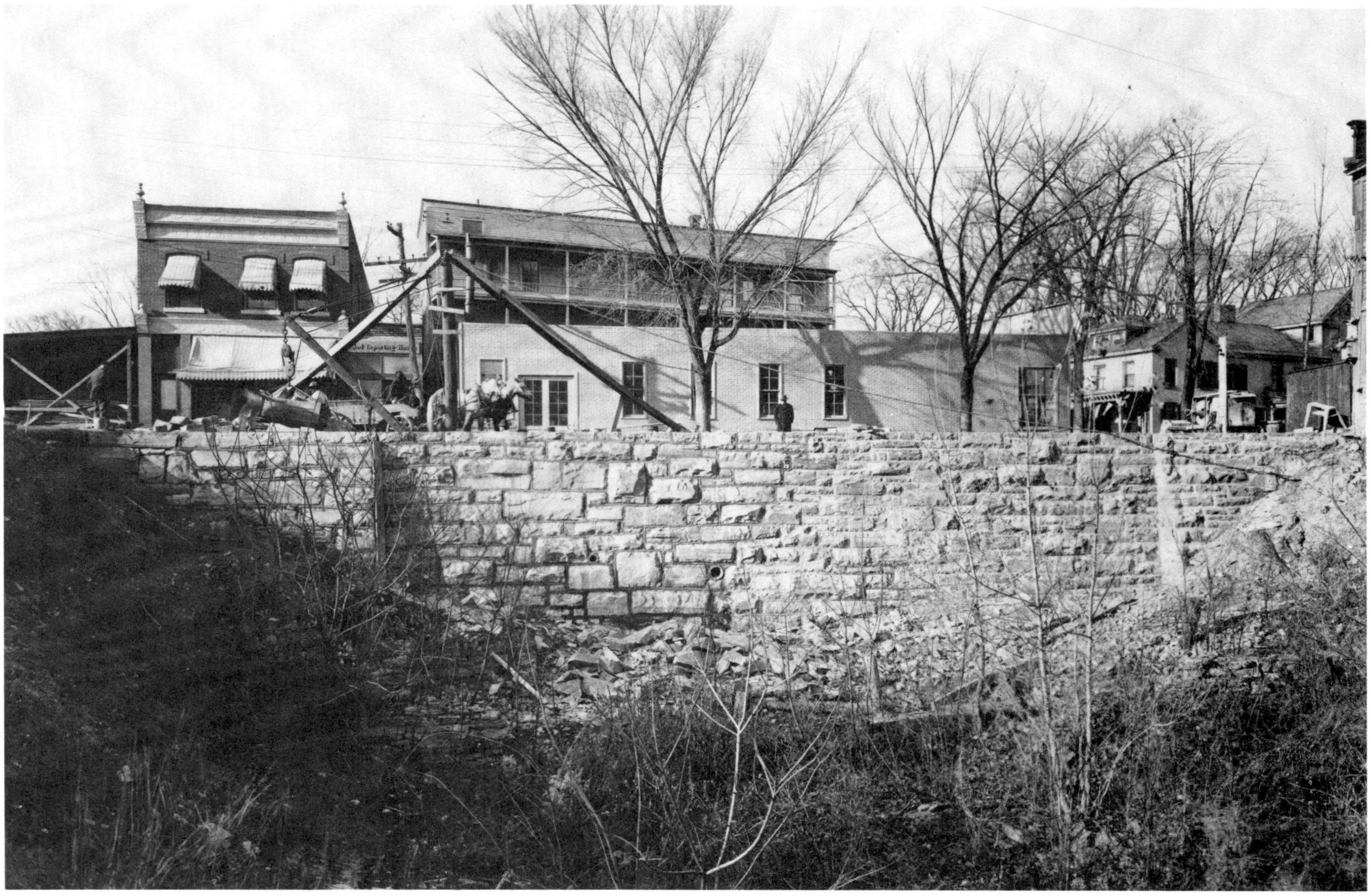

The Parks Hospital on Park Street, above, was the forerunner of Glens Falls Hospital. Solomon A. Parks gave his home for a community hospital in 1899. With the approval of the Parks family, the name was changed to its present one in 1909. Before establishment of Parks Hospital, operations were performed in physicians' offices or in small makeshift hospitals on Elm Street near Park, at the corner of South and Elm Streets, and in the residence that is now St. Mary's Rectory on Warren Street.

The late Solomon A. Parks gave his home on Park Street for a hospital in 1899 and thereby sowed the seeds of what has developed into the present 440-bed Glens Falls Hospital, one of the largest and best equipped in the state.

The Parks Hospital, as it was originally known, opened November 23, 1900, after the house was remodeled. It had facilities for 22 patients, six of whom could be accommodated in private rooms. It quickly outgrew the available space and a three-story building was erected at Park and Basin Streets, being opened December 7, 1910, with a capacity for 72 patients.

The Georgian structure was built of hand-molded clay brick with terra cotta and marble trimmings. The building and land cost $125,000 and a total of $101,000 was raised in a 20-day community campaign. The ward doors were of solid mahogany and the elevator was run by water power. There were 19 private rooms on the second floor, furnished with brass beds and mahogany or fumed oak furniture. A solarium on each floor was designed to be used for open-air treatment of pneumonia.

With the opening of the new building, the former Parks residence was converted into a nurses' home, connected by a bridge to the new hospital. A training school for nurses had been established in 1903 and continued to function until 1932.

Eventually the nurses' home had to be used as an annex to the hospital when the latter building could accommodate no more patients.

As the years passed and the hospital continued to be taxed far beyond its capacity, it became increasingly apparent that a new and larger building was imperative. There was considerable agitation for construction of a new hospital at a different location, and among the proposals advanced was one for a "skyscraper" type of building, twelve stories high, to be erected on the Foulds property on Ridge Street with the aid of a Public Works Administration grant and loan.

The "skyscraper" plan was discarded January 29, 1936, in favor of a proposal to build an addition south of the existing building. A campaign to raise $500,000 to pay the cost of the work went over the top in five days. The old nurses' home was razed. Part of the new building was placed in use July 6, 1938, and, as soon as patients could be moved into the new section, work was begun on remodeling the old building.

The new building was four stories high and faced the west, whereas the old hospital had been three stories high and faced the north. The main entrance was now on the west side. A west wing was added in 1949, with the main entrance again facing the north, and an east wing in 1962. The newest enlargement, completed in 1976, saw additions made all over the building, and the main entrance was once more placed on the west.

The pictures on the following pages show the progress of the building program over the years.

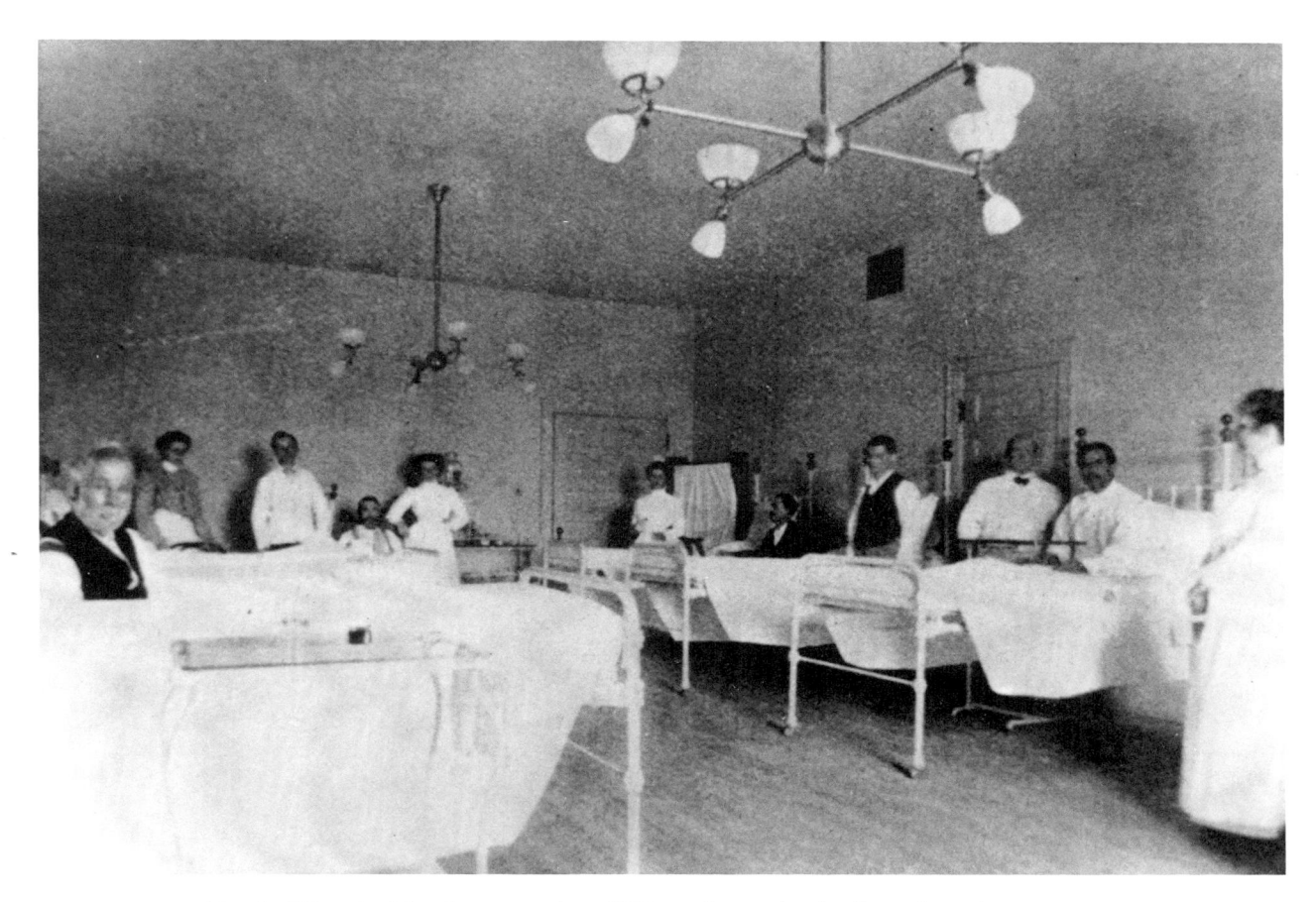

Parks Hospital had a capacity of 22 patients, including six private rooms. Above is one of the ward rooms. The cost of a private room in 1903 was between $12 and $20 per week. Parks Hospital also had an operating room, below, and an emergency room. When the north wing of the present hospital was built, Parks Hospital became a nurses' residence and later a patient annex. It was finally razed in connection with hospital expansion.

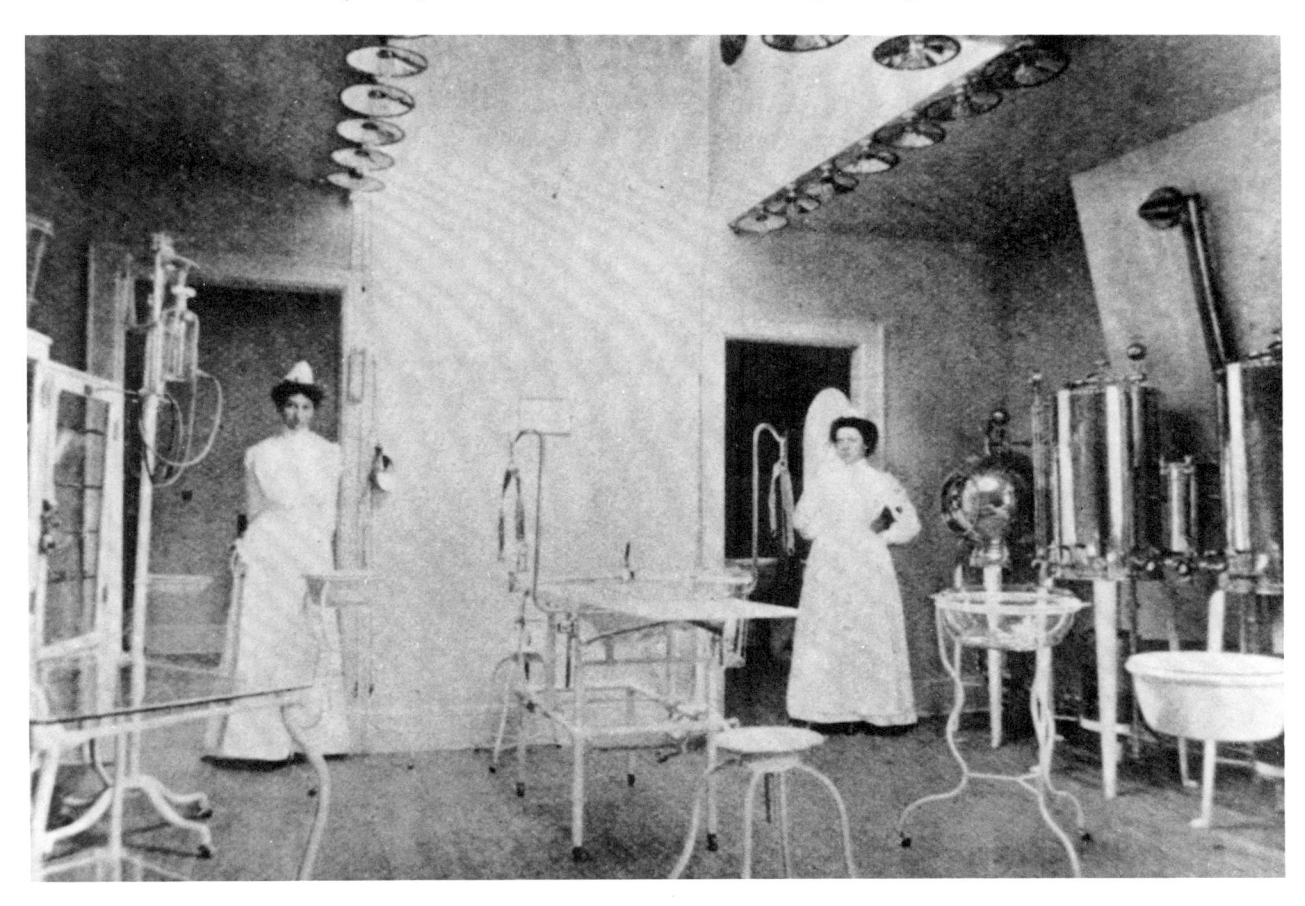

Erected in 1910, the original building of the present Glens Falls Hospital is shown above. The emergency entrance was under the marquee at the left. The south wing, shown below, was opened in 1938.

The west wing of Glens Falls Hospital, shown above, was added in 1949, with the original part of the building, now known as the north wing, at the left. Below, an aerial view of the hospital as it appears today following an extensive building program completed in 1976. The main entrance is at the left. The 1910 part of the building, the original wing, appears at the upper center of the photo, extending toward the white house on Park Street.

South Street from Glen Street toward Union Square has not changed a great deal since the above photo was taken in the early 1920's. Gone today are the Crandall Block at the left foreground and the small buildings on the north side of the street, between the Empire Theatre and the Bissell piano store. A landmark in the South Street section for more than 60 years was the house, below, at the corner of South and Elm Streets, home for a quarter of a century of Capt. Joseph J. Little and his family. It was built in 1836 and removed in 1900.

One of the earliest known photographs of South Street was the winter scene, above, taken from the middle of the block between Glen and Elm, looking toward Elm. The South Street engine house is at the far left. Below is one of the small hotels which once flourished in Glens Falls, known first as the Commercial and later as the Brick Manor. It was built as a private residence about 1879 at the corner of South Street and Columbia Avenue, and was converted into a cafe in 1893 and a hotel in 1903. It was torn down in recent years for the Henry Hudson Townhouses.

That the earliest residents of Glens Falls were conscious of the danger of fire is evident from the fact that at the town meeting in 1772, only nine years after the first settlers arrived, Ichabod Merritt and Jacob Hicks were elected town firemen. They were both sons-in-law of Abraham Wing, the founder.

Twice the community was burned — first in 1777 by General Burgoyne's army advancing on Saratoga and second in 1780 by Major Christopher Carleton's force of British troops, Tories and Indians.

The first attempt at organized fire protection was made in January, 1835, when a "vigilance committee" was appointed to "examine the apparatus of stoves and fireplaces" in the village. Each householder was requested to provide a ladder and one or more buckets. After the incorporation of the village in 1839, the village board had wells dug, acquired "two good pumps" and hooks, ladders and other equipment, and in 1842 purchased the first hand engine.

The first volunteer fire company, Glens Falls Fire Engine Company No. 1, was organized June 27, 1842. Others followed: Defiance Engine Co., Cataract Engine Co., M. B. Little Engine and Hose Co., Jerome Lapham Engine Co., J. L. Cunningham Hose Co., Eagle Hook and Ladder Co., James McDonald Hook and Ladder Co., and D. J. Finch Hook and Ladder Co.

An engine house was built in 1865 on Ridge Street, next to the present City Hall, followed shortly by another on South Street next to the present Hotel Madden. The paid department was organized in 1903. The old South Street engine house was replaced in

1913 by a new one on Broad Street, opposite St. Alphonsus Church. The old South Street building is still standing behind a one-story front next to the Madden. A new Ridge Street station was built in 1939 on the site of the Ridge Street School, at Ridge and May Streets, and the old one was torn down. A new Broad Street station was built in 1973 at the corner of Murray Street and the old one razed.

Highlights in the history of the fire department are shown in pictures on these pages: Clockwise starting at the upper left, (1) members of Cataract No. 2 with their hand engine in front of the Glens Falls Hotel, where the fire of 1864 started; (2) firemen and their horse-drawn equipment at the old Ridge Street station and (3) at the South Street station after organization of the paid department; (4) "The Exempts" hand engine, formerly the Defiance, which like Cataract helped to fight the fire of 1864 and later was used by exempt volunteer firemen for parades and contests; (5) the 1,360-pound bell upon which the village's fire alarms were sounded for many years is lowered from the tower of the Glens Falls Insurance Company building when the structure was moved in 1912 (the bell was stored until 1942 and then thrown on the World War II scrap pile); (6) Fireman Warren Bristol at the wheel of the department's first motor-driven apparatus, a converted Buick touring car, in 1915; (7) one of the department's modern trucks, Engine 2; (8) the present Broad Street station; (9) the Ridge Street station; (10) the Jerome Lapham Engine Company's parade cart, gayly decorated for a festive occasion in the 1880's.

Glens Falls Historical Association Museum

    The stately DeLong home, at the corner of Glen and Bacon Streets, was given to the Glens Falls Foundation by Juliet Goodman Chapman after the death of her husband, Frederick B. Chapman, in 1957. His expressed wish was that the beautiful home eventually be used for a charitable or cultural purpose. Through the dedicated efforts of the late Ralph M. Lapham, chairman of a museum committee, the Glens Falls Historical Association was designated by the Foundation to preserve and maintain the mansion for a museum and educational institution reflecting the heart of the community. Built about 1865 by Zopher Isaac DeLong, this fine example of a traditional Victorian mansion was "a marvelous gift from a very gracious lady." With Mr. Lapham as its first curator, the Glens Falls Historical Association Museum was opened to the public on July 6, 1967. A choice collection of local memorabilia has been assembled since that time. The museum presents rotating exhibits, educational programs for area schools and local history courses, and is now establishing a photographic research library. A major collection of Seneca Ray Stoddard material, recently acquired by the association, lends national significance to the photographic collection at the museum.

The two houses above were at the southwest corner of Glen and Pine Streets and were torn down in 1933 to make way for the present New York Telephone Company building. At left is the Dr. Charles S. McLaughlin house, one of the oldest in Glens Falls when it was razed. The home of William Cronkhite, who had a general store at Bank Square, is at right. This building was later purchased by Dr. McLaughlin and at one time housed the offices of Dr. Edsall D. B. Elliott. Below, one of the first automobile owners in Glens Falls, Patrick Moynehan, who was president of The Morning Post, *is shown in his chauffeur-driven vehicle with members of his family in front of his Glen Street home. A Grand Union store later occupied this site and was torn down to make way for the 11-story Continental Insurance Companies building.*

Above and below are two stages in the life of the Sherman house at the northwest corner of Glen Street and Sherman Avenue. Built in 1844 by businessman Augustus Sherman, it houses the Glens Falls Senior Citizens Center today and is owned by the First Presbyterian Church. It was the first building in the city to be named to the National Register of Historic Places.

Above, a glimpse down Grove Avenue about 1895. The street got a bit muddy in the spring, and some homeowners installed boardwalks over the dirt sidewalks. Below, one of the buildings housing the famous Bemis Sanitarium for the treatment of eye diseases from 1893 to 1902 was this gracious mansion at the southeast corner of Glen and Union Streets, with the old High School just north. Dr. Edward H. Bemis, who operated the sanitarium, lived for a time in the Sherman house, shown on the opposite page.

Construction of the plank road from Glens Falls to Lake George in 1848 was followed by many years of successful operation of stagecoaches between the two places, slowed only by extension of the railroad to the resort village in 1882. Photos above and at center of the opposite page show stages at the French Mountain tollgate near the Halfway House. At top right, another Tally-Ho stops at the Rockwell House in Glens Falls. Cronkhite's Newsroom is at the left. Below, 13 passengers and the driver fill all available space. The tollgate on the plank road near Glenwood Avenue is pictured at the bottom of the next page. This building is still standing on Glenwood Avenue. When the plank road passed out of existence in 1904 the toll from Glens Falls to Lake George was 12 cents for one horse and 24 cents for a team.

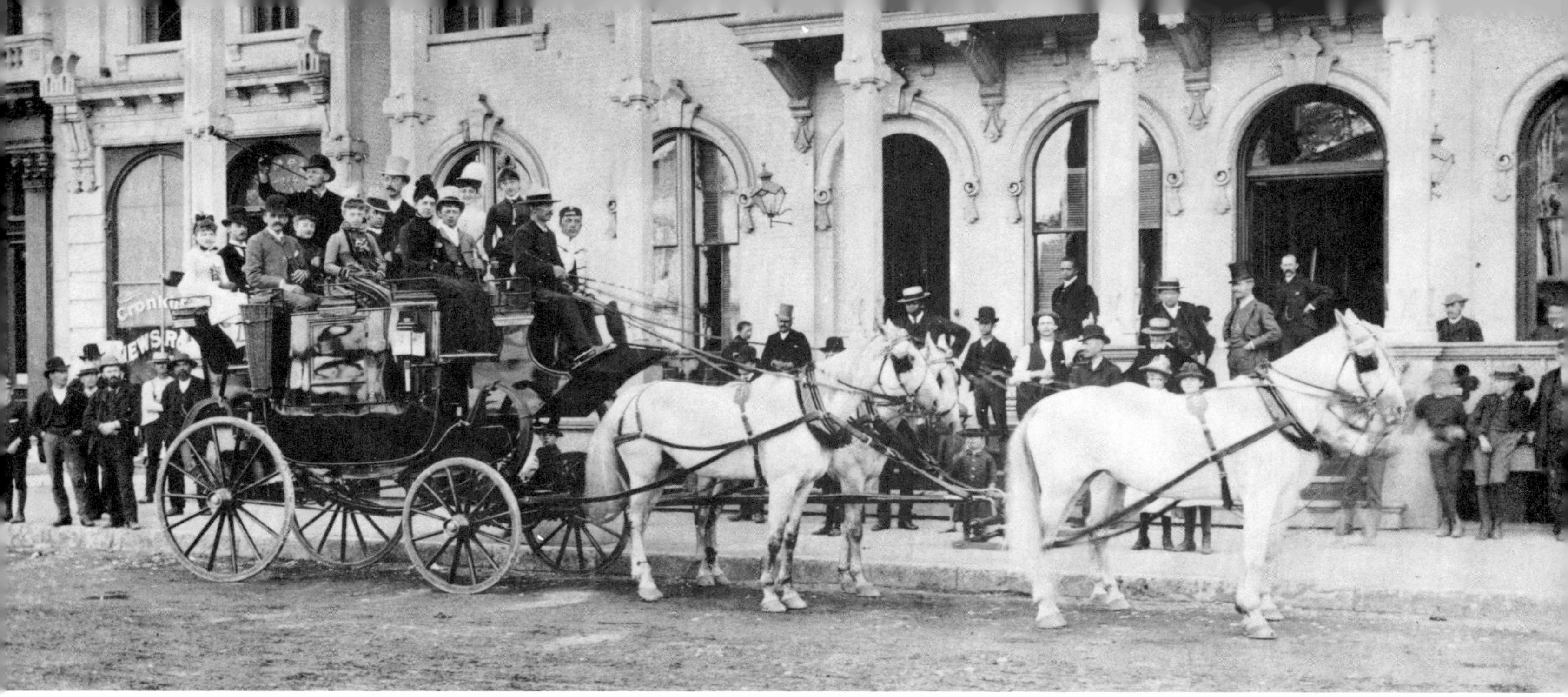

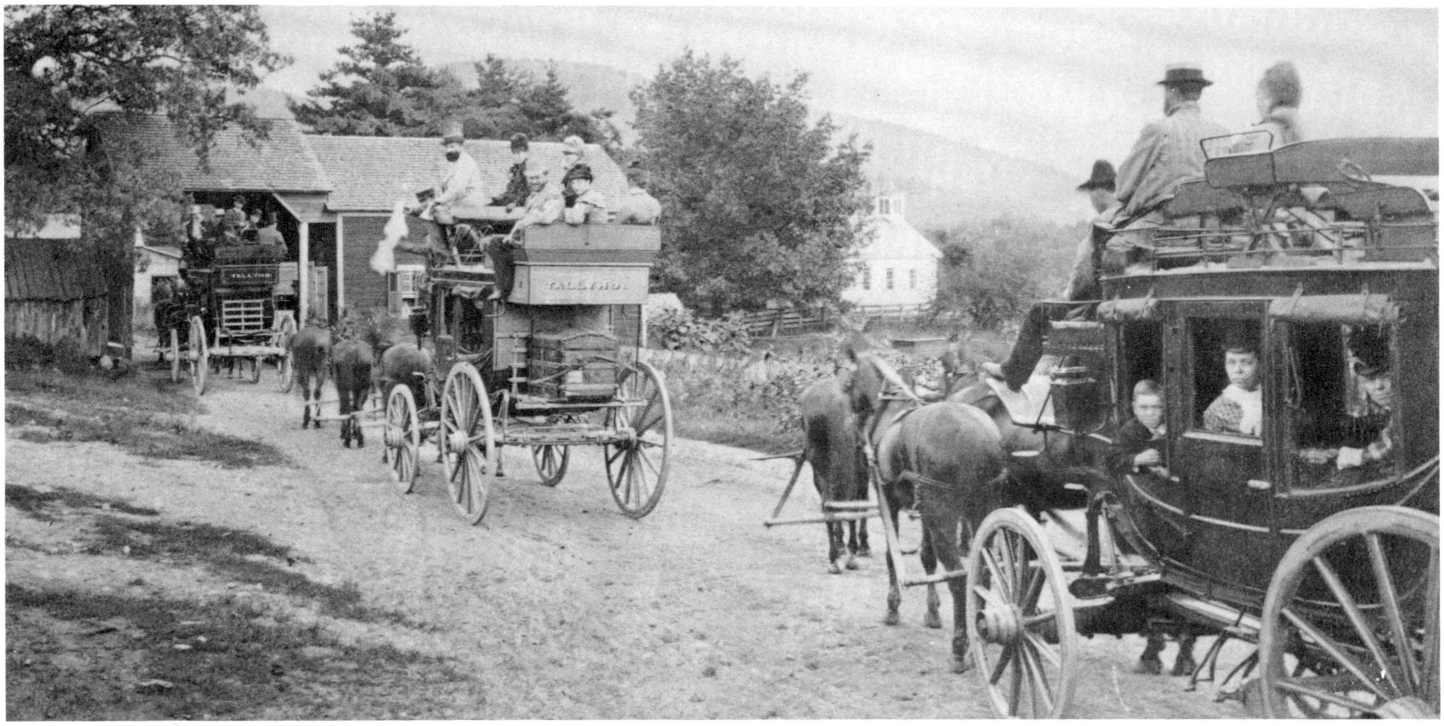
TALLYHO

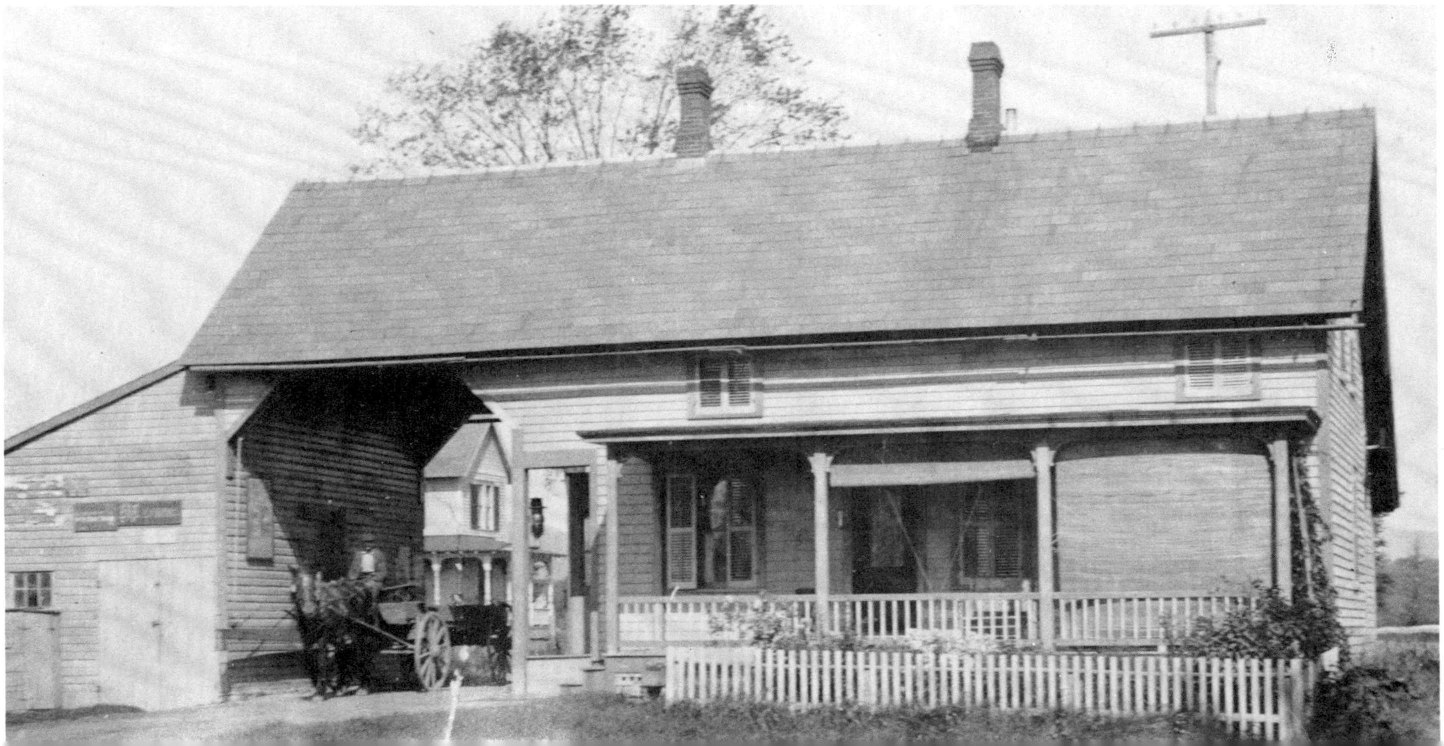

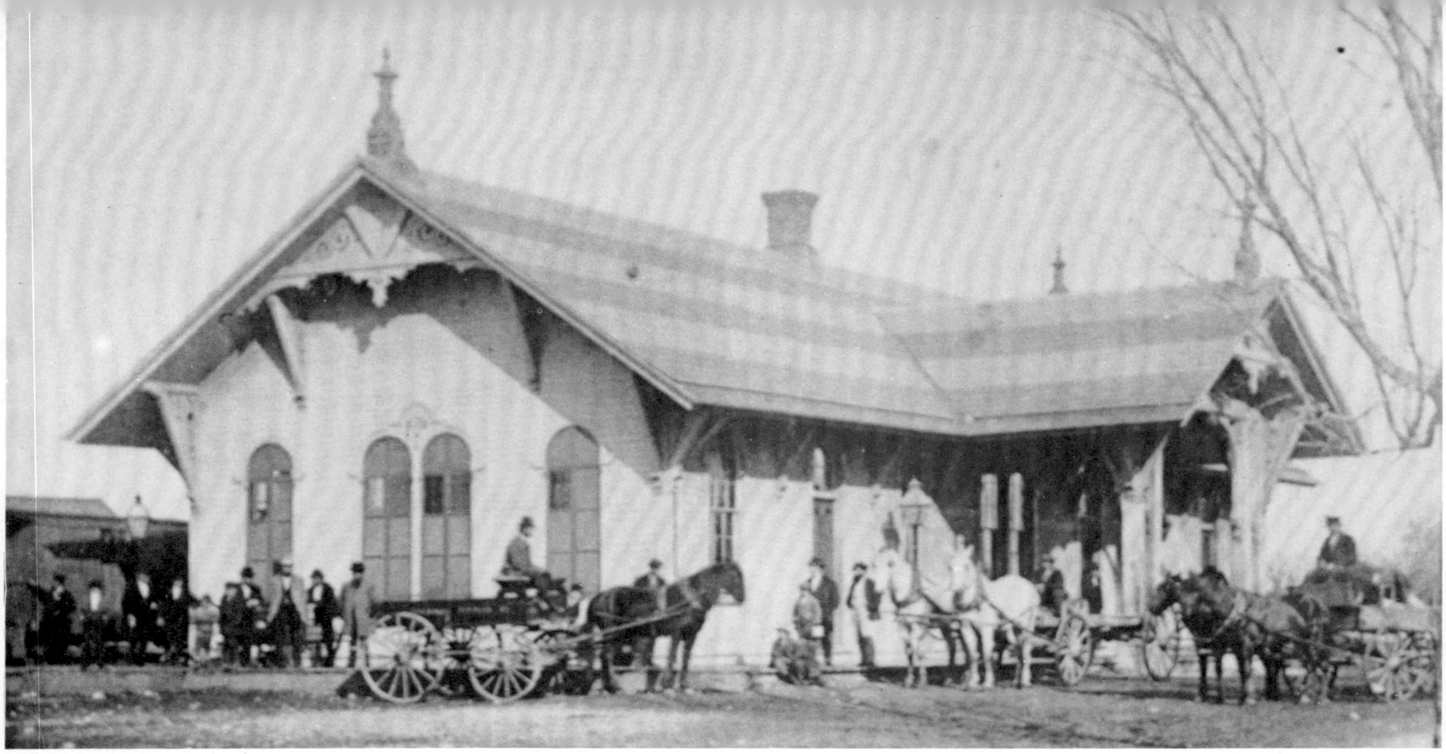

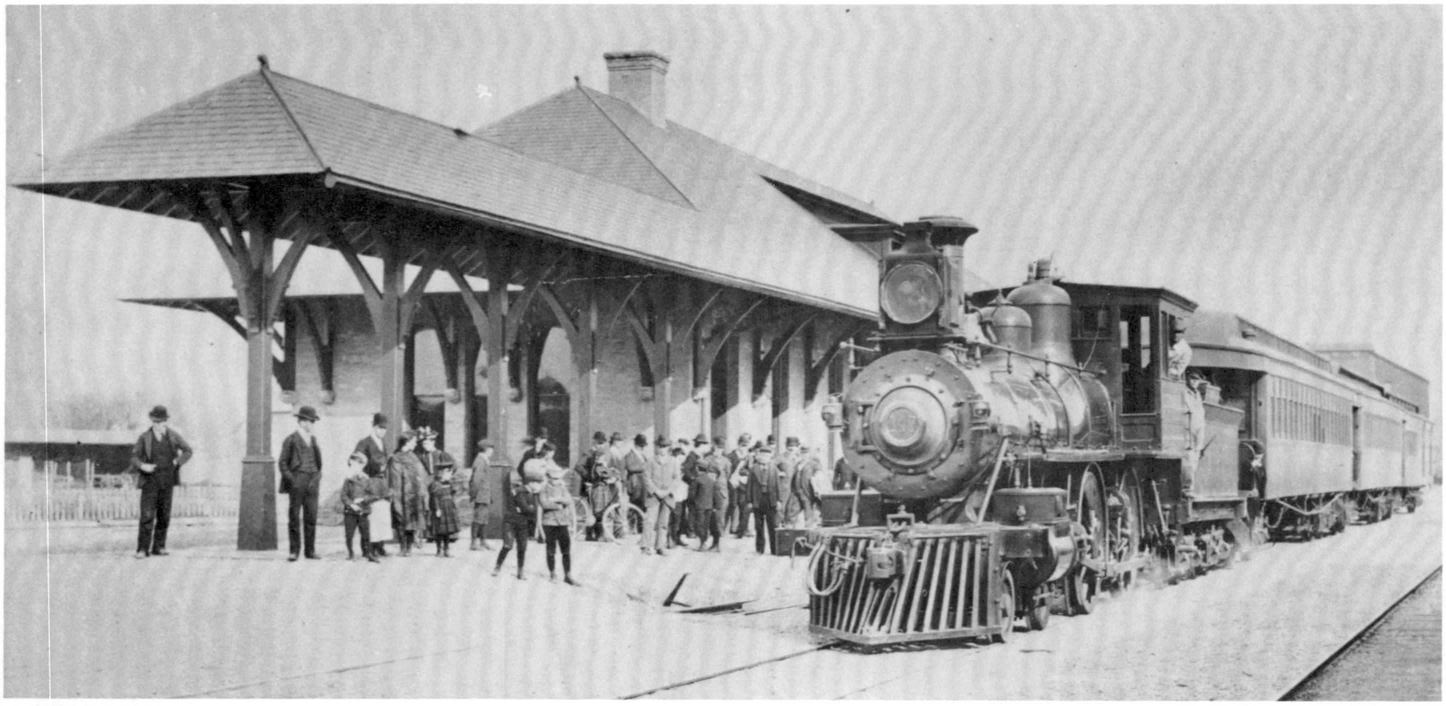

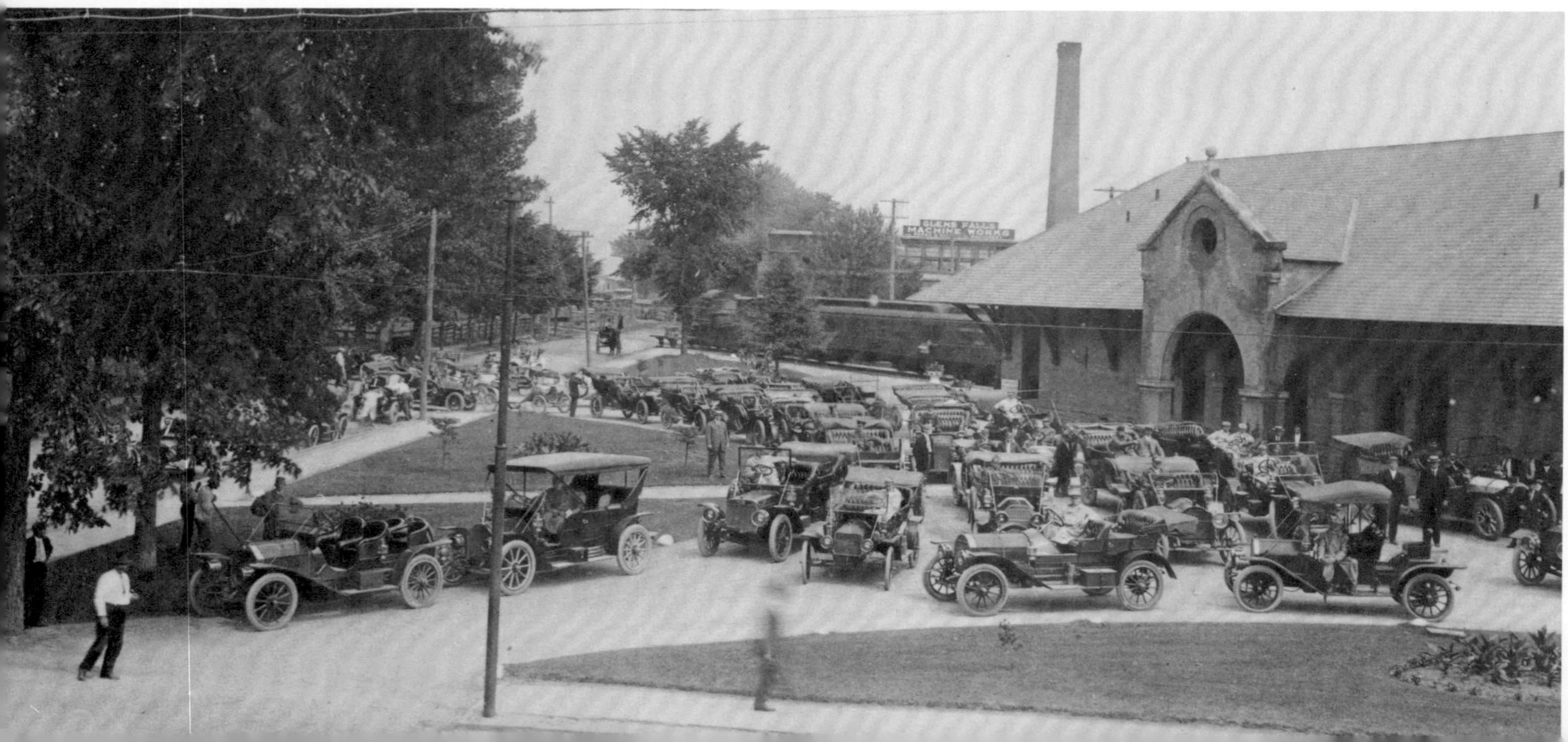

Glens Falls in its time has had two railroad passenger stations. Now it has none. The top photo on the preceding page shows the first station, erected in 1869 on the north side of Maple Street opposite Oak. This building was moved later to the rear of a lot on the same side of Maple Street opposite Locust, where it stood for many years. The center photo shows the second station, built in 1897 at the northeast corner of Lawrence and Cooper Streets. This was torn down in 1971 for construction of The Post-Star building.

The railroad into Glens Falls was completed and formally opened on July 4, 1869, when the Rensselaer and Saratoga Railway Company operated eleven round trips between this city and Fort Edward. Hundreds of Glens Falls, Sandy Hill (Hudson Falls) and Fort Edward residents rode free of charge all day long, many of them bringing lunches to eat on the train. The photo above shows the train's locomotive, decorated for the occasion, at the station. Passenger service to Glens Falls ended January 10, 1958.

Responding to an appeal for cars, nearly 50 automobile owners were at the Delaware and Hudson railroad station in Glens Falls, photo at left, on July 7, 1909, to greet members of the National Association of Railway Agents who arrived here by special train on a two-weeks Eastern States tour. The visitors were taken on a tour of the city and to Lake George. At the right, the Freedom Train visited Glens Falls 40 years later, on October 3, 1949. Thousands of local and vicinity residents inspected its priceless exhibits.

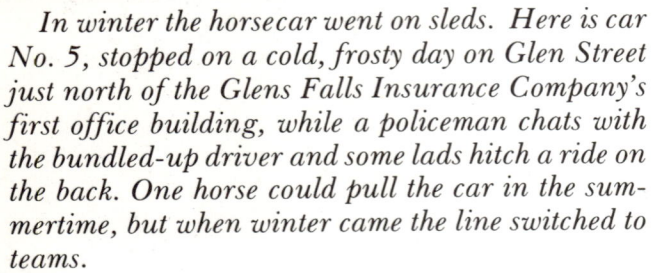

In winter the horsecar went on sleds. Here is car No. 5, stopped on a cold, frosty day on Glen Street just north of the Glens Falls Insurance Company's first office building, while a policeman chats with the bundled-up driver and some lads hitch a ride on the back. One horse could pull the car in the summertime, but when winter came the line switched to teams.

This was Glens Falls' version of the "Toonerville Trolley." In the summertime nothing was more enjoyable, nor less expensive, than a ride on an open trolley car. For a nickel you could ride to Sandy Hill (Hudson Falls), and another nickel would bring you back. The Glens Falls, Sandy Hill and Fort Edward Street Railway's car No. 24, a single-truck car built to carry about 30 passengers, is shown here on its way to Fort Edward.

Trolleys were for traveling, and the Hudson Valley Railway made it possible to travel not only all over Glens Falls but also to Hudson Falls, Fort Edward, South Glens Falls, Troy, Saratoga Springs, Lake George and Warrensburg and points in between. Connecting lines provided service to a much larger area. In the photo below, taken about 1907, the South Street-Depot line's car No. 4 makes the turn from Ridge Street into Glen at Bank Square. There are horse-drawn vehicles aplenty, but only one automobile, in front of the Colvin Building. Glen Street had not yet been double-tracked. A system of switches in Bank Square gave trolleys access to all lines at that point.

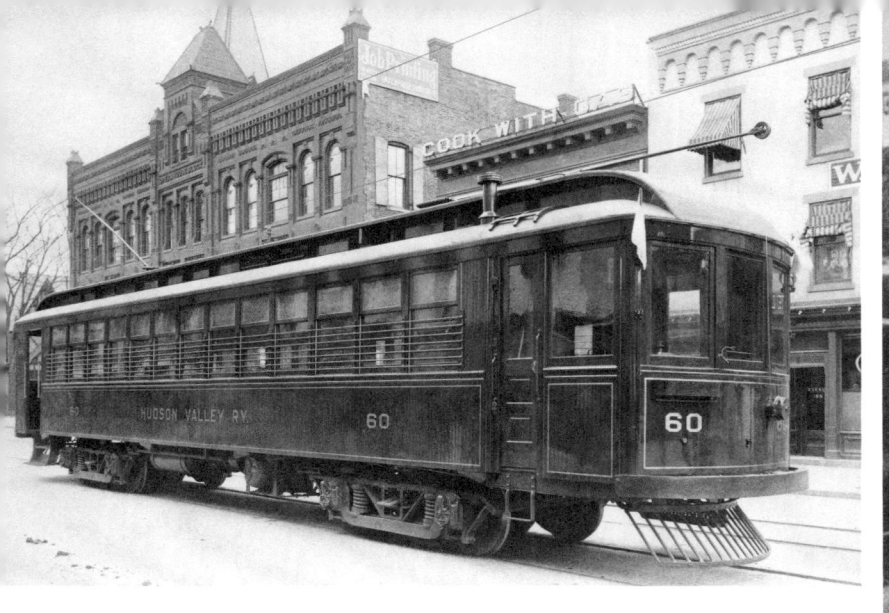

From the small single-truck cars used on the city lines, equipment used by the Hudson Valley ranged up through various sizes of cars to the big "60 series" operated between Glens Falls and Troy and Warrensburg and Saratoga Springs. The map below shows the Hudson Valley system and connecting lines to Albany, Schenectady, west to Fonda and south to Hudson.

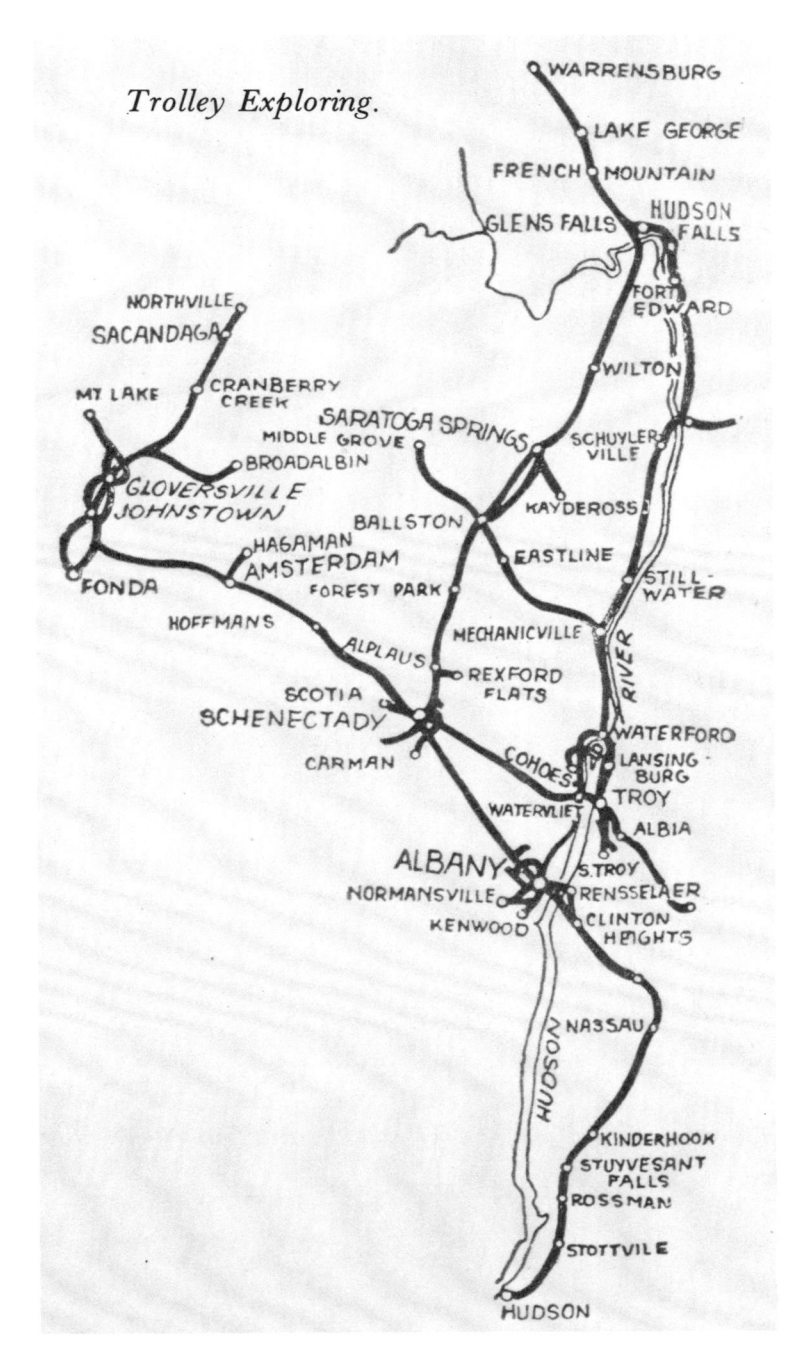

Trolley Exploring.

From the beginning of horsecars in 1885 to the end of electric cars in 1928 it was only 43 years, but that was the grand total of streetcar service in Glens Falls and vicinity.

The Glens Falls, Sandy Hill and Fort Edward Street Railway began operating horsecars in 1885 between Glens Falls and Fort Edward. In 1891 the line was electrified, rebuilt and extended. The Hudson Valley Railway, formed in 1901, went out of business December 1, 1928. Bus service replaced the trolleys and that, too, ended in time. There is no longer any public transportation in Glens Falls, except long-line buses and taxis.

One legend that survives the Hudson Valley concerns Dick, a small mongrel dog that became the company mascot. Shown in the photo above with four friends, he had given up a good home to become a "railroader." Among his friends was an express car motorman. One day Dick rode to Warrensburg with this friend and promptly became a trolley car aficionado. He adopted the Boulevard carbarn for a home and became a friend of all the trolley employes, who shared their lunches with him and purchased his license tags. He rode all over the system on both passenger and freight cars and often spent a night with a friend, but always came back to the carbarns, waiting along the tracks until a car approached and he was picked up.

A weakness for fighting with other dogs proved Dick's undoing. In June, 1914, such an encounter resulted in injuries so serious he had to be put to sleep. So deeply did his death affect employes all over the system that they raised a fund to pay for a tombstone, suitably inscribed, to mark his grave in front of the old dispatcher's office on the Boulevard.

One Sunday morning not long after 1879 this group gathered in front of the Quaker Church on Ridge Street.

170

The earliest churches serving the community were, for some reason, located away from Wing's Falls and the business center. The first Quakers worshipped at the 1786 meeting house, up Bay Road; the Baptists, at Lake Sunnyside and West Mountain; the Methodists, at Sanfords Ridge, and the Catholics, at Sandy Hill.

By 1864, however, with the settlement nearly a century old, there were Universalist, Methodist, Roman Catholic, Baptist and Presbyterian churches all within a few doors of each other on the edge of the business section, and not far away were Episcopal and French Catholic structures. Then, just a decade later, the Quakers moved back to town.

The tide appears to be moving away from the center of the community again, as Glens Falls goes into its third century with houses of worship of many sizes and persuasions dispersed throughout the city and its suburban and rural environs. A current religious directory lists a surprising total of 30 congregations.

No drawing or photograph exists of the Universalist Church or the second Methodist Church, both located on Warren Street and destroyed with two other houses of worship in the fire of 1864, nor of the Hicksite Quaker meeting house on Bay Street. Otherwise, the historian is fortunate that representations of all other early churches within the city have survived, and many are shown on the pages that follow.

Each congregation has its own fascinating story, with decline and growth, dissent and harmony, skepticism and revival. Some of those annals have been committed to writing from time to time; others are found in the bare congregational records and the memories of the faithful.

The community was settled by Quakers who first worshipped here in 1767. The earliest meeting house on Bay Road was replaced in 1802 by a "large frame building" on Ridge Road where the Friends Cemetery is located. The structure was moved later to The Oneida and today, right, houses that hamlet's community church. The third Quaker building, above, on the west side of Ridge Street between Fulton and Grand, was erected in 1875 at a cost of $1,300 and had no heat "except zeal, and coals brought in metal boxes." The former church is now headquarters for the Adirondack Mountain Club, and local Quakers worship at South Glens Falls.

This monument to Quaker pioneers is located at the southwest corner of Bay and Quaker Roads in Queensbury on the site of the town's first meeting house, school and cemetery. The first church and school, built in 1786 of logs, was a long, low edifice with two entrances, for men and women, and small windows near the roof.

The First Church of the Presbyterians or "Old White," 1808-1848

The Second Church, 1848-1864

The Third Church, 1864-1884

Interior of the Fourth Church

An 1803 community fund drive produced a union church, the first house of worship in Glens Falls. A number of those who had promised to donate later had to be sued. The frame structure, used from the start by Presbyterians, was located on the south side of Warren Street, between Glen and Church, and became known as "Old White." Its bell announced the presence of the messenger of death by tolling three times for a baby, six for a woman and nine for a man. The bell broke when tolled at the death of Governor Clinton in 1827. The building became dilapidated and was demolished in 1848. The second church was built of brick at a cost of $9,000. It was in this structure that spiritualism problems beset the congregation in 1858, and it burned in the fire of 1864. The third church, "with lines of chaste, pleasing design and having a very graceful tower," was dedicated in 1867. Fire again visited the site on the morning of April 28, 1884. As the church clock began to strike the hour of nine, only six strokes had sounded when the beautiful tower fell.

Remains of the Third Church After the Fire of 1884

In building their fourth edifice on the Warren Street site, the Presbyterians preserved as much as possible from the ruins of the third church. The structure was dedicated in 1886, and galleries were added in 1897. The interior is seen as it appeared on Children's Day, June 7, 1925, the last Sunday morning on which a service was held there. The site was then sold to Fred W. Mausert and became the State Theatre, a movie house.

The Fourth Church, 1886-1925

For their fifth and present home, the Presbyterians moved to the southwest corner of Glen and Notre Dame Streets. The Gothic structure was designed by Ralph Adams Cram and was dedicated in 1929. At that date, the church's membership had grown from nine in 1803 to 1,358, and the congregation was maintaining a neighborhood house for foreign children on Lower Warren Street, Sunday schools at Miller Hill and West Glens Falls, and rural parishes at Bay Road, The Oneida and West Mountain.

The little stone church behind the picket fence on the east side of Church Street was built by the Methodists in 1829 for $1,500. In 1848 it was sold to St. Mary's Parish for $850, as Methodist membership had grown from an original 12 communicants to 181. A new church was built on the Warren Street corner that is today the site of St. Mary's Academy, but this second home of Methodism was destroyed in the 1864 fire, being wholly uninsured. The third church was erected at the same location for $16,000 the next year, and an addition, for $21,000 in 1874. Through the last half of the 19th century, the Methodist congregation was the largest and wealthiest of the Protestant churches in the community, according to state census reports. The third church was sold to St. Mary's Parish for $25,000 in 1905 and today's Christ Church, United Methodist, was built on the southwest corner of Bay and Washington Streets in 1907.

The First Church of the Methodists, 1829-1847

Christ Church, United Methodist

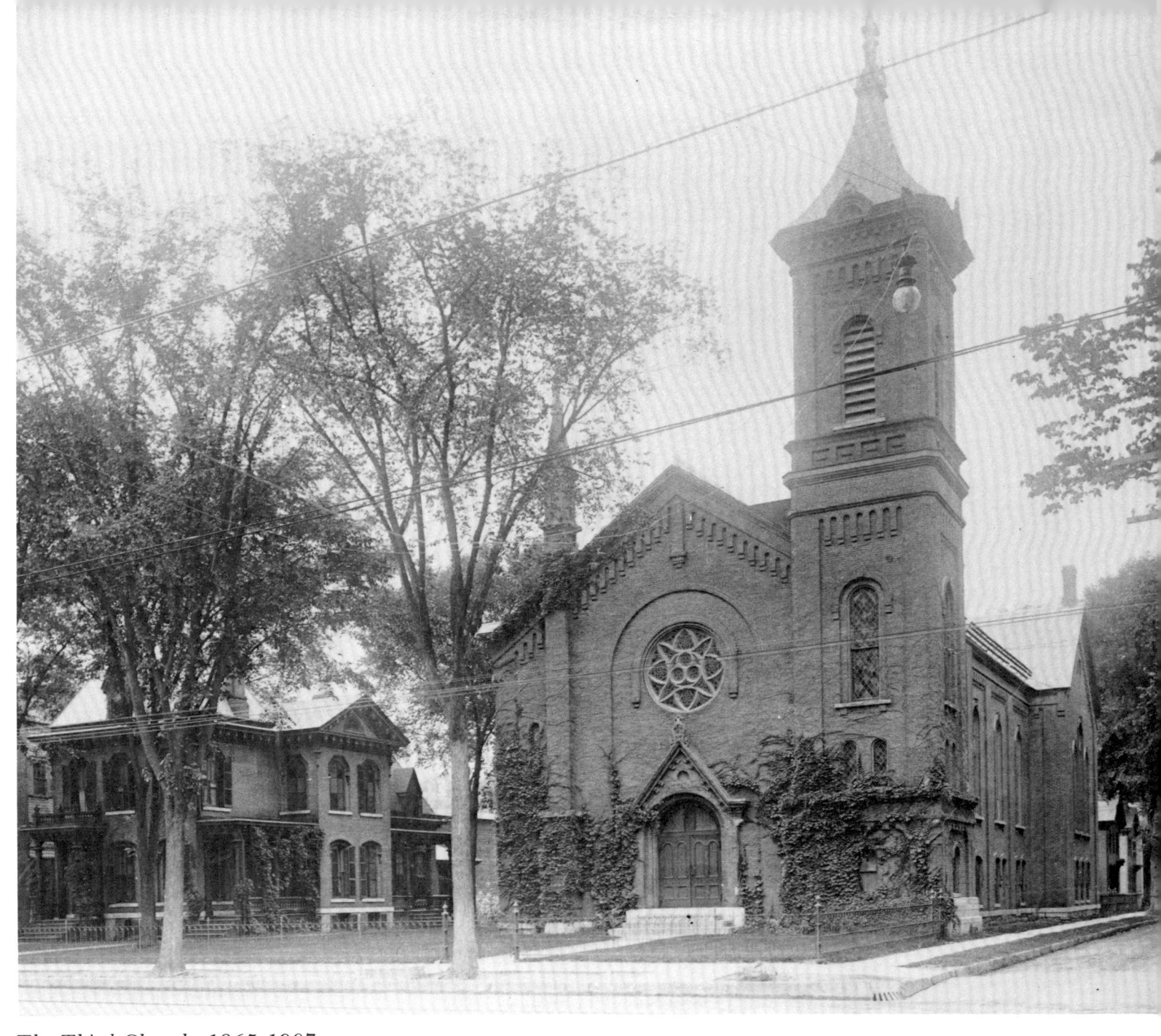

The Third Church, 1865-1907

Interior of the Third Church

An early Methodist church, completed in 1871, was located at West Mountain and is today a community church.

Construction of the First Baptist Church on the north side of Maple Street, opposite Church Street, above left, was undertaken in 1840, but actually it was the fourth Baptist Church in the Town of Queensbury. Earlier were a log structure at Lake Sunnyside; a frame church not far away, on the east side of Rockwell Road, and the Burnham meeting house, on Luzerne Road diagonally across from Mount Hermon Cemetery. The Baptists have the record, however, for worshipping at one location longer than any other religious body in Glens Falls, since the present church was completed in 1885 on the same Maple Street site. The photograph at right above was taken soon after construction, and the interior view is also an early one.

Episcopalians first met in the Methodist Church on Church Street and in schoolhouses, but a wooden chapel was erected in 1843 on the west side of Ridge Street, today the site of the Queensbury Hotel parking lot. A church historian recalls that "the first seats were simply rough slabs in the ends of which were inserted two round sticks as legs." The cornerstone of the present Church of the Messiah, located on the east side of Glen Street just north of the Monument, was laid in 1854, but the edifice was not consecrated until 1866, and even then it still lacked spire, chancel, bell, carpets and cushions. The interior view was taken during the Christmas season of 1879.

Changes in Glen Street are apparent in these three views of the Episcopal Church of the Messiah, the architectural jewel just north of Monument Square. The huge elms and picket fences are gone, as are the stately residences further up the street. Also among the missing today is the Glens Falls Insurance Company's five-story office building, which stood a few feet from the church on the south, overshadowing it from 1912 to 1976.

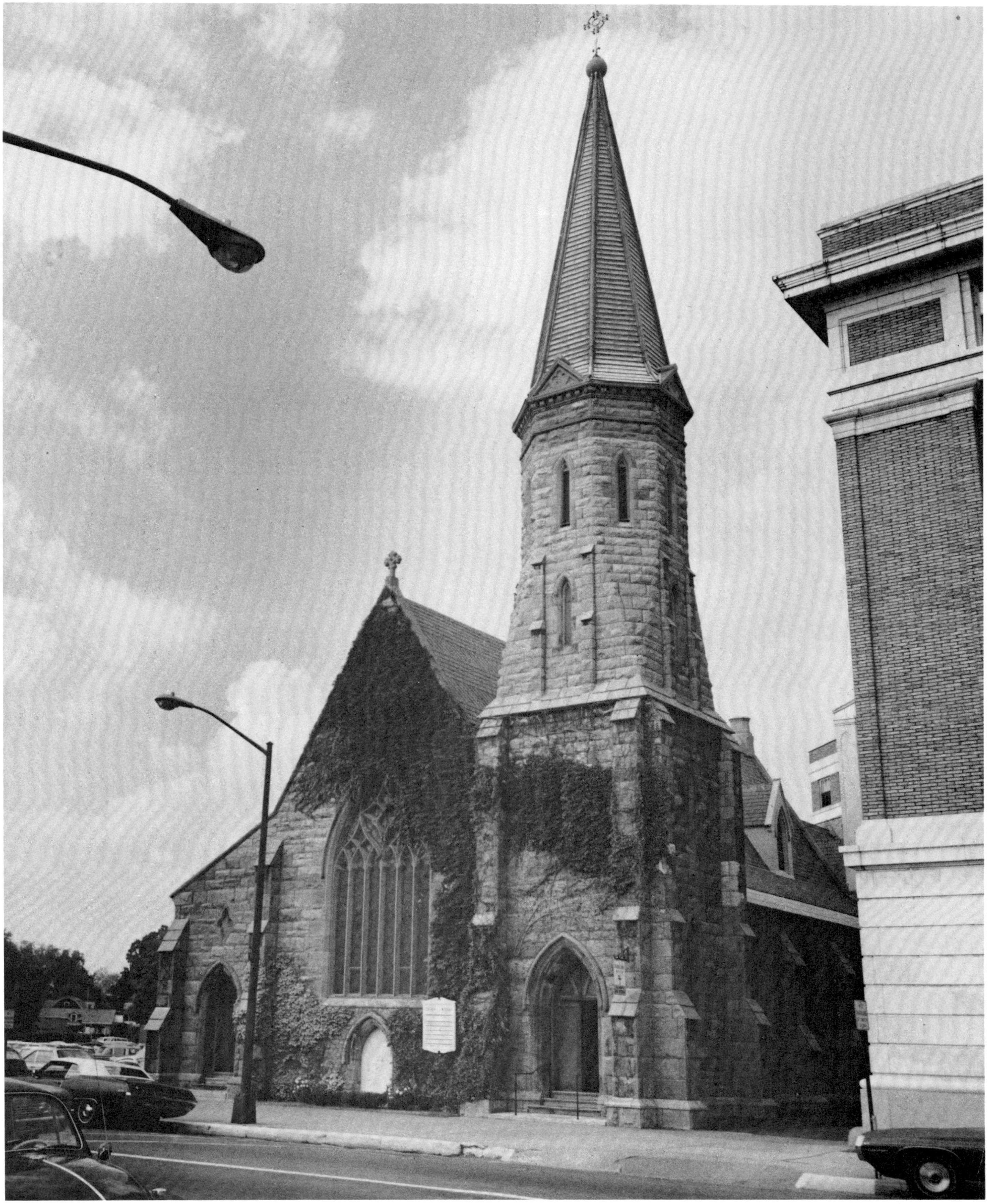

Catholics in Glens Falls worshipped at Hudson Falls until the old stone church of the Methodists on the east side of Church Street, near Berry, was transferred to the Bishop of Albany in 1849, and St. Mary's Parish was established. The pastor traditionally wore a black beaver top hat in those days. Construction of the present church on the southeast corner of Warren and Church Streets began in 1867 and was completed in 1869. The view on the opposite page is from 1871, showing the inevitable picket fences and gaslight of that period. The lofty spire is gone today.

185

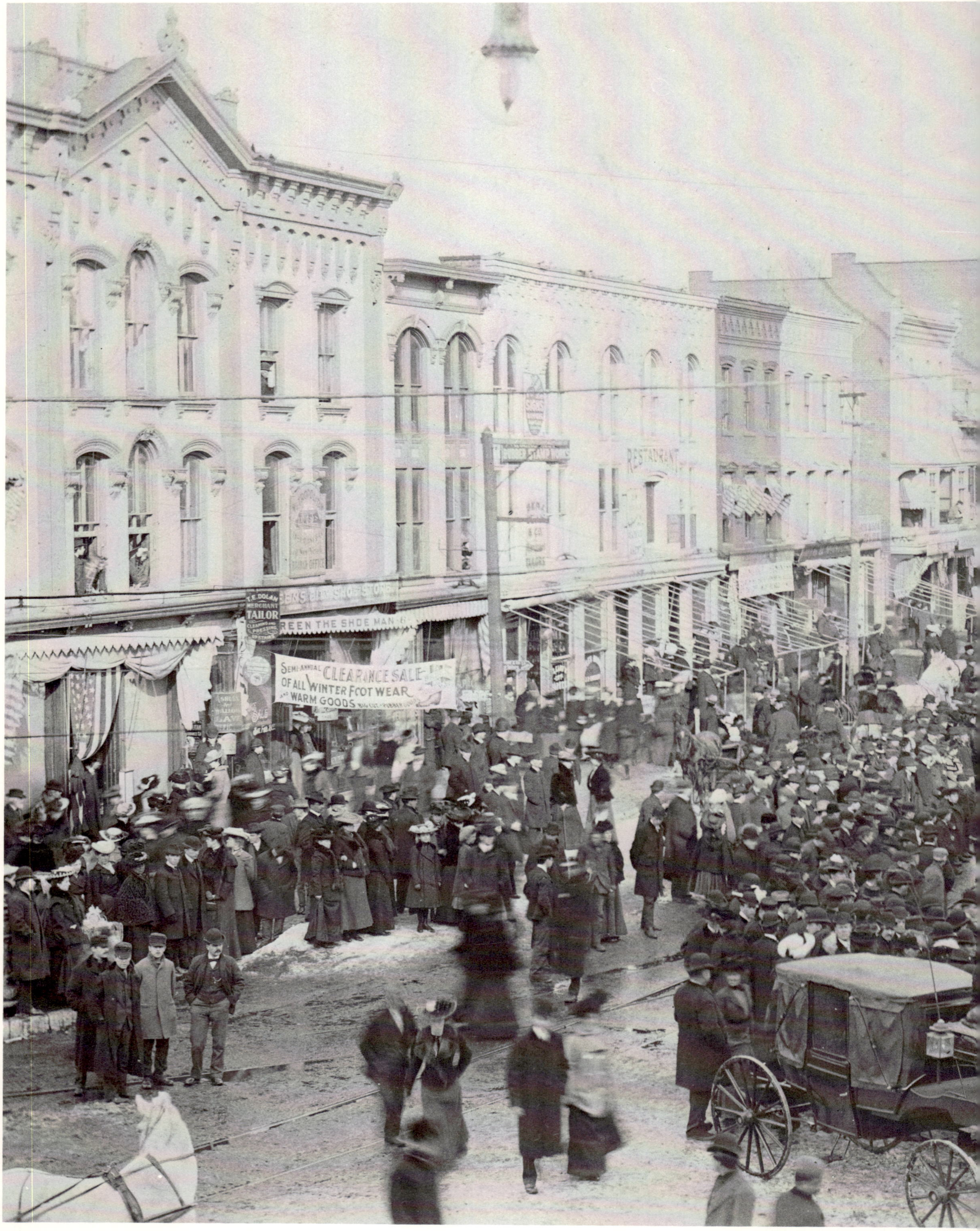

Bank Square is a solemn place February 20, 1903, as the funeral procession for the Rt. Rev. Msgr. James McDermott, pastor of St. Mary's Parish from 1865, moves from the church on Warren Street toward the cemetery at South Glens Falls. "Father Mac" had overseen building of the present church, a brick rectory just east on Warren Street and grammar school, high school and convent buildings on Church Street, in addition to administering to an ever increasing flock. It was estimated that 5,000 persons attended services at the grave, and all of the union schools, stores, banks and many businesses were closed for the occasion.

Catholic missionaries from Canada ministered to the French population here as early as 1837, and services were first held in private homes. What is today St. Alphonsus Parish began with the settlement of a resident pastor in the community about 1853. The census reports that his salary was $600 and the communicants numbered 700. The first church was built of wood at the northwest corner of Pine and Broad Streets, the present site, and was called St. John the Baptist Church. It was enlarged and galleries were added in 1873. St. Alphonsus Church, a magnificent brick structure, was erected on the site in 1888. It stood until January 12, 1955, when it was gutted by fire, and it has been replaced by a modern edifice shown at bottom right. The interior view is from the first church.

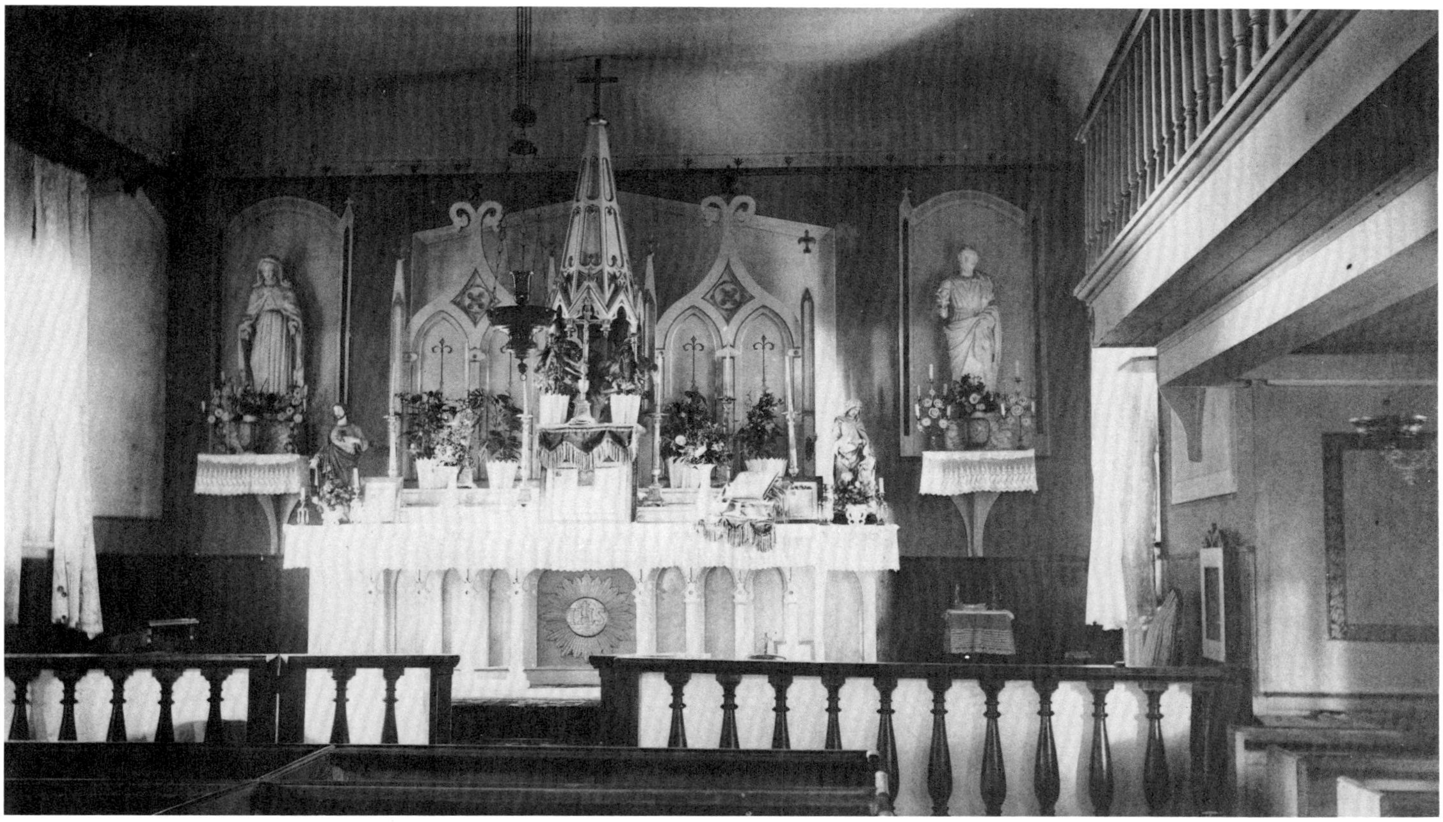

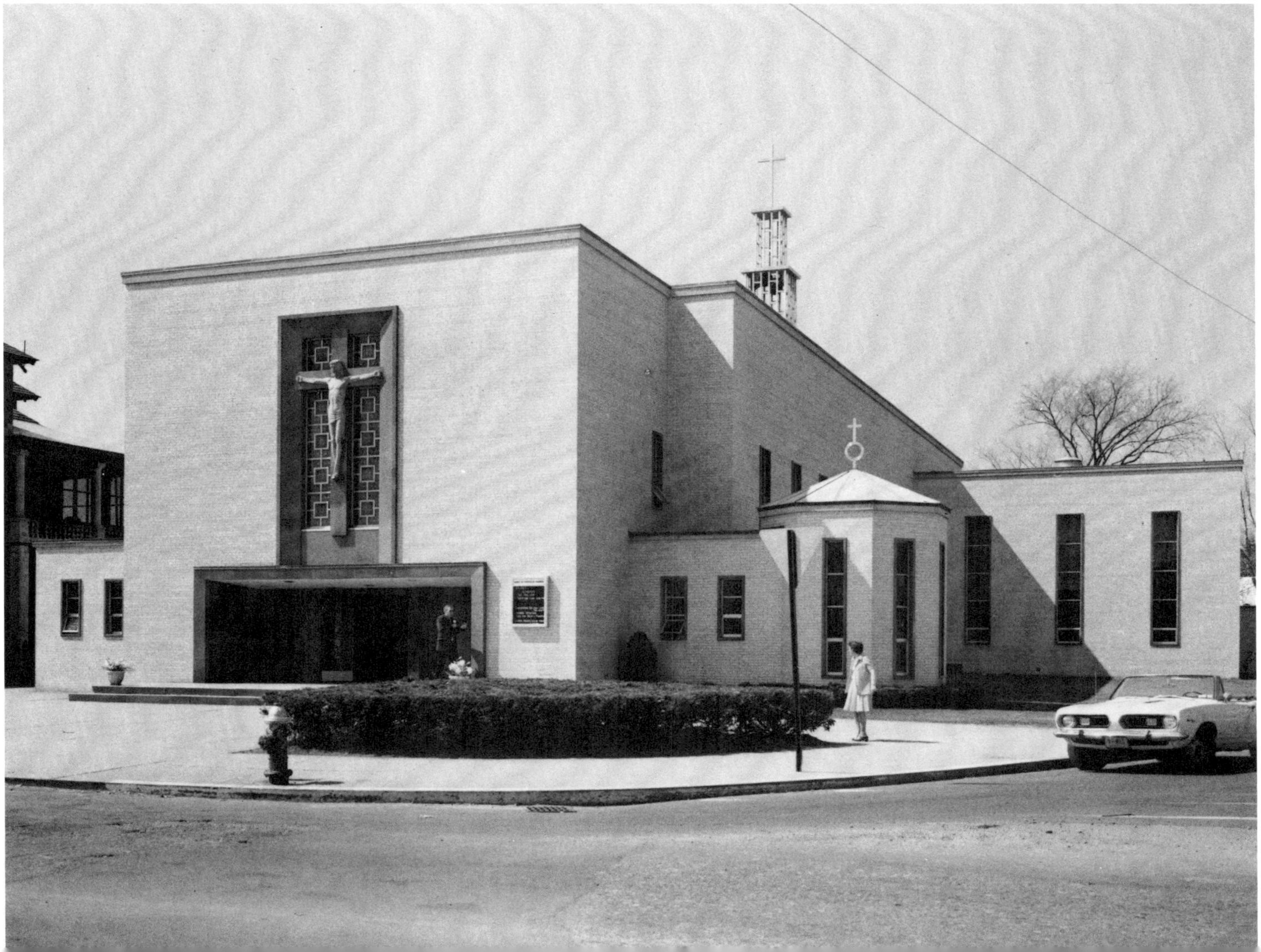

It was called St. Paul's Episcopal Church when this photo was taken. Today it is the Harrisena Community Church on Ridge Road.

The Orthodox Jewish Synagogue on the west side of Jay Street was erected about 1893 and used until the late 1920's. It later housed Calvary Tabernacle and then the Veterans of Foreign Wars and was razed for Urban Renewal.

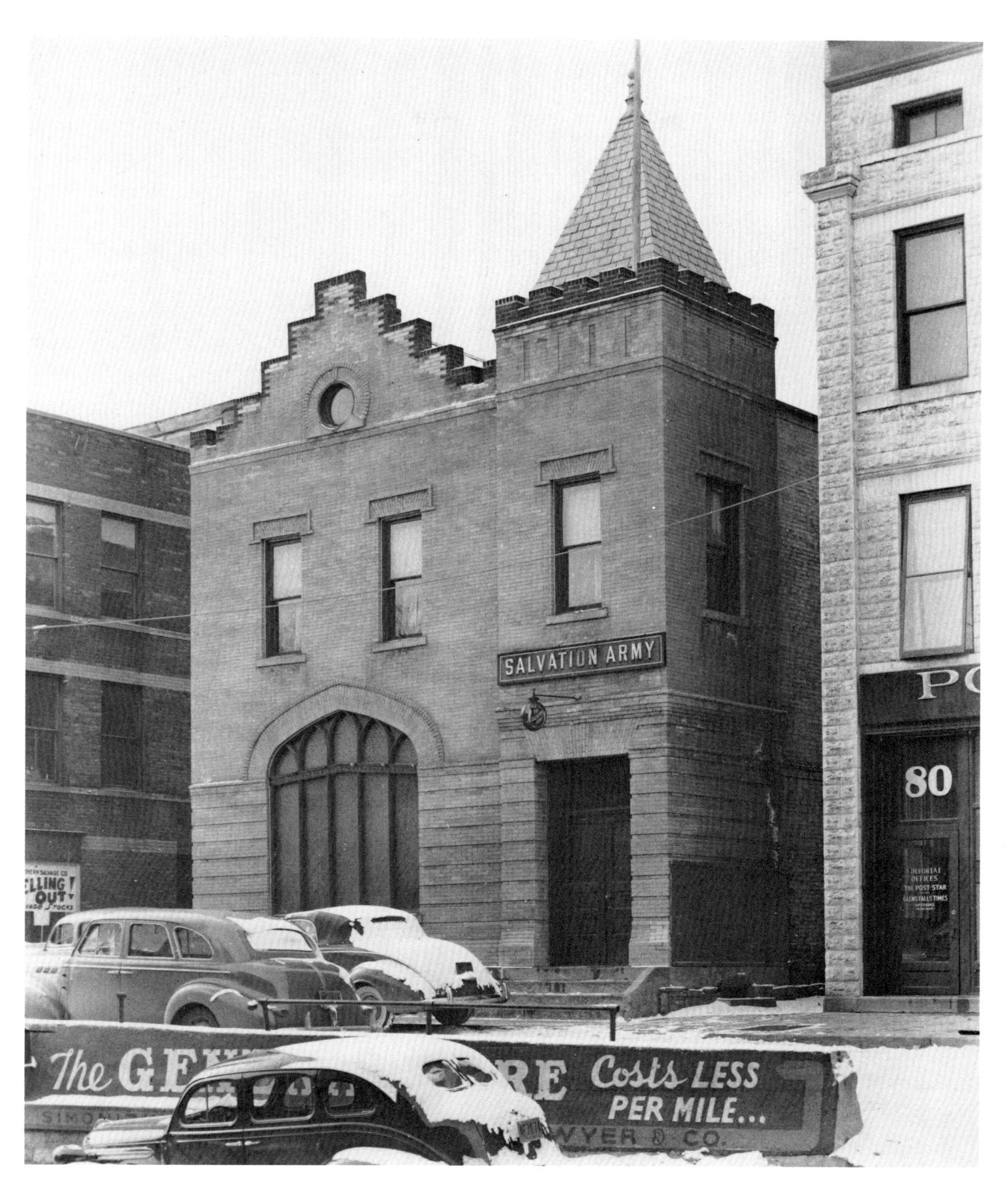

The Salvation Army dates from 1885 in Glens Falls, and this citadel, on the west side of Glen Street at the top of the hill, was built in 1905 for $10,000. The organization moved to the former Glens Falls Academy on Chester Street in 1956, and the old building was razed for parking in November of 1960.

Free Methodist Church

Christian and Missionary Alliance Church

Synagogue Center of Congregation Shaaray Tefila

Lutheran Church of the Good Shepherd

First Church of Christ, Scientist

Church of Christ

Calvary Assembly of God

Temple Beth-El

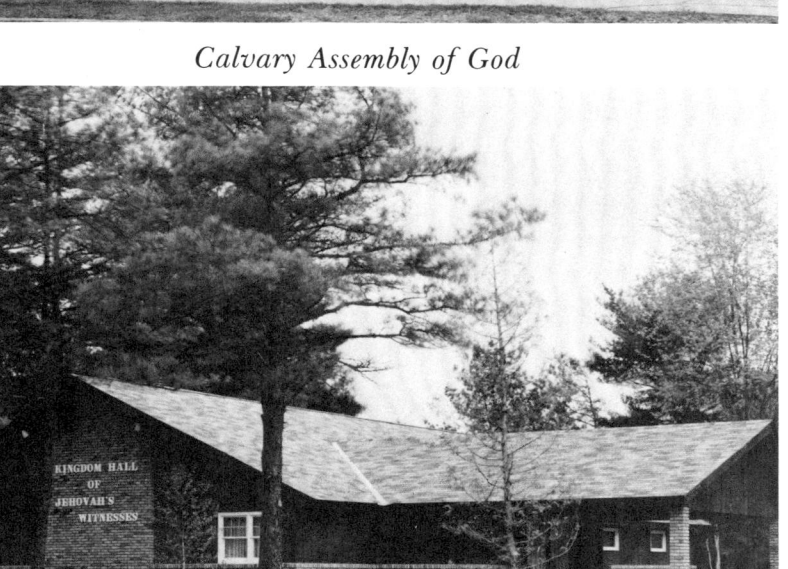

Kingdom Hall of Jehovah's Witnesses

Wesleyan Church

Church of Our Lady of the Annunciation

United Methodist Church of Queensbury

Elizabeth Call, a teacher in South and Broad Street Schools for more than 40 years, portrays the determined schoolmarm of early years in this 1965 painting by the noted artist Douglass Crockwell.

The first school in Queensbury met in the Quakers' log meeting house, built about 1785 at what is now the southwest corner of Bay and Quaker Roads. A. W. Holden states: "The first schoolhouse, if tradition may be relied upon, stood nearly at the site of the Soldiers' Monument, at the corner of Glen and Bay Streets." An article in an 1831 *Warren Messenger* describes a "small, rudely constructed schoolhouse now the residence of Mrs. Flannagan," built as early as 1786-7, later the home of A. W. Holden at 17 Elm Street. The Plank Road School, below, was a two-room building on Glen Street built in 1858 in a pine grove near Marion Avenue, that served until 1884.

Private schools of early times had advantages not available in public schools. In 1803 Reuben Peck employed two teachers to conduct a select school. This school on Elm Street was a one-story frame building with two rooms, each having a fireplace.

The center of advanced education was "The Old Academy" erected in 1812 on Ridge Street in present City Park. A large building served as both school and boarding house with dormitories above until 1840.

One of the more practical private schools in the 1860's was the Cronkhite Commercial School at 16 Park Street. James Cronkhite, imposing at six feet and 240 pounds, was a talented teacher and a stern disciplinarian. His students, teen-age boys, worked in the mills and on the canal in summer and attended school in winter. Parents said, "Take them to Cronkhite; he'll beat it into them." A former student reminisced in 1948, "Only one fault he had. He worked so seriously in the morning he would send one of his favorite pupils with a jug down to Mrs. Slade's grocery (?) and have it filled with vinegar (?). Result, Mrs. Cronkhite had to come in and teach in afternoons . . . He, with his sternness and ability; she with gentleness and capability certainly made a wonderful, successful teaching team."

In 1839 only three public schools existed in Glens Falls: the wood school of District 20 at South and West (now Broad) Streets, the brick school of District 2 on Ridge Street and the red school of District 19 on the corner of Warren and Canal (now Oakland Avenue) Streets. The Female Seminary on Church Street and the William Barnes School at 11 Ridge Street were major private schools. Public education was at a low level with no public high school, and low student attendance at all levels.

Typical of private schools was the Elmwood Seminary, a three-story boarding and day school on the northwest corner of Elm and Park Streets. It opened in 1862 with "a fine patronage of young women" and flourished during and after the Civil War. The curriculum included drawing, nature walks, current events, French, music, but especially deportment and manners. A deep ravine on Park Street gave the building a full "downstairs" with space for the first kindergarten. Elmwood Seminary operated successively as a ladies' seminary, a commercial school and a hotel before being destroyed by fire in 1889.

Professor J. M. Pilcher and wife pose with pupils in front of the Elmwood Seminary about 1885.

Students and teachers gather in front of the first Glens Falls Academy on Warren Street about 1860. The Academy provided a collegiate course "in the study of the Classics and Science" not available in the public schools. Headmaster D.C. Farr and professors are pictured on the side steps of the Academy about 1880.

With the demise of the Old Academy on Ridge Street, Holden reports the "more intelligent men of the community" became convinced that "if . . . adequate academic instruction were to be provided, a school should be built and supported by a sizeable group of sponsors." Accordingly, a meeting was convened in 1841, and 18 trustees were selected to establish the Glens Falls Academy. Its doors were opened that year, and a female department was soon added in the basement. For several decades it was the only secondary school in Glens Falls. With the support of leading families and the employment of outstanding teachers, the Academy provided quality education in the area for almost a century. Illustrative of the quality of its early program is the fact that the first New York State High School Regents Diplomas were awarded to three female graduates in 1880.

196

The "Extension" at the back of the Academy was built about 1870, doubling the seating room and accommodations. A. W. Holden reported in 1880 that graduates of the Academy entered college the most thoroughly prepared of any students in the state. This prestigious institution educated both men and women.

The heyday of the Academy began in 1894 with the building of a three-story addition in front of the original building. A side porch connected the new addition to the 1870 extension in back. Fire partially destroyed the building in 1912. The trustees, faced with reconstructing three old buildings, voted to build a modern school on Chester Street in the style of New England academies.

Students of the old Academy pose in front of the building around 1890.

A tire shop was built in front of the old Academy in 1925. The former school was converted into apartments. An attempt to remove "Glens Falls Academy" above the old entrance was not entirely successful; the words may still be faintly seen.

The last Glens Falls Academy, with J. Thacher Sears as headmaster and his wife, Katharine, as assistant, opened in 1914. Over the next two decades, increasing costs and declining enrollment led to its closing in 1937, ending almost a century of distinguished service. Following World War II, the Chester Street building served briefly as Skidmore College Extension, and in 1965 it was purchased by the Salvation Army, which still occupies it.

199

Citizens celebrate Columbus Day on the lawn of Union School No. 1 on Glen Street in 1884. This was the first new building of the Union Free School District consolidated three years previously. Under Dr. Sherman Williams, Union School No. 2, below left, was constructed at South and West (Broad) Streets in 1891, and Union School No. 3, below right, on Ridge Street in 1897. These three schools comprised the entire Glens Falls village public school system for the next three decades.

The Union Free School Act of 1853 permitted the consolidation of small school districts, but it was almost thirty years before action occurred in Glens Falls. On December 14, 1881, the Ridge Street School, South Street School, Seminary Hill School on Church Street and the Plank Road School were consolidated to form Union Free School District 1 of Queensbury. Dr. Sherman Williams, newly appointed superintendent, assessed the school system: "I had never known anything so poor, nor supposed it possible for such poor schools to exist anywhere, much less in a large and thriving town." Almost immediately new construction began. By 1897, all old schools had been replaced, a high school program and teacher-training class established.

The high school diploma of J. Ward Russell, later mayor of Glens Falls and a member of the Board of Education for 40 years, was awarded in 1898. From the signatures it may be noted that three members of the original 1881 board, Jerome Lapham, Samuel Pruyn, Daniel O'Leary, were still serving.

The Advanced Degree diploma of 1908.

Stark walls remain following the destruction of the Union School No. 1 by a disastrous fire on December 17, 1902. The school board and community under the leadership of the new superintendent, Dr. Elbert W. Griffith, reacted quickly. While classes continued on the third floor of Village Hall, a second high school was built close to the same location on Glen Street. The Glen Street High School welcomed its first students in 1906.

Changing educational practice and increasing numbers of students led to the building of a Junior High School on Union Street behind the High School in 1926. In 1966 the entire two buildings, now the Junior High School, were extended by the addition of a classroom and cafeteria wing.

The new high school built on Sherman Avenue and Quade Street in 1952 has a ten-acre campus that provides space for athletic fields. A classroom wing and girls' gymnasium were added in 1971 to the original building.

This four-room brick building on Walnut Street near the Delaware and Hudson railroad was built in 1867 by District 18 following the burning of the little red schoolhouse at Warren and Canal Streets. The student body gathered for the year-end picture below in the 1890's. Note the "S" iron supporting the brick wall near top of lower picture.

The Walnut Street School building was condemned as unsafe in 1934. School was held in a former factory at 227 Maple Street until the Abraham Wing School opened in 1937 at Lawrence and McDonald Streets. Abraham Wing School serves as the office for District 18 which has remained independent of the City School District for more than 150 years. Children below work on a geography project in the old Walnut Street School about 1930.

In January, 1883, thirty-five years after St. Mary's parish was established, six Sisters of St. Joseph opened classes for 300 children in the first St. Mary's School on Church Street, far right. A high school building, St. Mary's Academy Hall, left, was added in 1903. The Sisters of St. Joseph's convent stood between them.

Classes in St. Mary's Hall, the elementary school, one of which is shown here, were large and orderly. By 1924 the schools were crowded and in need of repair. St. Mary's chapel on the northwest corner of Warren and Church Streets was razed to prepare the site of a new St. Mary's Academy.

At the opening in 1932, the year of St. Mary's Golden Jubilee, a local newspaper called the new St. Mary's, below, a "temple of learning." St. Mary's enrollment of 1,400 students at the time made it the largest parochial school in the country. The architect, Ralph Adams Cram, designed a collegiate Gothic structure copied from England's Westminster Hall.

Twenty years after St. Alphonsus parish was established in 1853, the Academy of Our Lady building on the corner of Pine and Uncas (Crandall) Streets served as a school for children of French-speaking families. The building housed the first Catholic school in Glens Falls and the convent for the Sisters of Assumption until Ecole St. Alphonse was built in 1908 on Crandall Street. An early point of contention with the parishioners was that "Punch" Bannon's saloon occupied the land between the convent and school. The land was quickly purchased and the saloon leveled for a playground.

St. Alphonsus school offered a progam for students in grades one to eight only. Students then transferred to St. Mary's or the public school. Following the fire which destroyed the church in 1955, a new St. Alphonsus school building was planned for the corner of Broad Street and Cottage Place to replace the deteriorating Ecole St. Alphonse. The new school, with a Kindergarten, eight classrooms, library and cafeteria, opened in 1967. A new convent was also built on Crandall Street opposite the school.

Sanford Street School
Built in 1915

Jackson Heights School
Built in 1937

Big Cross Street School
Built in 1927-28

Broad Street School
Built in 1931

The present elementary school buildings of the Glens Falls City School System replaced all the schools of Superintendent Sherman Williams' era. Superintendent Elbert W. Griffith built Sanford Street School to take care of the overflow of elementary students attending Union School No.1 on Glen Street. Big Cross Street School was built to absorb students from the Haviland Avenue area. The remaining schools were built during the administration of Alexander W. Miller: Broad Street replaced the old Union School No. 2 on South Street, Jackson Heights replaced the aging Union School No. 3 on Ridge Street and Kensington Road School provided space for an increasing number of students in the northwest part of the city.

Kensington Road School
Built in 1958

In 1948 nine one or two-room district schools similar to the Harrisena school, left, were consolidated to form a new Union Free School District No. 2 of Queensbury. Two years later an elementary school was erected on the former Floyd Bennett airfield on Aviation Road. In 1953 high school and junior high wings were added.

A two-million dollar bond issue was approved to build and equip a 750-pupil high school west of the first building. It opened in 1963. A new elementary building and swimming pool were also opened in 1969. Completing the Queensbury School campus are athletic fields, tennis courts and a school bus garage.

As early as 1953 the citizens of Warren County sought a local community college. By 1958 an Action Committee of Warren and Washington County citizens was established. In 1959 a survey was conducted and finances and facilities discussed. In April of the next year both County Boards of Supervisors resolved "to join in forming a community college pursuant to the provisions of Article 126 of the Education Law."

A Board of Trustees was appointed and a budget of $225,000 established. Work proceeded at once on the selection of a temporary site and a president, and the name Adirondack Community College was chosen.

On September 12, 1961, the college opened in the former Griffin Lumber Co. building on Upper Broadway in Fort Edward, top right.

Steps were then taken by the trustees to build a permanent campus. A gift of 141 acres of land on the Bay Road by the Glens Falls Insurance Company was enthusiastically accepted by the trustees and supervisors in 1963. The college moved to its new $4.5 million seven-building campus in September of 1967, and it continues to operate there today. As of 1978 1,000 full-time and a larger number of part-time students attend for programs in liberal arts, nursing and occupations, with a tuition of $500 per year.

ACC's busy new campus on Bay Road

Theatres and music halls flourished in the community from before the Civil War. As early as 1835, the Presbyterian Session House was used for amateur theatricals. By the 1850's performances and concerts were given at Apollo Hall, Glen and Berry Streets; Fonda's Masonic Hall on Warren, just east of Bank Square, and at Numan's Hall, on the east side of Glen Street Hill. All three were destroyed in the fire of 1864.

Union Hall was built where Numan's had been located, more recently the site of Fitzgerald's Hotel and Restaurant. Built next door in 1869 was the Cosgrove Opera House, later the location of the Economy Store. The Cosgrove had a capacity of 1,000, with a stage 20 by 50 feet and a full set of scenery. It was later called Cosgrove Music Hall and burned in the fire of 1884, along with Union Hall. The Cosgrove was rebuilt as Keefe's Hall.

Foremost site of entertainment in the community for a substantial period was the Glens Falls Opera House on the south side of Warren Street, near Glen. With seating for 1,600, it opened in November of 1871 and brought to the community such fun as concerts, plays, lectures, walking matches and bicycle races. Destroyed in the fire of 1884, the Opera House was rebuilt and became the Rialto Theatre in 1918. The Rialto fell in Urban Renewal demolition of 1969.

The first downtown theatre to open on a site away from the present Civic Center area was the Empire, still standing as an office building at 11-15 South Street. From 1899, when it opened with "Way Down East," it brought the best of American theatre to local audiences for many years. It later became a movie house, eventually playing second-run programs, and was lost to the competition of television in 1950.

The development of silent movies resulted in several small and short-lived nickelodeons downtown: Wonderland, Majestic, and Capitol Music Hall, all on Ridge Street; Bijou, in Keefe's Hall; Fairyland, on Glen Street near Exchange; and World in Motion, in the Opera House Block.

Said to be the first theatre in northern New York especially built for motion picture productions was the Park, which lasted from 1911 to 1937 and was located on the south side of Park Street, near Glen, today the site of Guy Printing. The State, opening in 1925, was a movie house converted from the old Presbyterian Church on Warren Street. It closed in 1953, and the building was demolished in 1969. The commodious Paramount, a movie palace in the old tradition, opened in 1932 and is the only equipped theatre today standing in Glens Falls, although it is closed. The building has been purchased by Kamyr, Inc., and is scheduled to be converted into an office building.

212

The Glens Falls Opera House Block

The first Glens Falls Opera House opened in 1871 and is shown above as it appeared before destruction in the fire of 1884. The Presbyterian Church, later site of another theatre, the State, is at left. Below is the Opera House interior.

With motion pictures, the Opera House in 1918 became the Rialto Theatre. After a serious fire in 1925 the building was remodeled into a four-story structure and the theatre reopened, designed in the movie palace tradition. Above, the Rialto interior.

The Glens Falls Opera House was destroyed by fire on April 28, 1884. This view was taken from Bank Square, looking east, and the smoke-shrouded steeple is that of the Presbyterian Church. Both the Opera House and the church were rebuilt at the same locations.

History repeats itself. Taken from the same vantage point as the preceding photo, this view shows the Rialto Theatre and Hotel in flames on March 22, 1925. The Presbyterian Church steeple is behind the great clouds of smoke. The church was not damaged in this fire.

"Come when you like, stay as long as you like," all for five cents admission, was the invitation of the World in Motion, a nickelodeon opened in 1909 in the Opera House block. Another venture of the same ilk, shown after a 1914 fire, was the Bijou, at left, located in what was later to become the Economy Store building on Glen Street.

Built on the site of the old Glens Falls and Lake George Stage Company barns on South Street, the Empire Theatre opened October 6, 1899, with the play "Way Down East." For years the Empire was Glens Falls' leading playhouse, with such stars as George M. Cohan, Billie Burke, Al Jolson, Julia Sanderson, Fred Allen, the Barrymores and many others. Later it was part of the Schine movie chain. At bottom right of the preceding page is an early photo of the interior.

Two downtown movie houses remembered today are the State and the Park. Former patrons of the State, which was remodeled from the old Presbyterian Church, seen in the background, insist that much of the balcony seating consisted of wooden church pews. In its heyday, the Park boasted a piano player, a baritone singer, and its own theme song, "The Park Theatre March," which it modestly described as "one of the catchiest pieces of music ever played on a piano." It was the first theatre in this area to have an organ, installed in 1913.

The Paramount Theatre at Ridge and Maple Streets, opposite the Queensbury Hotel, was the last of several movie houses established in Glens Falls after the turn of the century. Built by the Paramount Publix Corporation and opened with fanfare on January 22, 1932, it was operated as a theatre until 1978, when it was sold to Kamyr, Inc., and closed. It will be converted into an office building. Motion pictures were being shown on Ridge Street within a decade after their invention by Thomas A. Edison in 1893, the Capitol Music Hall next door to the old Ridge Street engine house having advertised as early as 1902 "the latest Edison Kinetoscope comedy pictures" and films of the Jeffries-Fitzsimmons fight of 1899. In 1907, the Wonderland, a nickelodeon, opened in the store later occupied by Van the Shoeman.

Glens Falls' love of horse racing had an early start at the half-mile track of the Warren County Fair. The fair was conducted from 1862 to 1868 on grounds owned by George Brown south of his Halfway House on the Lake George Road.

In 1868 the Glens Falls Citizens Association purchased land west of the plank road just north of the village limits between what are now Lincoln and Horicon Avenues and moved the fair to its new location. An oval half-mile race track extended east-west from the plank road, now Glen Street, along the north side of Lincoln Avenue almost to the present location of Kensington Road. A spacious grandstand seated 2,000 spectators.

The main entrance to the fairgrounds, above, stood at what is now the corner of Glen Street and Lincoln Avenue. Fairs continued there until 1895 when Arthur W. Sherman and R. A. Little bought the property and laid out the residential area seen today. Coolidge Avenue was named for Sherman's wife, the former Gertrude Coolidge.

By 1890 horsemen and spectators alike were clamoring for a larger race track with better facilities.

Alexander W. Miller, reporting about the 1890's, stated: "Almost any afternoon there was a free show on Bay Street, when racing would be going on from Monument Square to the cemetery."

When the fairgrounds and half-mile track were closed, a group of citizens known as the Northern New York Horse Breeders Association bought 100 acres of land west of the old fairgrounds and Kensington Road and laid out the east-west Mile Track, later labeled by horsemen the fastest in the country. In August from 1895 until 1902, spectators would ride by trolley up Lincoln Avenue, dismount, and walk to the new grandstand, top, next page.

During the years 1896 to 1900 when the Mile Track was on the Grand Circuit, nearly every horse of note raced over it. On September 10, 1896, the world record for pacers was shattered by the great John R. Gentry in a matched race of three heats against the equally-famous Star Pointer. An estimated 10,000 tense spectators watched from the grandstand, and along the rail.

The Mile Track, perhaps overshadowed by racing in Saratoga Springs, lasted a mere seven years. The land was reluctantly sold and later developed into the BroadAcres residential area. No evidence of the Mile Track, save the curve of Horicon Avenue, remains today.

Not a part of the fairgrounds, but a favorite resort of horsemen and their friends, was the Club House, below, on Sanford Street. The building originally stood on the northeast corner of Glen and Sanford Streets and was known as the Glen Park Hotel. In the 1890's it was moved to the present site of the Sanford Street School and, though listed officially as the Granger House, was popularly known as the Club House.

The Club House was operated from 1891 to 1895 by Marcus E. Granger, father of the colorful Kattskill Bay innkeeper, Claude C. Granger. Marcus, a jovial man, was a popular fiddler for local square dances all his life. Under new management in 1895, the building again became the Glen Park Hotel and was eventually destroyed by fire on December 1, 1913. Sanford Street School was erected on the site shortly thereafter. The barns were torn down to make way for a playground.

A columnist in *The Morning Star* of August 22, 1887, discussed an ever present and disagreeable subject, the behavior of Glens Falls youth: "Knots of boys hang on, . . . engage in rough 'horse play,' . . . swear and blaspheme and talk obscenely at all times . . . Some of the 'chippies' who parade up Glen and Bay Streets have lately taken to forcing people off the sidewalk."

He suggested a public reading room or a Young Men's Christian Association to offset the lure of "new saloons being opened weekly . . . with gilding, cut glass and polished brass . . ." Later he wrote, "It seemed strange, and yet pleasant to me, after writing last week" to learn that "the prospects of a Young Men's Christian Association being formed here are at present very bright." And indeed they were.

Katharine Cunningham reminisced that the first person actively to do something about a YMCA was the Rev. George Collyer, minister of the Methodist Church, who talked his ideas over with her grandfather, William McEchron. A citizens' meeting was held in the basement Sunday School room of the Methodist Church where "not even the somewhat musty atmosphere could dampen the enthusiasm of the group."

After several meetings, the Glens Falls YMCA was organized and incorporated in December of 1888. Classes were begun in the winter of 1889 in the Sol Russell building over J. E. Sawyer's store, 26 Warren Street. A 250-volume library was also collected for use. So great was the interest of young people that the facility was quickly outgrown.

In January, 1890, a wealthy lumberman, Jones Ordway, at the urging of William McEchron and friends, contributed $50,000 for the purchase of the Glens Falls Insurance Company property on Glen Street and the construction of a YMCA building. In September, 1891, the cornerstone was laid. The building, Ordway Hall, above, was dedicated on June 14, 1892, and was first lighted with gas. The first basketball games in the village were played in the new YMCA soon after its opening. Only one basketball was available and peach baskets served as goals. In spite of intricate rules, interest in the new sport grew and many outstanding local teams were organized.

In 1909 the William McEchron family donated a gymnasium, swimming pool, locker room and bowling alley that was built behind Ordway Hall. This downtown YMCA building was in active use until 1969.

The bicycle craze, like the jogging craze today, was at its height in the 1890's. Clubs were organized and bicycle paths built along side roads in many directions. Here a typical, all-male bicycle club that boasts a priest, center, as a member, poses in front of the new YMCA building before setting off on a trip.

After 75 years of continued use, it was determined that the downtown YMCA building would have to be replaced. In 1966 land was purchased in the north part of Crandall Park; construction of a new YMCA building commenced two years later. The new Family YMCA officially opened its doors on October 5, 1971. The new building, below, houses gymnasiums, swimming pool, game and activity rooms providing for a year-round program of family activities.

This early view of the tennis courts in Crandall Park reminds us that parks and recreation facilities were not always available. The generosity of Henry Crandall made possible both City Park and Crandall Park, two of his favorite projects. He bequeathed a trust fund in 1913 "creating, continuing, enlarging and maintaining" the parks. New trees were planted, ponds cleared and play areas begun. Crandall is said to have dredged one of the ponds for boating. In 1919 the Chamber of Commerce contributed funds to improve the baseball diamond and build bleachers. Five years later, Mayor Charles W. Cool appointed the first city recreation commission to develop playgrounds and tennis courts. The city purchased other properties during the 1920's and '30's. Through the joint efforts of the Outing Club and the Recreation Commission, Crandall Park, Haviland's Cove and East Field were developed as community facilities.

Baseball has been a major sport for young and old since the 1900's, whether played on sandlot with a pickup team, or in a League Park on the Boulevard between Glens Falls and Hudson Falls. The Ancient Order of Hibernians team, seen below, boasted a record of defeating all comers in 1905. One strategy used by the players when a batter dropped a short hit in outfield and a runner was scoring from second was to take a short cut through the pitcher's mound while the umpire was watching the play at home plate! Two years later the Sunsets played for large crowds in a field on the Luzerne Road near Broad Street. Other popular teams of early days were the Tigers, West Glens Falls, Ridgewoods and the Glens Falls semi-professionals. Little League baseball organized in the 1950's and a baseball field was opened in Crandall Park for the League in 1955, complete with dugouts, bleachers and fencing. The Glens Falls Independents, a semi-professional team, still compete with area teams in Crandall Park.

Haviland's Cove Beach House was built on Pruyn's Island in 1926 with funds provided by the Zonta Club. A boom in the Hudson River prevented logs from floating into the swimming area.

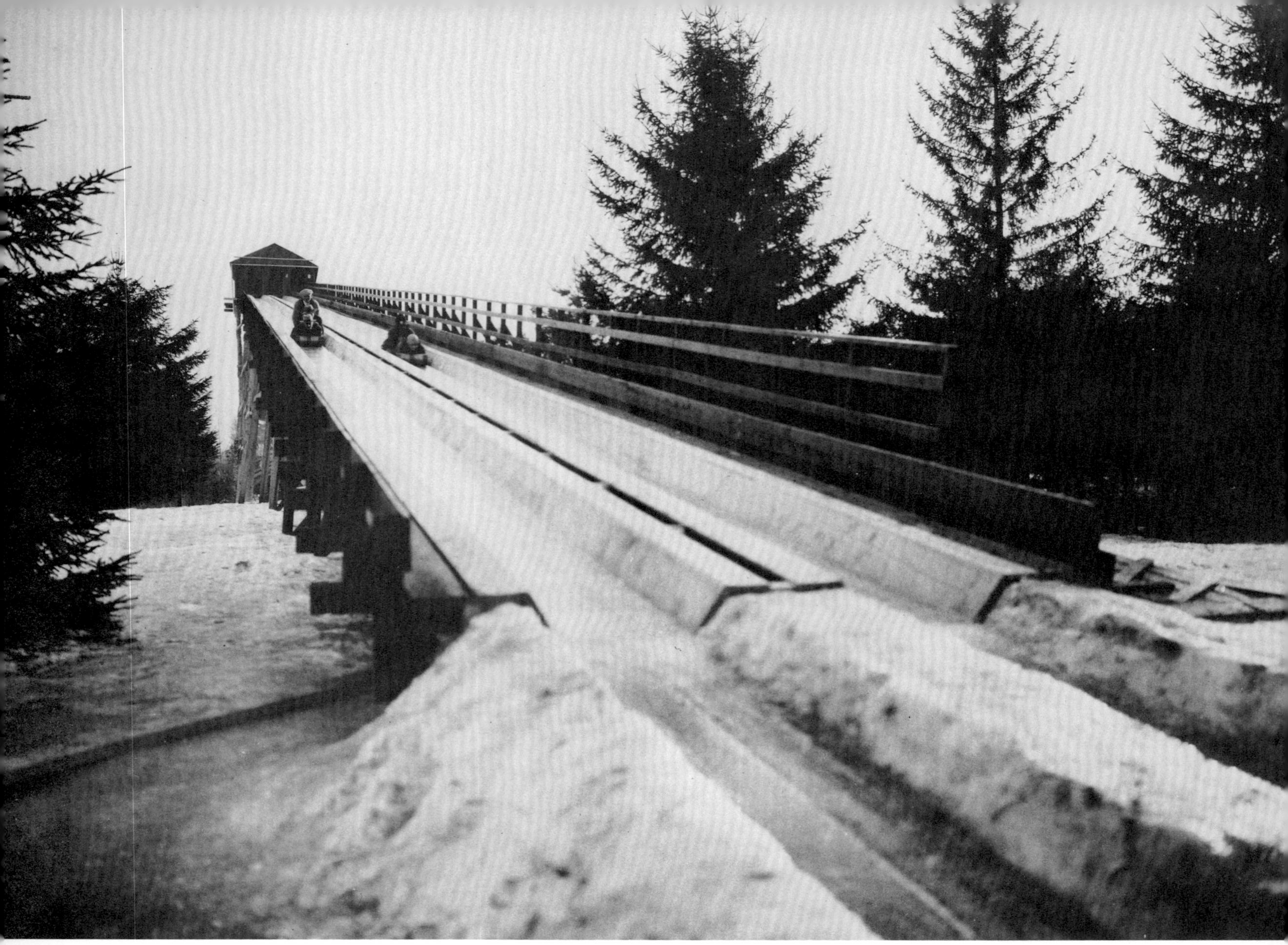

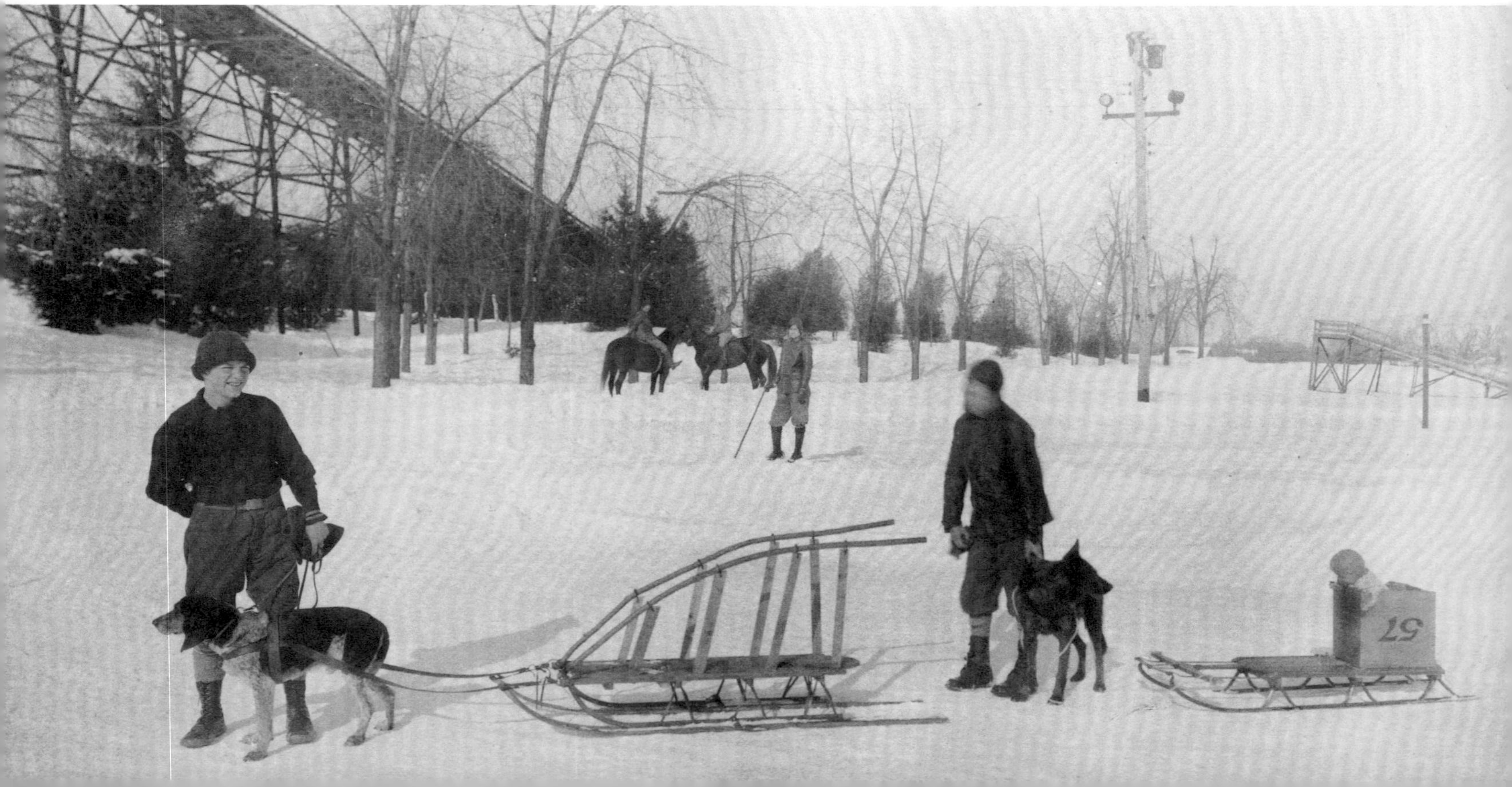

The Outing Club was organized by prominent citizens in 1927 to promote Glens Falls as a sports and recreation center with "skating rinks, toboggan slides and ski jumps." Crandall Park fields and ponds made a natural setting for winter activities. A small building was moved from the shore of the pond, placed in back of third base on the baseball diamond and converted to a warm fieldhouse. The Glens Falls High School manual training class constructed a 50-foot-high, 250-foot-long slide with a runway extending from the fieldhouse almost a quarter of a mile to Halfway Brook.

The first Winter Carnival conducted by the Outing Club in February, 1928, offered speed skating, figure skating, hockey, tobogganing, even dog-sledding. The festivities included a gala parade, floats, the coronation of a king and queen and a Winter Ball. One national sports magazine reported that the three-day Winter Carnival linked Glens Falls "with Lake Placid and Tupper Lake as a winter sports center in New York State." The Winter Carnival continued in full array until 1932 when it gradually declined. The depression and uncertain weather led to its demise.

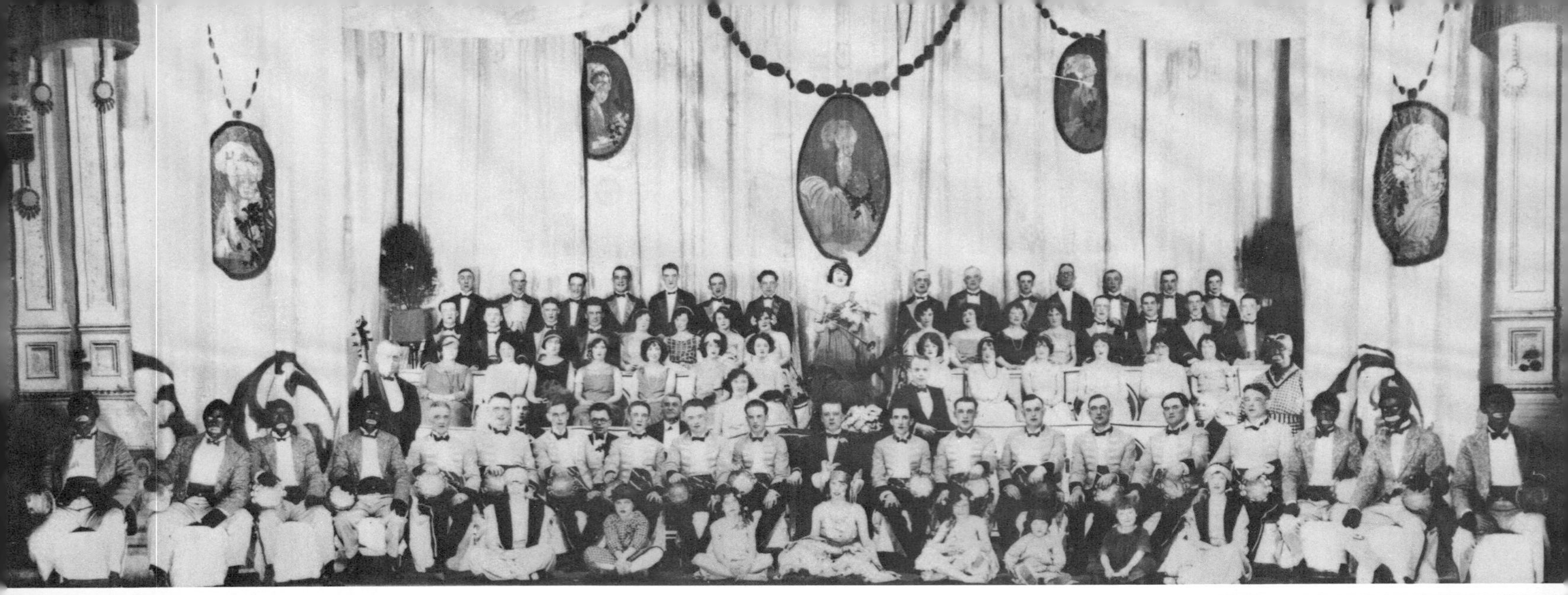

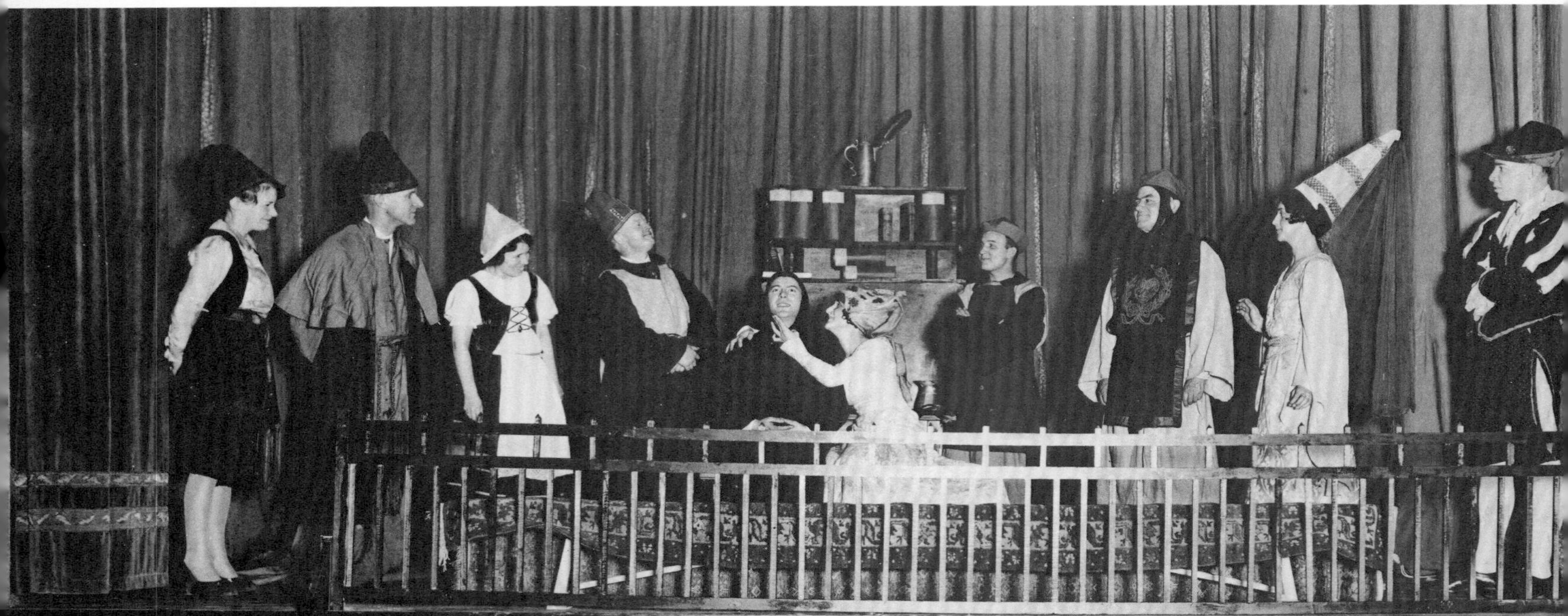

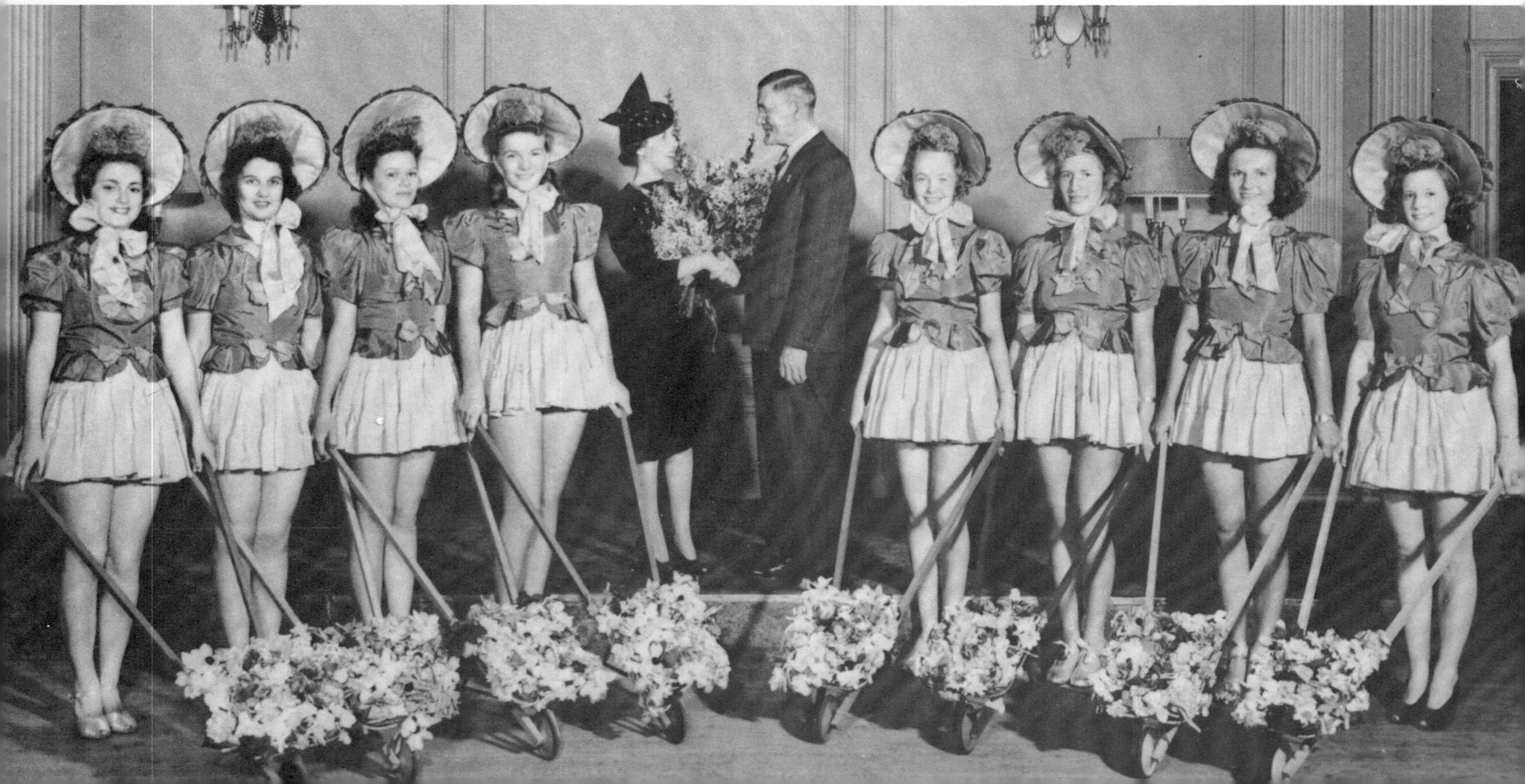

Amateur theatricals have been an important activity in Glens Falls for many years. As early as 1834 the Glens Falls Thespian Society staged a number of dramatic entertainments. During the early 1920's, the Knights of Columbus minstrels were a popular annual feature in town. The 1926 cast, shown upper left, performed on the Empire Theatre stage. In 1928 the Outing Club organized a Little Theatre Group and presented three or four plays annually at the Junior High School. A tense situation in a 1928 production, "The Man Who Married a Dumb Wife," appears middle left.

Community organizations also presented amateur musicals. In the early 1940's the Woman's Civic Club provided several years of "Fall Frolics" to large and enthusiastic crowds at the Junior High School. Mayor John Bazinet greets the 1941 program chairman amidst members of the dancing chorus at bottom left.

An amateur group that has delighted local audiences over the past 42 years is the Glens Falls Operetta Club. Two Glens Falls school teachers organized the group in 1935 to provide "an artistic outlet for musical and dramatic talents of several hundred vocalists, instrumentalists, actors, dancers and technicians in the Glens Falls area." As directors of dramatics and music, they presented "HMS Pinafore," seen above, as a benefit for the Glens Falls Hospital Guild. Other Gilbert and Sullivan shows followed in subsequent years. The club moved into Victor Herbert and finally into recent Broadway productions like "Oklahoma," "Sound of Music," "Fiddler on the Roof" and "Hello, Dolly."

An oratorio group, organized in 1939, sang Handel's "Messiah" in the First Presbyterian Church. Similar classical works have been performed each year since. A Little Theatre group, formed in 1940, will be remembered for such plays as "Our Town" and "Death of a Salesman." The Operetta Club with its present budget exceeding $20,000 boasts a supporting associate membership of over 600 persons in spite of increasing numbers of professional companies in the area.

In July, 1975, the Brigade of the American Revolution, 150 strong, camped for two days in full regalia in Crandall Park west of the pond, and each day reenacted a battle. Above, the opposing commanders meet on the battlefield, the baseball grounds, to negotiate a settlement.

The Glens Falls Operetta Club presented a historical musical, "1776," in January, 1976. Benjamin Franklin and a member of the Continental Congress are portrayed in a tense moment. The musical was one of the highlights of the Bicentennial observance.

Three soldiers of the Seth Warner Regiment who conducted the ceremonial salute on the morning of July 4, 1976, in Monument Square stand below. Area church bells were rung and special services held throughout the day.

In years past Glens Falls faced celebrations with vitality and style. The Bicentennial was no exception. In January, 1974, the Common Council of the City of Glens Falls appointed the Glens Falls Historical Association as the official representative and three months later the association selected a Bicentennial Committee.

The purposes of the Bicentennial celebration as developed by the committee were: "To honor those who gave us what is, with all its faults, a superb system of government and a splendid way of life; to take renewed courage, at a time of crisis, from increased understanding of the past, and to look forward to a future, based upon that past and present, when the promises of 1776 and 1976, the promises of *Common Sense,* and the Declaration of Independence, of the United Nations Charter and 'I Have a Dream' of Martin Luther King will all be fulfilled."

The printed program of the Centennial in 1876, right, located in Crandall Library, gave impetus to many events and activities in 1976, from the rebuilding of a bandstand to a balloon ascension. The culmination of the celebration was the week-long Hometown Days '76 event, including an all-day arts festival, a gala parade, a community family day, a fireworks display and on July 4th, a ceremony at Monument Square.

An early event in 1975 was a fire hydrant painting contest portraying soldiers, women and woodsmen, much to the delight of citizens and canines alike. The Bicentennial logo, a Quaker, in recognition of our heritage, appeared on many projects: a calendar, a plate and a 4-foot wood carving in City Park.

On June 21, 1976, a sealed time capsule containing articles and mementoes collected by school children in the public and parochial schools was buried in the back yard of the Historical Association Museum, left. It is hoped that the capsule will be opened by school children a century hence for the Tricentennial celebration.

233

One observer of the Hometown Days '76 parade and family day in Crandall Park on June 26, 1976, wrote:

"Crandall Park luxuriates in fragrances I'd nearly forgotten but could never forget. Some are customary — the aroma of the thriving pines, the thick, rich odor of the pond. Others are just wafting through — burgers charred on open fires.

"Onstage performances attract a flow of spectators and listeners; the audience never stays the same."

On Saturday morning the Bicentennial Parade marched from Ridge Street and Bank Square to Crandall Park. "For almost two whole hours, the parade marches and rolls on by. Adult legs ache by the time it's over. A tired youngster turns finally and asks: 'Is this the same parade, Daddy?'

"Maybe it was the longest parade ever in the Tri-Counties. Certainly my longest . . ."

The floats were not as glamorous as the ones seen on TV, but they were a greater accomplishment. The old-time fire engine, left, a replica pulled by Broad Street school children, passes the reviewing stand with the Crandall monument in the background.

Saturday afternoon in Crandall Park provided games, music, entertainment and all kinds of food, such as the ox roast. "It all took time. Seventy deep were customers lined up for roasted ox sandwiches. Patience lasted longer than the ox did."

On the Recreation Field backstop, a banner proclaimed "Hometown Days June 19 - July 4," above right. The "4" was backwards, but like everything else in the Bicentennial celebration, no one wanted it changed.

A "camp follower" of the Brigade of the American Revolution prepares bread colonial style during the encampment in Crandall Park in May, 1975. All members of the Brigade wore authentic dress and lived as the troops of early days.

The Bicentennial was greeted on May 16, 1976, by the hot air balloon, "Gregarious Pilgrim," carrying the "world's biggest birthday card," a 60 foot square nylon sheet, signed by hundreds of area residents.

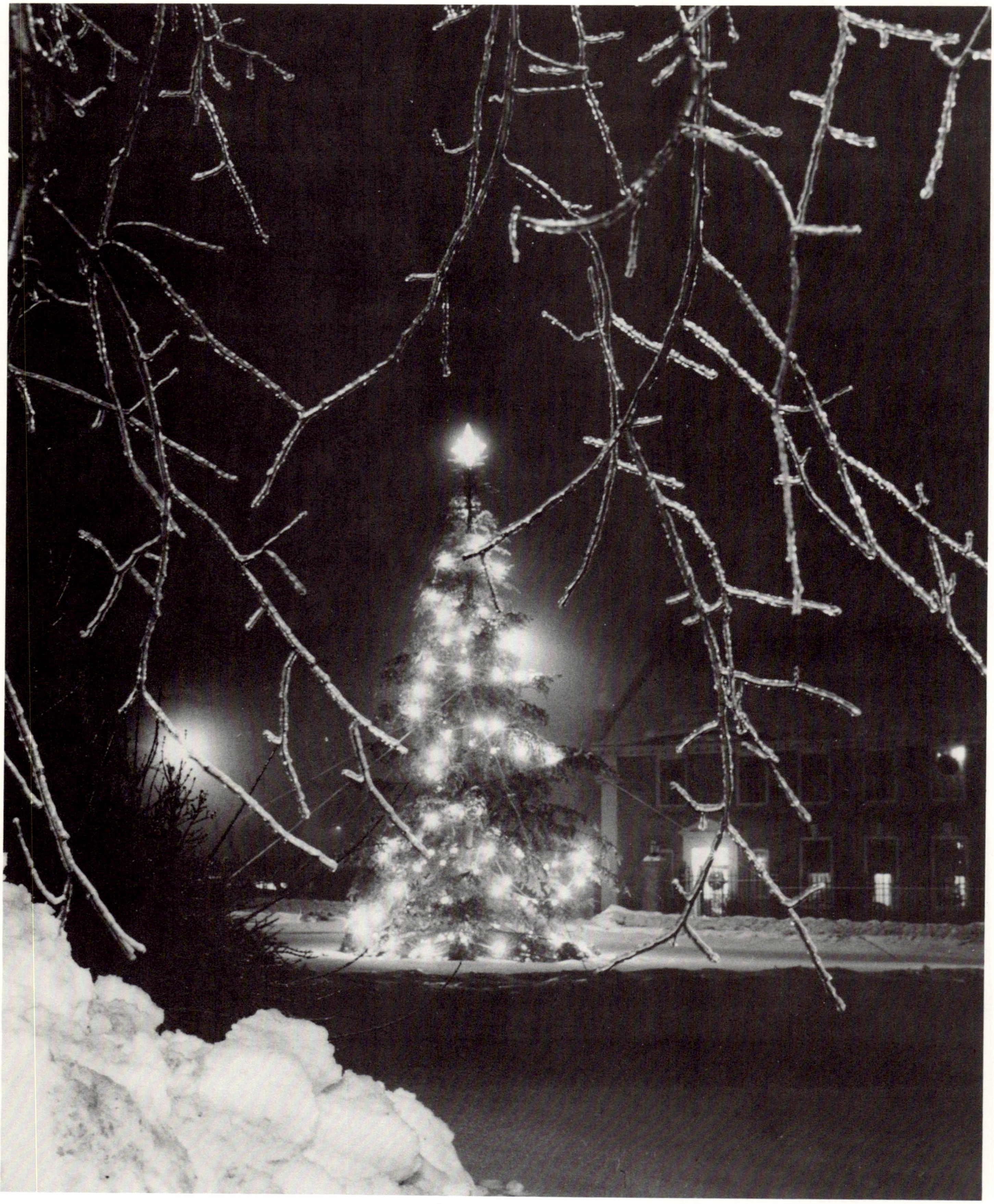

Glens Falls.

It is children at play in summer's twilight, a crackling fire on a snowy eve.

It is busy schools and friendly churches, beautiful homes and cozy cottages, wars and fires, picnics and parades.

It is the noise of a hospital, the hush of a funeral home.

It is the beauty of spring buds, summer flowers, and autumn leaves.

In winter, the lights of Christmas shine through a cold and drab season to express the warmth and joy of life in the community so many have loved.

Glens Falls.

Acknowledgments

We are deeply indebted to the many professional and amateur photographers of yesterday and today who have brought to life the image and mood of our community. The legacy of Seneca Ray Stoddard is invaluable. Other local photographers now deceased whose works have endured include George W. Conkey, Bernie A. Degnan, William W. Kennedy, Ralph M. Lapham, Charles Oblenis, Harry Pangburn, Karl R. Rissland, George P. Sauter, Frank M. Taft and many unidentified camera artists. Among those recording the scene in recent years, and whose work has been used extensively, are Carl N. Atiyeh, Francis L. Bayle, Everett Bowie, Monty Calvert, Richard K. Dean, Edward and Richard Durling, Walter W. Grishkot and the North Country Photographers.

This essay would not have been possible without the dedicated efforts and publications of past historians: Dr. Austin W. Holden's history of Queensbury, a primary source of local lore; Smith's history of Warren County; Hyde's history of Glens Falls, and the sesquicentennial Warren County history, edited by William H. Brown with the chapter on Glens Falls written by Alexander W. Miller. Source materials were found in the Glens Falls City Hall, the Queensbury Town Office Building, and in the Warren County Municipal Center at the Clerk's Office, Historian's Office, Surrogate's Court and the Records Storage Center. Access to an abundance of photographs, manuscripts and publications, as well as research assistance, was generously provided by Crandall Library and the Glens Falls Historical Association.

Below are listed some of the many who provided photographs or information or assisted in any way. So much material was made available that only a portion could be used. The committee is grateful to everyone who helped.

Adirondack Community College
Mrs. Olive G. Arsenault
Mrs. Frederick G. Bascom
Miss Genevieve Bazinet
Frank Beattie
Mr. and Mrs. Lyman A. Beeman
Lyman A. Beeman Jr.
Mark Behan
Erminie Smith Benz
Juli Bermann
Mrs. Minnie E. Bidwell
Joseph J. Blaze
Mrs. Dorothy W. Bowden
Mrs. John L. Bowman
Harold Bradley
Mrs. Clarence Bradway
Harold Brothers
Hubert C. Brown
Gerald T. Buckley
Mrs. Dora Bullock
Mrs. Russell M. L. Carson
Mrs. H. Allen Center
Donald Clements
Richard C. Collins
Continental Employees Club
Continental Insurance Companies
Theodore G. Corbett
Mrs. M. C. Cornwell
James K. Cotter
Crandall Library Trustees
Mrs. Douglass Crockwell
George E. Daley
Irving Dean
Mrs. Emile Deguire
Maitland C. DeSormo
Arlene DeTemple
Peter T. Donnelly

John A. Wilcox
Robert J. Dorey
Mrs. Robin Early
Graham R. Easson
Robert L. Eddy
Finch, Pruyn and Company, Inc.
First National Bank of Glens Falls
Peter L. Fisher
Thomas I. Ford
Claude Fox
Mark W. Freeman
Friends of Crandall Library
Mark Frost
Dr. Richard D. Garrett
Stanley O. Gericke
Mrs. Mary Gleason
Glens Falls Camera Club
Glens Falls City School District
Glens Falls National Bank and Trust Company
Glens Falls Operetta Club, Inc.
Glens Falls Recreation Commission
Albert F. M. Granger
Gordon Granger
Mrs. Carol Greenough
Mrs. Myrtle Hamilton
Gerald Hammond
Mrs. Lena Harris
William H. Helm
Harry P. Herbold
Miss Peggy Herrick
Mrs. Myron H. Howk
Harold L. Hubert
Mr. and Mrs. Arthur P. Irving
Kamyr, Inc.
Mrs. Billie Kidwell
Jean A. King
Joseph A. King

Mr. and Mrs. Robert M. King
Mrs. Royal E. Knowles
Miss Mary LaMoy
Mrs. Jerome F. Lapham
Arthur LaPorte
Leland LaVoy
Arthur A. Light
Henry Lindstrand
Mrs. Gabrielle Lohret
G. Nelson Lowe
John R. Lustyik
Thomas C. Mahoney
Mrs. Dorothy Mannigan
James Marsh
Miss Sarah McEchron
Miss Hilma McIlvaine
Alexander W. Miller
Edward Moon
Victor Morgan
Walter Munger
K. Douglas Neely
Niagara Mohawk Power Corporation
Mrs. Kathryn O'Brien
Lawrence E. O'Hara
Norwood W. Olmsted
Mrs. Rita Oudekerk
Burr A. Patten
Francis P. Poutre
Queensbury School District
Daniel L. Reardon
Walter P. Reichert
Mrs. Violet B. Rhodes
Mrs. Blanche Richardson
Adelbert R. Root
Elmer B. Rowley
Steve and Rita Saskiewicz
Mrs. George P. Sauter
Senior Citizens Center
Ralph R. Shapiro
Jean C. Smith
William M. Smith
Southern Adirondack Library System
Robert A. Starbuck
Miss Ernestine G. Stoddard
Rev. C. Henri Tessier
The Post-Star
Garner C. Tripp Jr.
Addison M. Varney
Mrs. Pamela Vogel
Mrs. Helen Whaley

Sources and Resources

The following books and other materials were quoted or used to verify the information in this essay:

BOOKS

History of the Town of Queensbury by Austin W. Holden. Albany, N.Y. Joel Munsell Company, 1874.

History of Glens Falls, New York and Its Settlement by Louis Fiske Hyde. Glens Falls, N.Y. Glens Falls Post Company, 1936.

History of Warren County, New York, William H. Brown, editor. Board of Supervisors of Warren County. Glens Falls Post Company, 1963.

William McEchron 1831-1906: Homely Recollections by Katharine Cunningham. Woodstock, Vermont. Elm Tree Press, 1962.

History of the Lumber Industry in the State of New York by William F. Fox. Harbor Hill Books, 1976.

The History of St. Mary's Parish, Glens Falls, New York. 1848-1949 by the Rev. Joseph P. Kelly S.T.D. Glens Falls, N.Y. Glens Falls Post Company, 1950.

Glimpses of the Past. Historical Museum Notes by Richard C. VanDusen. Walter P. Reichert and Harold M. Long, editors. Glens Falls, N.Y. Ridgecraft Books, 1970.

Backward Glances by Howard C. Mason. Glens Falls, N.Y. Vols. 1, 2, 3. Webster Mimeo Services, 1963, 1964, 1965.

Under the Bridge, An Autobiography by Ferris Greenslet. New York, N.Y. Literary Classics Inc., 1943.

History of Warren County by H.P. Smith. Syracuse, N.Y. D. Mason and Company, 1885.

Warren County, a History and a Guide, American Guide Series, Writers Program of the Work Projects Administration, Warren County Board of Supervisors. Glens Falls Post Company, 1942.

Saratoga Through Car: A History of the Hudson Valley Railway by David F. Nestle, 1967.

The Natural Thing: The Land and Its Citizens by Pieter W. Fosburgh, New York, N.Y. Macmillan, 1959.

OTHER MATERIALS

Glens Falls, New York, The Empire City. Glens Falls Publishing Co., 1908.

Annual Reports of the Glens Falls Union Free School District, 1897-1903.

The Scout, house publication of Finch, Pruyn and Company, Inc., Glens Falls, N.Y.

Historical Manual of the Presbyterian Church of Glens Falls. Messenger Printing Establishment, 1876.

In the Days of Old Glens Falls by Samuel G. Boyd. Zonta Club of Glens Falls, N.Y. 1927.

The Eagle Trolley Exploring Guide. Brooklyn Daily Eagle, Brooklyn, N.Y. 1917.

The Church in Glens Falls and Its Neighborhood by Mrs. William A. Wait. Glens Falls, N.Y. 1899.

"The Last of the Mohicans, Cooper's Historical Inventions and His Cave" by James A. Holden. *Proceedings* of the New York State Historical Association, Vol. 16, 1917.

"History of Education in the City of Glens Falls" by Mary DeLong West.

"The Story of Canals of New York State" by John P. Cashion, 1963.

"The Lime Industry in Glens Falls, 1832-1938" by J. Thacher Sears.

"Manuscript History of Glens Falls, 1834, 1835, 1836" by the Rev. Ephraim Newton.

"Recollections" by Harlow (pseud.) in *The Warren Messenger,* 1831.

Miscellaneous manuscript materials prepared by Marian A. Chitty, Alexander W. Miller and others, deposited in Crandall Library and at the museum of the Glens Falls Historical Association.

Back issues of *The Post-Star, The Glens Falls Times, The Morning Star, The Glens Falls Republican, The Glens Falls Messenger, The Warren Messenger* and other newspapers, many on microfilm, at Crandall Library.

About the Authors

Members of the group responsible for compilation of this portrait of Glens Falls, New York, share an interest in the lore of the community. All are active in the Glens Falls Historical Association, which maintains a museum in a Victorian home, formerly the DeLong residence, at 348 Glen Street. This volume has been published with the cooperation of Crandall Library, a rich source for local and regional history.

Publications Committee members:

• Robert N. King, Chairman, is vice-president of the Historical Association and a long-time local teacher and school administrator, now associated with the State Department of Education. He served as general chairman of the Glens Falls observance of the American Bicentennial, and this volume is a product of that celebration.

• John D. Austin Jr., a local attorney and former newspaperman, was for some time editor of *The New England Historical and Genealogical Register* and has long been interested in early Glens Falls.

• Susan E. Buffington acted as research assistant and professional coordinator for local American Bicentennial activities and wrote a column, "Museum Notes," for *The Post-Star*. She is now a Warren County Children's Service caseworker.

• Arthur S. Fisher, retired managing editor of *The Glens Falls Times,* has assembled an outstanding collection of facts, photographs and lore of old Glens Falls. He served several years as secretary of the Historical Association.

• Florence M. King, a member of the Glens Falls Bicentennial Committee, has served as business and production adviser for the publication.

• Elizabeth S. McAndrew is assistant director and head of reference services at Crandall Library. She is active with both Glens Falls and Washington County historical groups.

• Pauline S. Smith, retired from a public relations position with Finch, Pruyn and Company, Inc., was editor of the house publication, *The Scout.* Her special interest has been early logging and river drive material.

Index

Abraham Wing School District	18, 204, 205
Academy of Our Lady	207
Adirondack Community College	18, 211
Adirondack logs	58, 59
Adirondack Mountain Club	172
Adirondack Northway	16, 17, 43, 104
Adirondack timberlands	15, 54, 59
Adirondack (Upper Hudson) waterways system	15, 59
Adirondacks, the	11, 15
Aerial views —	
Adirondack Northway	17
Big Boom area	17
Finch, Pruyn and Co., Inc., plant and vicinity	36-37, 65
Hudson River	36-37, 52, 56, 62-65
Downtown Glens Falls	74-75, 143
Continental Insurance Co. building and vicinity	123
Monument Square and vicinity	132
Glens Falls Hospital	155
Glens Falls High School campus	203
Queensbury School campus	210
Adirondack Community College campus	211
Ahlstrom Company	139
Airport, Warren County	16
Albany	15, 16
Albany County	16
Albany Savings Bank	132, 133
Allen, James M.	101
American House	112-113, 115, 125, 145
Amherst, Gen. Jeffrey	11
Ancient water route	11
Apollo Hall	212
Arlington Hotel	47, 52
Armando candle factory	146
Armory	149
Army National Guard	149
Arthur, Chester A.	107
Auringer, Rev. O. C.	47
Automobile	122, 124, 146, 159, 161, 166, 167
Aviation Rd.	210
Balloons, hot air	6, 134, 233, 235
Band, French Cornet	21
Band, Glens Falls City	21
Bandstand, City Park	134, 135
Banks (see listing under name)	
Bank Square	16, 19, 71, 73-85, 91-99, 102, 136, 138, 168, 186-187, 216, 217
Bannon, "Punch"	207
Baptist Church	18, 180
Barrel manufacturing	57
Bartlett, William Henry	25
Basin St.	152
Baxter, R. T.	116
Bay St.	4-5, 12, 75, 114, 116-122, 124-128, 132, 133
Bayle, G. F. and Co.	103
Bazinet, Mayor John	231
Bemis, Dr. Edward H.	163
Bemis Sanitarium	145, 163
Benack, John saloon	47
Bentley, W. F.	150
Berry, Capt. Sidney W.	68
Berry St.	68, 79
Betty, Benjamin	131
Bicentennial Celebrations	134, 232-235
Bicycle Club	225
Big Bend	15, 17, 58-59, 62
Big Boom	15, 17, 48, 50, 58-63
Big Cross St. School	208-209
Bijou Theatre	212, 218
Bishop, Charles Reed	21
Bissell, W. F.	219
Black marble industry	15, 47, 55
Blackwell's	58
Blockhouse, Halfway Brook	11, 12
Blue Ledge	58
Borden's	132, 134
Boreas River	58
Boston Store	103
Boulevard carbarn	169
Boyd, Samuel G.	47, 54

241

Boys' Savings Club	130
Bradley Opera House	111
Braley, P. P. and Co.	103
Braydon and Chapman	83
Brick Manor	157
Bridges —	
First Bridge (1788-1792)	23
Second Bridge (1792-1802)	23
Toll Bridge (1803-1833)	23, 24
Free Bridge (1833-1842)	25
Covered Bridge (1842-1890)	inside covers, 22-23, 26-27, 50, 60
Arch, The (1842-1913)	27-29
Iron Bridge (1890-1913)	30-33, 50-51
Loaned Bridge (1913-1915)	34, 35
Concrete Viaduct (1915 to present)	2, 35-39, 42, 43, 67
Brigade of the American Revolution	232, 235
Briggs, Walter	12
Bristol, Warren	159
Broad St. fire station	159
Broad St. School	209
Brown, George	222
Brown's Hotel	81, 102
Buckingham, J. S.	41
Bullard Press	134
Bullock, Dora	131
Burglary, bank	82
Burgoyne, General	158
Burns, J. J. Newsroom	77, 81, 88
Burns Wines and Liquors	104
Buses	16, 110, 111, 145, 146
Butler Brook	12, 14
Call, Elizabeth	194
Call Hardware	224
Calvary Assembly of God	193
Canal boats	53, 54
Canal St.	47, 68
Canavan's Tire Shop	199
Capitol Music Hall	212, 221
Carleton, Major Christopher	158
Carpenter, Wait S.	73, 91
Cataract Engine Co.	73, 158
Centennial (1876)	233
Chamber of Commerce	18, 226
Champlain Canal	52, 53
Chapman, Frederick B.	160
Chapman, Juliet Goodman	160
Charlotte County	16
Cheney and Arms gristmill	28
Chepontuc	15
Chitty house	124

Christ Church (see Methodist churches)	
Christian and Missionary Alliance Church	193
Churches (see listing under name)	
Church of Christ	192
Church of the Messiah	4, 18, 116, 120-123, 181-183
Church of Our Lady of the Annunciation	193
Church St.	79, 147
Cigarmakers Union	18
Cisterns, water	73, 84
City Hall	128, 134-136, 158
City Hotel	142
City Park	6, 84, 118, 119, 124-126, 128, 134-136
Civic Center	67, 68, 79, 142, 212
Civil War monument (see Soldiers' Monument)	
Civil War veterans	73
Club House, The	223
Coale, Griffith Bailey	40
Collins House	102
Collyer, Rev. George	224
Columbia Ave.	157
Colvin, Addison B.	131
Colvin Building	168
Commercial Bank	83
Commercial Hotel	157
Commercial training school	18
Communications	16, 81
Company K, Army National Guard	18, 149
Conkling, Mary A.	149
Conklingville Dam	51
Connecticut	11
Continental Insurance Co.	16, 75, 120, 122, 123, 161
Cool Insuring Agency	134
Cool, Mayor Charles W.	226
Coolidge, Gertrude (Mrs. Arthur W. Sherman)	222
Cooper, James Fenimore	24, 39, 41
Cooper St.	166, 167
Cooper's Cave	40, 41
Corey's store	112-113
Corners, The (see also Wing's Corners)	71, 82, 83
Cosgrove Opera House	78, 212
Cowles, D. H. and Co. building	89, 120, 138
Cowper, Jeffrey	11, 12
Cram, Ralph Adams	177, 206
Crandall Block	110-114, 156
Crandall, Henry	21, 118-119, 122, 124, 128, 130, 131, 134, 226
Crandall Library	21, 119, 124, 126, 128-130
Crandall monument	128, 234
Crandall Park	12, 21, 63, 84, 128, 130, 131, 144-145, 225, 226, 229, 232, 234, 235
Crandell, John Bradshaw	2, 25
Crockwell, Douglass	21, 194
Cronin, Robert J. High-Rise	137
Cronkhite Commercial School	194

242

Cronkhite, James	194
Cronkhite, William	142, 161
Cronkhite's Newsroom	164, 165
Crown Point	12
Cultural and entertainment facilities	18, 21
Culvert St.	140
Cunningham, J. L. Hose Co.	158
Cunningham, Katharine	53, 73, 145, 224
de Chastellux, Marquis	23
Decoration Day celebration	119, 124
Deer Den	58
Defiance Engine Co.	73, 158
Delaware and Hudson Railroad	35, 166, 167
DeLong, Zopher Isaac	160
Derby's Hotel	18
Dix, Gov. John A.	21
Dolan Building	77
Dutchess County	11, 12
Eagle Hook and Ladder Co.	158
East End	145
East Field	226
East Washington St.	130
Economy Store	212, 218
Eden Park Nursing Home	146
Electricity	18, 150
Elks Club (Benevolent and Protective Order of Elks)	18, 85
Elliott, Dr. Edsall D. B.	161
Elm St.	73, 150, 156, 157
Elmwood Seminary	195
Empire Automobile Co.	111, 146
"Empire City, The"	15
Empire Hotel	127
Empire Theatre	21, 127, 212, 218, 219, 231
Englander Men's Store	101
English, William H.	107
Episcopal Church (see Church of the Messiah)	
Erie Canal	53
Exchange Building	120
Exchange St.	73, 96, 109, 120, 124
Fairgrounds	12, 21, 222, 223
Fairyland Theatre	212
Falls, the	10, 33, 34, 48, 50-51
Family Service Association	137
Farmers' Market	124, 125
Farmers' Sheds	150, 151
Farr, D. C.	196
Feeder Canal	15, 36-37, 42-47, 52, 53, 56, 57, 59, 61, 65, 149
Feeder Canal bridges	42, 43, 46-47, 52, 53, 66, 67
Feeder Dam	15, 18, 47, 52, 53, 61, 62
Fenimore Bridge	63
Ferris, J. L. G.	12
Ferris, John A.	91
Ferriss, Alfred	132, 133
Finch, Daniel J.	54
Finch, D. J. Hook and Ladder Co.	158
Finch, George R.	146
Finch, Jeremiah W.	54, 109, 111
Finch, Pruyn and Co., Inc.	38, 42, 47, 51, 53-55, 61-65, 148
Finch Pruyn Sales	54
Firemen's Muster	86
Fire protection	18, 158, 159
Fires —	
Fires of 1777 and 1780	158
Fire of 1864	18, 70-75
Fire of 1884	76, 78
Fire of 1902	101, 108, 109
Union School No. 1	202
Rialto Theatre and Hotel	217
Fitzgerald's Hotel and Restaurant	79
Hotel Towers	92, 93
St. Alphonsus Church	188
Woolworth and Lerner stores	105
Crandall Block	113
First Baptist Church (see also Baptist Church)	18, 180
First Church of Christ, Scientist	192
First National Bank of Glens Falls	77, 81-83, 107, 126, 134, 135
First Presbyterian Church (see Presbyterian churches)	
Fisher, Alvan	24
Fitzgerald, David J.	79
Fitzgerald's Hotel and Restaurant	79, 212
"Five Points" area	21
Floating bridge	61
Floating sawmill	60-61
Flood of 1869	27, 48-50
Flood of 1913	30-33, 50
Flower, Gov. Roswell P.	80, 98
Floyd Bennett Field	16, 210
Fonda's Masonic Hall	212
Fort Edward	11, 15, 16, 73
Fort William Henry	11
Fosburgh, Pieter	58
Foulds, Dr. and Mrs. Thomas Hammond	139
Foulds property	152
Fountain	71, 84, 87, 89, 90, 94, 141
Fountain Square	71, 76-77, 80, 82, 84, 86, 87, 89, 90, 94-95, 98
Fowler, B. B. store	96, 98, 100, 101
Fowler, Joseph	106-107

Fowler, Joseph Shirt and Collar Co.	108, 109
Fox brothers	59
Franklin, Benjamin	71, 232
Freedom Train	167
Freeman, George W.	47
Free Methodist Church	192
French and Indian War	11
French-Canadians	13, 145
French Mountain	164
Friends, Society of (see also Quakers)	11-13, 18, 170-173, 233
Garfield, James A.	107
Gas and gaslights	18, 67, 71, 184, 185
Glen, Col. Johannes	13
Glen House	47, 68
Glen Park Hotel	223
Glens Falls	10, 11, 15, 16, 233
Glens Falls Academy	18, 196-199
Glens Falls Bank	74, 82
Glens Falls Citizens Association	222
Glens Falls Company	47, 54, 64, 66
Glens Falls Dividend Mutual Insurance Co.	16, 120
Glens Falls, early names of	13, 15
Glens Falls Electric Installation Co.	134
Glens Falls Fire Engine Co.	158
Glens Falls Foundation	160
Glens Falls High School	200-203
Glens Falls Historical Association	18, 25, 160, 233, 239
Glens Falls Home for Aged Women	148-149
Glens Falls Hospital	150, 152-155
Glens Falls Hotel	68, 73, 91, 158, 159
Glens Falls Insurance Co.	12, 16, 19, 29, 106-107, 116, 118-125, 132, 159, 168, 237
Glens Falls-Lake George Stage Co.	164, 165, 219
Glens Falls Lime Co.	57
Glens Falls Lyceum	21
Glens Falls Market	74
Glens Falls National Bank	82
Glens Falls National Bank and Trust Co.	12, 76-77, 81, 82, 111, 113, 114, 237
Glens Falls Opera House	21, 78, 91, 140, 149, 212-216
Glens Falls Operetta Club	21, 231, 232
Glens Falls Oratorio Society	21
Glens Falls Outing Club	21, 228-231
Glens Falls Portland Cement Co.	53, 56
Glens Falls Post Office	15, 147
Glens Falls, Sandy Hill and Fort Edward Street Railway	168, 169
Glens Falls Savings and Loan Association	133, 135
Glens Falls Thespian Association	21, 231
Glens Falls Trades and Labor Assembly	18
Glens Falls Trust Co.	82

Glens Falls, Village of	16, 21, 71
Glen St.	4, 11, 12, 19, 20, 31, 36, 38, 42, 47, 66-68, 70-86, 91-127, 160-163, 165, 168, 237
Glenwood Ave.	164, 165
Goodman, Samuel B.	150
Goodspeed, Thomas W.	21
Goodspeedville (see also West Glens Falls)	53
Gordon, LeRoy J.	150
Grand Union store	161
Granger, Claude C.	223
Granger House	223
Granger, Marcus E.	223
Grant, W. T. and Co.	19, 92, 93, 105
Great Carrying Place	11
Greek-American Fruit Co.	81, 102
Green, Ira	47
Greeno's lunch wagon	111
Greenslet, Ferris	11, 21, 23
Griffin Lumber Co.	211
Griffing and Leland	68
Griffith, Elbert W.	202, 209
Grove Ave.	163
Gurney Lane	145
Guy Printing	212
Halfway Brook	9, 11-14
Halfway House	164
Hall Ice Cream Co.	133, 134
Hancock, Winfield S.	107
Hannan, Joseph	130
Harrisena Community Church	190
Harrisena School	210
Haviland, Abraham	12, 114
Haviland's Cove	227
Health Center	137
Henry Hudson Townhouses	157
Henry St. sawmill	64
Hercules plant	63
Hibernians, Ancient Order of	226
Hicks, Jacob	158
Hicksite Quaker Church	171
Hoag's service station	150, 151
Holden, Dr. Austin W.	12, 13, 48, 55, 56, 194, 196, 197
Holden, James A.	9, 15, 29, 30, 37
Hometown Days 1976	234, 235
Honigsbaum's	136
Horsecars	16, 110-113, 168
Horse racing	222, 223
Hotels (see also listing under name of hotel) —	
Hotel Bennett	115
Hotel Champlain	146
Hotel Madden	127, 158
Hotel Ruliff	112, 113, 115, 121
Hotel Towers	85, 91-93

244

Hudson Ave.	74-75, 80, 83, 91-93, 147
Hudson Falls (see also Sandy Hill)	52, 56
Hudson River	10-15, 17, 23, 34-35, 43, 48, 50-51, 58-65, 227
Hudson River Boom Association	15
Hudson River drives	58-64
Hudson River Regulating District	51
Hudson River Telephone Co.	18
Hudson River Water Power Co.	18
Hudson Valley Railway	35, 168, 169
Hughes, Charles Evans	16, 21
Hughes Light Guards	149
Hurley, James store	47
Hyde Collection	21, 148
Hyde Museum	148
Indian River	58
Indians	11
Industries	15, 16
Irish	13, 145
Italians	145
Jackson Heights School	208
Jay St.	147
Jehovah's Witnesses, Kingdom Hall	193
Jointa Lime Co.	56, 57
Joubert and White buckboards	15, 146
Junior High School	203
Jurisdiction	16
Juvet, L. P., optician and jeweler	128
Kamyr, Inc.	139, 145, 212, 221
Kamyr Valves	139
Kansas Coffee Shop	220
Keefe's Hall	149, 212
Keenan, John	57
Kennebec River	62
Kensington Rd. School	209
Kettle Mountain	58
King George III	11
Kingsbury	11
Knights of Columbus	135, 230, 231
Labor Unions	18
Lake Ave.	12
Lake Champlain	11
Lake George	11, 12, 16, 71
Lake George Opera Festival	21
Lapham, Benjamin	136
Lapham, Jerome	128, 129, 136, 201

Lapham, Jerome Engine Co.	158
Lapham Place	136
Lapham, Ralph M.	160
Lapham and Parks gristmill	28
LaPointe, Peter saloon	47
LARAC Festival (see also Lower Adirondack Regional Arts Council)	124, 125
Lasher, Rufus	119
Lawn Cottage	119
Lawrence St.	166
League Park	226-227
Leggett and Bush	103
Leggett and Peddie	103
Lerner store	105
Liberty Building	98
Lime industry	15, 47, 56, 57
Lincoln Ave.	12
Linehan, D. J. saloon	47
Little, Capt. Joseph J.	156
Little, Dr. George W.	137
Little League	226
Little, M. B. Engine and Hose Co.	158
Little, Russell A.	222
Little, Russell Mack	120
Little Theatre Group	230, 231
Locke shop and house	119
Locust St.	166, 167
Loeb Rhoades Hornblower and Co.	134
Log cabin, typical	9
Logging industry (see lumber industry)	
Log marks	60, 63
Lower Adirondack Regional Arts Council (see also LARAC Festival)	124, 125
Lucas, Dr. Francis F.	21
Lumber industry	15, 54, 58-65
Lumberjacks and rivermen	21, 47, 58-63
Lutheran Church of the Good Shepherd	192
Majestic Theatre	212
Mansion House	73
Maple St.	132-135, 137, 145, 166, 167
Maps —	
Burleigh lithograph 1884	endpapers
Halfway Brook	9
Province of New York — Part of Charlotte and Albany Counties	8
Queensbury before the Revolution	14
Stoddard and Spencer's map of Glens Falls (1874)	44-45
Trolley routes	169
Masonic Temple	120, 121
Mausert, Fred W.	176
May St.	159
Mead, Gideon F.	118

Mead, Joseph	118
Mechanical Association	18
Memorial Day (see Decoration Day)	
Merchants National Bank	19, 77, 81
Merritt, Ichabod	158
Methodist churches	18, 73, 86, 124, 178, 179, 192, 193, 224
Metropolitan Museum of Art	139
Milbert, Jacques-Gerard	24
Mile Track	21, 222, 223
Military Road, Old	12, 71, 75
Militia	18
Miller, Alexander W.	21, 209, 222
Miller Brothers Garage	134
Montgomery Ward & Co.	111
Monty's Bridge	57
Monument, Soldiers' (see Soldiers' Monument)	
Monument Square	4-5, 12, 16, 20, 75, 82, 95, 111, 114-133
Moreau Station	24
Morf and Galusha	134
Morgan Mills	47
Mott, Isaac	135
Moulton Bars	58
Moynehan Building	81, 91
Moynehan, Patrick	161
Murray St.	53, 61, 147, 159
McDermott, Rt. Rev. Msgr. James P.	186-187
McDonald, James Hook and Ladder Co.	158
McDonald, William	148, 149
McEchron, Bertha	73
McEchron, Maggie	73
McEchron, William	53, 73, 137, 149, 224
McGregor, Duncan	68
McLaughlin, Dr. Charles S.	161
McLaughlin, Helen	201
National Association of Railway Agents	167
National Auto Stores	111
National Bank of Glens Falls	81, 82
National Register of Historic Places	162
Newberry's	105
Newcomb	58
New England	11
New Fountain Square, Ltd.	138, 141
New Hall House	47
Newspapers —	
Glens Falls Messenger, The	16, 47, 48, 52, 54
Glens Falls Republican, The	16
Glens Falls Times, The	16, 83
Morning Post, The	16, 161
Morning Star, The	16, 224
Post-Star, The	16, 82, 167
Warren Messenger, The	194
Warren Republican, The	16
Newton, Dr. Ephraim H.	68
New Union Telephone Co.	18
New York City	11, 15
New York National Guard	149
New York Telephone Company	161
Niagara Mohawk Power Corp.	52, 134
Nickelodeons	212, 218, 220
North Creek	62
Northern New York Horse Breeders Association	222
Northway	16, 17, 43, 104
Northway Hotel	115
Numan's Hall	212
Oak St.	166, 167
Oakland Ave.	42, 47
Oblong, The	11
"Old and Tried"	120
Old Brownstone	82
Old Glens Falls Club	18
Old Military Road	12
"Old White" Church	174, 175
O'Leary, Daniel	201
Oneida Community Church	172
Opera House (see Glens Falls Opera House)	
Ordway Hall	224, 225
Ordway, Jones	224
Orthodox Jewish Synagogue	190
Outlet store	96
Palmer, Mrs. W. H., millinery	103
Paramount Theatre	212, 221
Pardo, George	115
Parkman, Francis	23
Parks Hospital (see Glens Falls Hospital)	
Parks, Solomon A.	152
Park St.	150-152, 155
Park Theatre	212, 220
Patterson, Robert P.	21
Peabody's Hotel	102
Pearl St.	139
Pearsall and Gray cigar store	81
Peck, D., grocery	77
Peck, Reuben	194
Pettit, Micajah	47
Pilcher, Prof. and Mrs. J. M.	195
Pine St.	161
Plank Road	16, 164, 165
Plank Road School	194, 201
Plaza Hotel	115
Police	127
Post Office	15, 147
Presbyterian churches	18, 68, 73, 74, 78, 86, 91, 145, 162, 174-177, 212, 214, 216, 217, 220

Prospect Mountain	145
Prospect St.	146, 149
Pruyn, Samuel	54, 148, 201
Pruyn's Island	64, 139, 227
Pulp and paper	15, 16, 64, 65, 139
Quaker Church (see also Friends)	132
Quaker Rd.	16, 132, 173
Quakers (see Friends)	
Queensbury	11, 12, 14-17, 158
Queensbury Hotel	25, 40, 91, 134, 181, 221
Queensbury Patent	48
Queensbury Schools	18, 194, 201, 210
Queensbury Town Meeting	12, 158
Race tracks	21, 222, 223
Railroads (see also Delaware and Hudson)	16, 145, 166, 167
Ranger, Squire	119
Recreation (see also Sports)	62, 222-229
Recreation Commission	226
Red schoolhouse	194, 204
Regents diplomas	196, 201
Religious life	18
Rensselaer and Saratoga Railway Co. (see also Railroads)	167
Revolutionary War	11, 71
Rialto Hotel	217
Rialto Theatre	85, 212, 215, 217
Ridge St.	12, 18, 71, 75, 77, 80-81, 88, 89, 91, 120, 128, 137, 138, 139, 152, 158, 159, 201
Ridge St. engine house	158, 159
Ridge St. School	144, 159, 200
Robbins, Calvin	67
Rochester Clothing Store	100, 225
Rockwell House (Hotel)	71, 75, 77, 80-81, 83, 84, 90-93, 145, 164, 165
Rogers Building	124, 132, 133
Rosekrans, Enoch	57
Rugg and Moren	224
Russell, J. Ward	201
Sacandaga Reservoir	51
St. Alphonsus Church	159, 188, 189
St. Alphonsus School	18, 207
St. John the Baptist Church	188
St. Lawrence River	11
St. Mary's Academy	18, 145, 147, 206
St. Mary's Church	86, 147, 178, 184, 185
St. Paul's Episcopal Church	190
Salvation Army	191, 199
Sands, George	47
Sandy Hill (see also Hudson Falls)	52, 56, 73
Sanford St.	223
Sanford St. School	208, 223
Sanfords Ridge	149
Sawmills	15, 47, 54
Sawyer, J. E. and Co., Inc.	67, 68, 224
Schenectady	13
School St.	150
Sears, J. Thacher	57, 199
Seminary Hill School	201
Senior Citizens Center	162
Seth Warner Regiment	232
Settlers, early	11-13
Sewer system	18, 71
Sherman, Arthur W.	222
Sherman, Augustus	53, 162
Sherman Lime Co.	57
Sherman Lumber Co.	52, 53
Sherman, William	53
Shermantown	57
Sisson house	12, 116-118, 120, 121, 132
Sisters of St. Joseph Convent	206
Skidmore College Extension	18, 199
Smiths Basin	57
Soldiers' Monument	4-5, 114, 116-119, 122-128, 132
South End Livery	127
Southern Adirondack Library System	128
South Glens Falls	32, 71
South St.	12, 75, 112, 113, 115, 127, 130, 156-159
South St. engine house	158, 159
South St. School	200
Spier Falls dam and hydro-electric station	18
Spiral stairway on Hudson River bridge	39
Sports (see Recreation)	
Square Nail Gift Shop	67
Stage coaches	115, 164, 165
Staples, Anson	74
State Armory (see Armory)	
State Theatre	176, 212, 220
Stichman Towers	79, 147
Stilwell and Allen hardware store	100, 101
Stilwell, Thomas C.	101
Stoddard and Spencer	44-45, 57
Stoddard, Seneca Ray	68, 80, 112-113, 118, 147, 160
Streetcars (see Trolley cars)	
Street system, establishment of	16
Sullivan and Minahan Funeral Home	150
Synagogue Center of Congregation Shaaray Tefila	192
Synagogue, Orthodox Jewish	190
Taylor, C. A. store	103
Temperance movement	18
Temple Beth-El	193

Threehouse, Peter D.	73, 91
Tollgates	164, 165
Towner, Zaccheus	11
Town Meeting, Queensbury	12, 158
Trade union movement	18
Transportation improvements	16
Trolley cars	16, 19, 30, 71, 81, 84, 97, 110, 111, 121, 124, 127, 168, 169, 187
Troy Public Works Co.	97
Union Bag and Paper Corp.	63
Union Free School Dist. 1	18, 200-202, 209
Union Free School Dist. 2	201, 210
Union Hall	78, 212
Union Square	156
United Methodist Church of Queensbury	193
Universalist Church	171
Urban Renewal	76, 79, 98, 138
Van Dusen, Col. Zenas	47, 53
Van Dusen mills	52, 53
Vaughn, Eleazer	57
Veterans of Foreign Wars	135
Vigilance Committee	158
Voluntary Action Center	18, 137
Wall, William Guy	24
Walnut St. School	18, 204, 205
Warren County	15, 16, 59, 82
Warren County Agricultural Society	18
Warren County Airport	16
Warren County Fair	12, 21, 222, 223
Warren St.	12, 18, 71, 73-75, 78-80, 86, 87, 89, 91, 120, 138, 140-142, 146-149
Warrensburg	58
Washington County	16
Washington, Gen. George	12, 13
Washington Monument	55
Washington St.	178
Water system	18, 71
Wellington Hotel	135
Wesleyan Church	193
West End	145
West Glens Falls (see also Goodspeedville)	53, 135
West Mountain	71, 145, 179
West Mountain reservoirs	18, 71
Wheeler and Wilson Mfg. Co.	103
White Water Derby (see Recreation)	
William Barnes School	194
William St.	119
Williams, Sherman	128, 200, 201, 209
Williams Tire and Rubber Co.	133
Willis, N. P.	25
Wilson's, "Penny," store	119
Wing, Abraham	11-16, 23, 48, 71, 89, 138, 149, 158, 173
Wing, Abraham III	15, 59
Wing, Edward	12, 173
Wing family monument	173
Wing farm	149
Wing, Halsey	57
Wing sawmill and gristmill	12, 15, 38, 47, 48, 54, 64
Wing's Corners (see also The Corners)	71
Wing's Falls	13, 16, 23, 171
Wing's Tavern	12, 18, 71, 75, 89, 138
Winter Carnival (see Recreation)	
Woman's Civic Club	230, 231
Wonderland nickelodeon	221
World in Motion nickelodeon	212, 218
World War II	15, 21, 136
Young Men's Christian Association	106-107, 120, 123, 126, 224, 225

The assistance of Virginia E. Combs and Ruby Combs in the preparation of this index is deeply appreciated.

Glens Falls, N.Y.